PE⊕PLE
in Time and Place

PROFESSIONAL GUIDE

WEDNESDAY

THURSDAY

FRIDAY

...SDAY

Monuments — Memorials

Famous Places in Washington, D.C.

In your Cooperative
Learning groups
Remember to:
• Give your ideas
• Listen to others ideas
• Plan your work with the group
• Present your project
• Discuss how your group worked

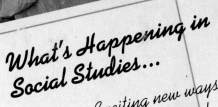

What's Happening in Social Studies...

History: Exciting new ways to let **ALL** students see themselves as makers of history

Geography: Effective new ways to help **ALL** students grow up to be geographically literate in a changing world

Citizenship: Inspiring new ways to involve **ALL** students actively in citizenship — starting **now**

And more ...

SILVER BURDETT & GINN

We Bring It All Together

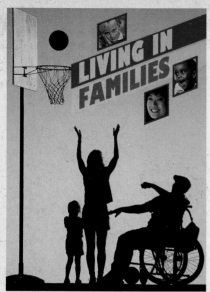

LIVING IN FAMILIES

LIVING IN COMMUNITIES

COMPARING COMMUNITIES

COMPARING REGIONS

OUR COUNTRY

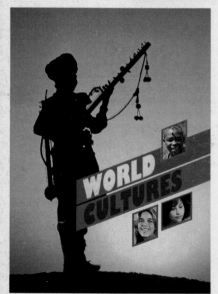

WORLD CULTURES

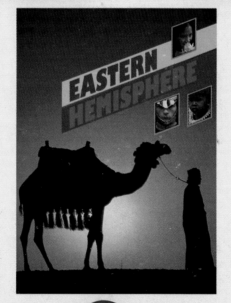

EASTERN HEMISPHERE

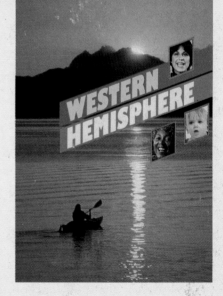

WESTERN HEMISPHERE

PEOPLE
in Time and Place

Silver Burdett Ginn

1

Our Bill of Beliefs

1. **We believe that every moment spent on social studies education is precious time well spent, for it is primarily through social studies that students learn the knowledge, skills, and values they need for a lifetime of full and productive citizenship.**

...That is why we provide a social studies program that reaches ALL students.

2. **We believe that the twin cornerstones of social studies are history and geography.**

...That is why our authors are talented historians and geographers, capable of presenting solid content as an engaging story of people in time and place.

3. **We believe that citizenship education must emphasize active participation in school and community.**

...That is why we provide ample opportunities for students to put into practice the knowledge, skills, and values they are learning.

4. **We believe that social studies reaches ALL students through a multicultural perspective.**

...That is why we have structured the program so that every child feels dignified as an active participant in the ongoing story of people in time and place.

5. **We believe that the story of people in time and place is enriched by the social sciences, fine arts, and humanities.**

...That is why we have integrated appropriate literature passages, fine arts reproductions, and other primary and secondary materials.

6. **We believe that social studies must provide each child with the opportunity to grow in self-awareness and self-confidence.**

...That is why we have built in opportunities for learning, practicing, and applying thinking and other skills, including skills for effective interpersonal relationships.

7. **We believe that the story of people in time and place becomes more memorable and exciting when students are actively involved.**

...That is why we have included a variety of "hands-on/minds-on" activities, cooperative learning, and ways to make thinking more visual.

8. **We believe that social studies takes on added meaning, maximizing time spent on social studies, when students make connections between social studies and other subjects.**

...That is why we have incorporated content-area reading strategies, writing across the curriculum, and multidisciplinary activities.

9. **We believe that the textbook program comes to life through the classroom teacher.**

...That is why we have involved classroom teachers in every step of the development of this program and in the writing of the Teacher-to-Teacher Edition.

10. **We believe that classroom teachers have the right to expect the very best support when they teach social studies.**

...That is why we have brought together in one program everything teachers need to make social studies a successful experience for ALL students: textbook, ancillary materials, and personnel committed to providing top-quality in-service.

PE○PLE
in Time and Place

Silver Burdett Ginn

HISTORY
as a Well-Told Story

How good writing draws students into the study of history

Dr. Herbert J. Bass

All teachers know that getting students involved is a key to learning. Well-written history helps teachers do just that. Writing that is clear and direct, that employs eye-catching detail to flesh out characters and relate events, that helps young readers create mental images of the past — that kind of writing brings history to life for students.

History brims with suspense and drama

Someone once described history as a "cracking good story." That's the way it should be written. Certainly history

doesn't lack for rich story materials. Who could imagine a more wildly improbable tale than that of Pizarro and his band of 168 men conquering the huge empire of the Incas? Is there a more inspiring story than that of the American colonists' struggle for independence against the greatest military power of the age? Or a more suspenseful one than Harriet Tubman's risking her life to guide slaves to freedom? Surely the true stories of the explorers and the pioneers rival the best adventure novels. Such stories have a vast potential for involving the young reader.

Well-written history encourages acts of imagination

To understand history, students have to put themselves into a time very different from their own. That's not easy to do. There is no time machine to carry young readers back to the first Thanksgiving, the American Revolution, or life in the early days of their communities. No time machine, that is, except the one that is within ALL students — imagination.

We encourage acts of imagination when we present history not as a collection of dry, isolated facts but as a story filled with vivid descriptions of what the eye would have seen and the ear would have heard. For example, we could simply state, *City streets in America in 1850 were crowded.* Or we might write this instead:

> *If you visited an American city in the year 1850, you would quickly notice how crowded the streets were. Soon after the sun rose, wagons, carriages, horses, and mules jammed the streets. Few cities had sidewalks, so people walked in the street or along the side of it with the rest of the traffic. There were no laws about which side of the street to ride on, so people traveled on both sides of the street in both directions!*

Each version conveys the facts about crowded city streets, but the second one can also get students' time machines "up and running."

Visuals support the well-told story

Today's "visual generation" is used to getting information from TV and other visual images. Making use of well-chosen visuals such as photographs and paintings, along with plenty of maps and well-constructed time lines, can capitalize on that fact. Teachers will often use films, slides, and videos to stimulate thinking and discussion. That is all to the good.

4

But in the end, it is the written word that matters most in learning history. And since that is so, it is the well-told story that offers us the greatest opportunity to turn students into interested, active learners.

Dr. Herbert J. Bass, Professor of History, Temple University, Philadelphia, Pennsylvania, has written or edited a half dozen books on American history, several of them for use by elementary students. A recipient of an award for outstanding teaching, Dr. Bass is one of the professional historian-authors of PEOPLE IN TIME AND PLACE.

PEOPLE IN TIME AND PLACE helps to draw students into the study of history.

- **An engaging writing style** presents history as the story of people in time and place

- **Understanding Source Material** engages students in learning about the past and present through interesting print and nonprint sources of information

- **Literature excerpts and selections** *about* historical periods and *of* historical periods give students an illuminated view of the people, places, and events they are learning about

- **Quotations** from people who lived in a particular time and place, as well as quotes about those people, when woven into the text, provide students with a sense of historical perspective

- **Historical maps, time lines, graphs, diagrams, tables, and other graphics** provide integrated visual support for the text, as well as another mode of presentation for historical information

- **Citizenship and American Values** features enable students to understand the history of democracy

- **Five Themes of Geography questions** in the teacher edition help students connect history and geography, time and place

- **Comprehensive vocabulary treatment** provides students with a knowledge of the key terms that bring more understanding to their reading about history

- **Skillbuilders** provide opportunities for students to learn skills that help them unlock the story of people in time and place

- **Current Events** activities in the teacher edition increase student interest in history-in-the-making

- **Multidisciplinary Activity** features help students connect history with the social sciences and other subject areas

History

as a well-told story of people in time and place inspires ALL students to see themselves as makers of history.

From *Our Country*, p. 289

They are unknown to history. They were the Minutemen on Lexington green. They were the soldiers who shivered at Valley Forge. They were the men who dashed out of their swamp hideouts to strike at the British. They were the women who brought food and water to the men in battle, took care of the wounded and the sick, and kept farms and shops running. They were the farm families who shared their food with the soldiers and the townspeople who gave the soldiers housing and made weapons and gunpowder for them. They were the boys and girls who helped produce the food and the clothing that the American soldiers needed.

When the war was over, people everywhere asked, "How could the American colonies have won a war against one of the great military powers in the world?" The answer to this question was really not difficult to find. The main reason that the Revolutionary War was won is that ordinary Americans refused to lose it.

for more HISTORY look for
- **Visuals with captions**
- **Using Source Material**
- **Literature excerpts and selections**
  and in the Teacher-to-Teacher Edition
- **Current Events**

PE⬤PLE
in Time and Place

We bring it all together

Promoting Geography Literacy

The five themes of geography help all students make more sense out of their world

Dr. Gail S. Ludwig

Geographers, teachers, and parents share a common goal: to make students more geographically literate. To help make this happen, professional geographers have shared with classroom teachers a conceptual framework to use in discussing geography. That framework is called the five themes of geography.

The following description of the five themes includes sample discussion questions based on Timbuktu, an African city that I enjoy using to illustrate the five themes of geography in presentations to teachers and students.

The Five Themes of Geography

Theme 1. Location

Location consists of **absolute location** and **relative location.** Every place has an absolute location that can be pinpointed on a map, using latitude and longitude. Every place also has relative location in relation to its surroundings.

To help students think in terms of absolute location, discuss in reference to latitude and longitude on a map or in a gazetteer: *What is the latitude and longitude of Timbuktu?* To help students understand relative location, discuss in reference to a map or globe: *Where is Timbuktu in relation to the Sahara Desert?*

Theme 2. Place

The sense of place includes the combination of physical and human characteristics that makes one location unique from all others. Physical characteristics include climate, soil, and vegetation; human characteristics include values, ideas, and architecture.

To help students think in terms of place, discuss with them in relation to maps, text, and visuals: *There is only one Timbuktu. What are some physical and human characteristics that make Timbuktu different from every other place?*

Theme 3. Human – Environment Interactions (Relationships Within Places)

Relationships within places include the ways humans have been affected by their physical environment. It also includes the ways humans have affected their physical environment.

To help students think in terms of relationships within places, both past and present, discuss in reference to maps, text, and visuals: *Why did Timbuktu grow and develop where it did? In the past, how have the people of Timbuktu changed their environment? What environmental problems do the people of Timbuktu face today? What solutions are they trying?*

Theme 4. Movement

Movement relates to the flow of people, goods, and ideas. The most obvious signs of movement are transportation systems — rivers, railroads and roads — and communication systems — word of mouth, television, newspapers, and so on.

To help students think in terms of movement, discuss in relation to maps, text, and visuals: *How do goods, people, and ideas travel within and in and out of Timbuktu?*

Theme 5. Regions

As a basic unit of study, regions are areas that can be defined on the basis of unifying characteristics, either physical or human (cultural, economic, social, and/or political).

Help students think in terms of regions by discussing: *To which region — or regions — does Timbuktu belong? How is this region different from the region where you live?*

Teaching with the Five Themes of Geography

Strategies For many years, classroom teachers have been using the five themes intuitively as a questioning strategy. Today, classroom teachers are using them more consciously in connection with a strong map and globe skills program. Because they overlap, the five themes do not have to be used in strict order, although the location theme logically is a good starting point. You may adapt the five themes to fit your teaching style and the needs of all your students.

Benefits   The five themes can help **ALL** students, especially students at risk of failing, make more sense out of the world around them. Thinking like geographers, students can use the five themes to see connections among history, geography, the social sciences, the arts, and the humanities. These connections help students remember information, observe, analyze, speculate, and do other kinds of critical thinking that enhances geography literacy.

Dr. Gail S. Ludwig currently serves as the Geographer-in-Residence for the National Geographic Society's Geography Education Program. An experienced social studies classroom teacher, Dr. Ludwig coordinated the first state-level National Geography Bee and has served as president of the National Council for Geographic Education. Dr. Ludwig is one of the professional geographer-authors of PEOPLE IN TIME AND PLACE.

PEOPLE IN TIME AND PLACE builds geography literacy.

- Consistent map and globe skills program is integrated throughout the text:
  - Maps have a caption question in the student text and a five-themes discussion question in the teacher edition, provoking geographic thinking
  - End-of-lesson map skills checks provide constant reinforcement

- Built-in reference tools support geographic exploration:
  - Map Skills Handbook, strategically positioned at the start of the text, reviews and previews important map skills and provides reference throughout the course of study
  - Atlas, Gazetteer, and Dictionary of Places in the Resource Section in the back of the student texts provide ready access to geographic information

- Extensive variety of clearly detailed special-purpose maps, including relief, physical, political, product, population, historical, and transportation maps, provide a rich basis for five-themes discussions

- Wealth of other graphic resources — charts, tables, photographs, and drawings — support five-themes discussions

- Content-rich geography, integrated with history and the other social sciences, the arts, and the humanities, provides the solid information and cultural literacy background that students need to discuss the five themes

Geography

literacy is built when maps, content, and skills come together through reading, thinking, and discussing.

From *World Cultures*, p. 286

C. Trading Kingdoms in West Africa

Gold-for-Salt During this period, trading kingdoms in West Africa grew from the gold-for-salt trade. Trading gold for salt may sound ridiculous to us today. In Africa south of the Sahara, salt was very important but it was very hard to find. In the hot climates, people needed salt in their bodies to keep from dehydrating. Salt was also needed to season some foods and preserve others, especially meats. Gold was abundant in many parts of Africa.

How did the gold-for-salt trade work? Arab traders loaded their camels with fancy silks and cottons and expensive leather goods. They traveled to North Africa to trade these goods for salt. Salt was abundant in North Africa, especially in the Sahara. The Arabs then took the salt to West Africa, where they traded it for gold. The king of Ghana made traders pay taxes and tributes. As a result, Ghana was a very wealthy kingdom

Muslim Invaders Gh... ...d to prosper until the end ...tury, when Muslims people of Ghana to ... fused to convert, th... Although Ghana's ar... able to push the ... their kingdom, th... all but ended. G... regain the power

The Kingdom o... of Ghana, the ki... trol of the gold... large kingdo... Mali was suc... said to take ... tal, the city ... had around

286

EARLY WEST AFRICAN KINGDOMS

GEOGRAPHY THEMES

Location

■ Have students look at the map on this page to help them answer the following questions: Of which kingdoms was Timbuktu a part?
(Mali and Songhai)

What is there about Timbuktu's location that contributed to its growth?
(It is located on the Niger River.)

To which African desert is Timbuktu close?
(The Sahara Desert)

From *World Cultures* T.E., p. 286

for GEOGRAPHY tools look for
- Gazetteer
- Map Skills Handbook
- Atlas
- Dictionary of Places

PE●PLE in Time and Place

We bring it all together

What's New in Citizenship Education?

Seven Strands Support Real-life Citizenship Participation

Dr. Theodore Kaltsounis

The goal of citizenship education is clear: to prepare all youngsters for their future roles as full and productive citizens, committed to the American values that protect us as a nation rich in individual differences and ethnic diversity. Traditionally, citizenship education has focused on teaching *for* and *about* adult citizenship. Today, the emphasis is on actively involving youngsters in *participating* in citizenship, **both in school and in their communities.** In this way, citizenship education is more than a dress rehearsal!

Seven Strands of Citizenship

The following seven basic strands of citizenship provide a framework for structuring activities that enable students to participate in real-life citizenship while learning the traditional information, skills, and values that provide the foundation for citizenship education.

1. **Participate in the democratic process**

2. **Develop patriotism and American values**

3. **Develop an awareness of and skills in interdependence**

4. **Develop an awareness of and skills in resolving social issues**

5. **Develop an awareness of and skills in relating to public officials**

6. **Learn how to use resources wisely**

7. **Develop strong personal integrity and positive self-image**

Real-life Citizenship Activities

Here are some examples of easily manageable real-life activities that illustrate seven basic strands of citizenship. Through these and similar activities, teachers play a vital role in preparing students for full adult citizenship by providing them with the opportunity, guidance, and encouragement they need to be active citizens **today.** Students don't just read about citizenship, they participate in it in ways that are commensurate with their ages, abilities, and interests.

1. Participate in the democratic process by	• Holding class elections • Writing classroom rules • Conducting mock trials
2. Develop patriotism and American values by	• Celebrating patriotic holidays • Pledging allegiance
3. Develop an awareness of and skills in interdependence by	• Engaging in cooperative learning • Making a farm-to-table foods flowchart
4. Develop an awareness of and skills in resolving social issues by	• Discussing current events • Conducting debates • Writing letters to the editor
5. Develop an awareness of and skills in relating to public officials by	• Writing to public officials • Interviewing public officials • Visiting town hall

6. Learn how to use resources wisely by

- Participating in recycling
- Holding a conservation-theme social studies fair

7. Develop strong personal integrity and positive self-image by

- Serving as a safety patrol
- Volunteering as a peer tutor
- Participating in scouting, 4-H

Dr. Theodore Kaltsounis, *Professor of Social Studies, College of Education, University of Washington, Seattle, Washington, is an experienced elementary teacher and author of a methods book on citizenship education. A former president of the National Council for the Social Studies, Dr. Kaltsounis is the social studies series consultant for PEOPLE IN TIME AND PLACE.*

PEOPLE IN TIME AND PLACE provides built-in ways to activate citizenship participation.

- **Citizenship and American Values** models for students seven citizenship strands including developing patriotism and American values and developing strong personal integrity

- **Citizenship and American Values: You Decide** enables students to evaluate alternatives, weigh evidence, and make decisions — skills that are needed for resolving social issues

- **Cooperative Learning** activities help students develop skills in interdependence, while also developing positive self-image

- **Skillbuilder** lessons enable students to practice a variety of thinking, social studies, and communication skills needed for citizenship, including skills for interdependence, resolving social issues, and relating to public officials

- **Current Events** activities in the teacher edition provide opportunities for students to develop an awareness of interdependence, resolving social issues, and relating to public officials

- **Five-themes-of-geography discussion questions** in the teacher edition encourage students to use resources more wisely

- **How To** features in the teacher edition provide guidelines for conducting activities that help students learn to participate in the democratic process

Citizenship

education puts the accent on active involvement by ALL students.

From *Living in Communities,* p. 184

CITIZENSHIP AND AMERICAN VALUES

Conserving Natural Resources

Adam wanted a drink of water. He turned on the faucet. He let the water run and run. Adam's mother heard the water running.

"Why is the water running for so long?" asked his mother.

"I want it to get cold before I drink it," replied Adam.

His mother said, "Water is an important resource. We must use only what we need. This way we can conserve it."

"What does conserve mean?" asked Adam.

"Conserve means we must not spoil or waste, but use wisely," said his mother.

Then Adam's mother gave him water from the refrigerator. She told Adam how it is important to conserve all of our resources.

Water is one of our most important natural resources. Air, land, and forests are also very important. We use many natural resources every

Current Events Activity

Ask students to bring in newspaper or magazine articles about organizations or individuals trying to conserve natural resources. Make a bulletin board and classify articles by the natural resources in question. Discuss ways students in the class can help specifically to preserve each of the resources mentioned.

From *Living in Communities* T.E., p. 184

for more CITIZENSHIP look for
- **Skillbuilder**
- **Using Source Material**

and in the Teacher-to-Teacher Edition
- **How To**
- **Cooperative Learning**

PE PLE
in Time and Place

We bring it all together

MULTICULTURAL PERSPECTIVES

in
Social Studies

Addressing content issues, process issues, and equity issues helps make ALL students winners

Dr. James A. Banks

A respected authority on multicultural education, Dr. James A. Banks served as chairperson and senior author on the National Council for the Social Studies Task Force that issued "Curriculum Guidelines for Multi-ethnic Education." A former elementary teacher, Dr. Banks has authored numerous books and articles on strategies for teaching multicultural education in the social studies. Dr. Banks is Professor of Education, University of Washington, Seattle, Washington.

Nowhere else are more of the world's culturally diverse people housed under one roof, so to speak, than in our own country. More than any other society, Americans have the opportunity to enjoy the full richness of cultural diversity — customs, traditions, values, and literature. Multicultural education brings that richness into the classroom, creating equal educational opportunities for students from different racial, ethnic, cultural and gender groups. The social studies classroom — where the story of people in time and place is told — provides the ideal setting to engage students in the practice of multicultural education in terms of (1) content issues; (2) process issues; (3) equity issues.

Content Issues

Content issues deal with the extent to which examples from a variety of cultures and groups are used to illustrate key concepts that are part of the social studies curriculum, such as culture, family, community, and nation. When families are studied, the examples in the textbook and other student materials can be extended by asking the students to prepare reports on the histories and cultures of their families. When preparing their reports, the students can interview their parents and other relatives. By asking the students to share the stories of their families, the teacher can highlight, dignify, and celebrate the diverse cultures and family experiences represented in the classroom, the school, or the community.

Process Issues

Process issues relate to the extent to which a multicultural approach is used — that is the extent to which students are helped to view concepts, issues, problems, and events from the points of view of ALL the groups involved: racial, ethnic, and gender. For example, in the study of United States history, students can be helped to view the westward movement from the point of view of the American Indian groups that were already living in the West as well as from the perspective of the European American settlers. By helping the students to view the westward movement from the perspectives of both groups, the teacher can help the students to develop a more accurate and compassionate understanding of the development of our nation.

Equity Issues

Equity issues relate to teaching and instructional strategies that facilitate the academic achievement of students

from diverse racial, ethnic, and cultural groups. While some researchers suggest that certain groups of students respond more positively when instruction is personalized, cooperative, and actively engaging, the reality is that the same strategies can help **ALL** students to increase their academic achievement and develop more interest in the social studies. Thus, implementing content issues, process issues, and equity issues in multicultural education is an effective strategy for making **ALL** students winners.

PEOPLE IN TIME AND PLACE addresses content, process, and equity issues to provide a multicultural perspective.

- **Content rich in the story of ALL people in time and place** — their history, geography, social institutions, customs, religion, music, art, literature, government and so forth — enable students to appreciate cultural diversity among the earth's peoples

- **Visuals** such as fine arts reproductions, pictures of artifacts, and photographs of ethnic celebrations that integrate with the text help students recognize and appreciate the contributions of culturally diverse peoples

- **Pen Pals** provide an opportunity for students to learn about the lifestyles of children in other countries

- **Using Source Material** questions engage students in looking at the experiences of people in time and place from the viewpoints of those who actually had the experiences

- **Thinking About Literature** questions stimulate students to reflect on the experiences of men, women, and children of different racial, religious, and ethnic groups

- **Citizenship and American Values** features help students appreciate the cultural diversity of our nation's people by presenting American democracy in terms of its history, its procedures, and its ideals

- **Citizenship and American Values: You Decide** features provide students with an opportunity to examine both sides of an issue

- **Meeting Individual Needs** activities ensure that **ALL** students have an opportunity to learn difficult concepts

- **Cooperative Learning** activities in the student text and teacher edition provide opportunities for **ALL** students to experience increased self-esteem and growth in positive interdependence

- **Writing skills check** questions in the student text and **Writing to Learn** activities in the teacher edition provide opportunities that enable students to personalize social studies

- **Multidisciplinary Activity** features, **How To** projects and activities, and a wide variety of **Optional Activities** in the teacher edition actively engage **ALL** students in learning social studies

Multicultural

perspectives enable ALL students to identify with the story of people in time and place.

From *Living in Families*, pp. 18/19

for more MULTICULTURAL perspectives look for
- Visuals with captions
- Literature excerpts and selections

and in the Teacher-to-Teacher Edition
- Meeting Individual Needs
- Current Events

PE●PLE
in Time and Place

We bring it all together

READING

IN THE CONTENT AREAS

Key Before-Reading Strategies That Prepare Your Students for Success in Social Studies

Dr. James F. Baumann

"I think social studies is boring," says Miguel.
"And I never do well on the tests," admits Susie.
Chances are these students are struggling content-area readers — perhaps because they haven't recalled what they already know, don't see the point of what they're reading, or haven't gotten a handle on critical vocabulary. We can help turn things around for them; we can set the stage for reading success in social studies. How? By helping students learn some key before-reading strategies that will provide a rich backdrop against which the content information will make a lot more sense — and be much more enjoyable!

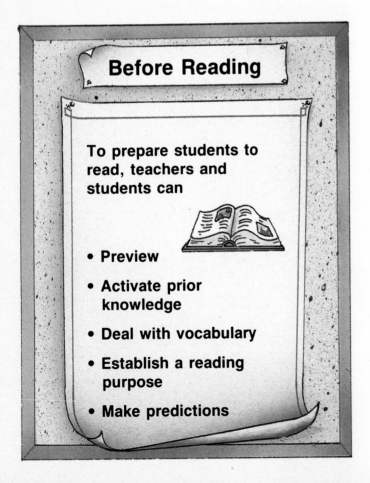

Before Reading

To prepare students to read, teachers and students can

- Preview

- Activate prior knowledge

- Deal with vocabulary

- Establish a reading purpose

- Make predictions

Five Before-Reading Strategies

Preview the Lesson

One nonthreatening before-reading strategy is previewing. You may help students preview by directing their attention to the lesson title and the boldfaced headings and subheadings. Then have students look at the graphic materials — the photographs, maps, charts, illustrations, and so forth — and have them read the accompanying caption questions. Previewing gives students an overall sense of what the lesson is about and provides a general context for the information they will be reading.

Activate Prior Knowledge

Another strategy for preparing students for reading is to help them activate their prior knowledge. One way to accomplish this is to ask questions that help students think about what they already know about the lesson topic. Activating prior knowledge enables students to link existing knowledge to new information. Having such a link provides students with a reference point for assimilating new material, thus adding greater meaning to the new content.

Deal with Vocabulary

Unlocking the meaning of unfamiliar specialized vocabulary terms is critical in preparing students to comprehend what they will be reading. Definitional, contextual, and associational activities provide sound ways to familiarize students with key new vocabulary terms. Helping students deal with key vocabulary terms prior to reading increases comprehension and motivation and decreases frustration and confusion.

Establish a Reading Purpose

Reading makes more sense when students know why they are reading — when their reading has purpose. You can involve students in setting the purpose for their reading or you can provide the reason for reading by providing a question for them to keep in mind.

Make Predictions

Having a stake in the reading increases student interest and motivation. Encouraging students to make predictions about the lesson content is one way to provide such a stake. You can help students make predictions by having them use section headings and visuals.

Is it necessary to use all the before-reading strategies every time my students read in the content areas?

Absolutely not! Based on the type of information being presented in a particular lesson, the overall purpose for reading the lesson, and the students' unique reading abilities and needs, you should select only the most appropriate before-reading strategies that will help your students become better content-area readers.

Dr. James F. Baumann, Professor and Head of the Department of Reading Education, College of Education, The University of Georgia, Athens, Georgia, is a former elementary teacher whose research on strategies that improve reading comprehension have helped classroom teachers teach reading in the content areas. Currently serving as editor of The Reading Teacher, *Dr. Baumann is the reading-language arts series consultant for* PEOPLE IN TIME AND PLACE.

PEOPLE IN TIME AND PLACE makes it easy to use before-reading strategies.

- **Carefully worded titles and headings** provide a sense of the lesson content, prompting students to preview and make predictions.

- **A variety of highly appealing visuals and caption questions,** and **Visual Thinking skill** questions provide a highly motivating way to get all students, particularly reluctant readers, to preview and make predictions.

- **Think About What You Know** questions and **Motivation** activities help students activate prior knowledge

- **Key new vocabulary words are thoroughly developed:** identified before each lesson, highlighted and defined in context the first time they appear in the lesson, defined in the **Glossary** and the **Picture Glossary,** extended through activities in the teacher edition, practiced on worksheets, and assessed in tests

- **Focus Your Reading** questions help students establish a reading purpose

Reading Strategies

build success in social studies for ALL students — right from the start of the lesson.

From Our Country, p. 235

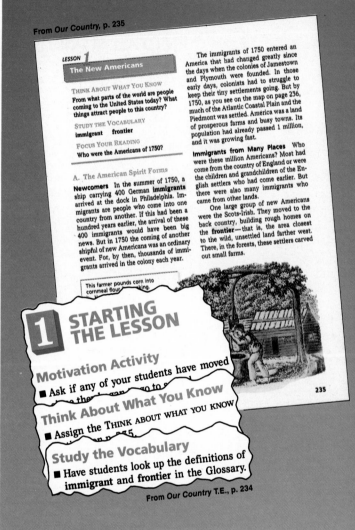

From Our Country T.E., p. 234

for more READING STRATEGIES look for

- **Visuals with caption questions**
- **Skillbuilder**

  and in the Teacher-to-Teacher Edition

- **Thinking Critically**
- **Read and Think**

We bring it all together

Sharpen Thinking Skills —

with

Graphic Organizers

Help ALL students visualize their thinking

Dr. James F. Baumann

Date: Election Day, 2020
Setting: Voting booths across America

The children currently sitting in your class are casting their votes, making decisions that will to a large extent shape American life in the upcoming years. Are they ready? Can they analyze the issues? Can they make accurate observations about the candidates, and summarize the stance of each? Do they know how to compare the platforms? Can they infer the probable effects of each plank?

As teachers of social studies, we can do a great deal to increase the likelihood that the answer to each of these questions is a resounding Yes, for social studies is the ideal arena for building the thinking skills that effective citizens need.

Getting the Big Picture

How do we teach youngsters to think clearly? A crucial step is to show them how to organize information, a prerequisite to making considered decisions. An easy way for children to get the hang of organizing ideas is to teach them to use graphic organizers. Graphic whats? Relax — they're really old friends: time lines, tables, and flowcharts are a few. *Graphic organizers* are simply visual displays that show relationships among ideas, conveying "the big picture." In addition, they allow users to see their thoughts unfolding in patterns as they construct them. Youngsters who learn to use graphic organizers become more aware of their own thinking processes, more metacognitive.

A Variety of Visuals

Specific types of graphic organizers facilitate particular kinds of thinking. For instance, wheels with spokes, as shown in the diagram that follows, help children make observations about things. In this case, on the spokes of each wheel students add observations about the colony indicated in the middle of the wheel.

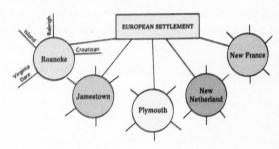

Branch diagrams assist children in selecting important ideas and analyzing the relationships among them. The graphic organizer shown below, for example, helps students process information about colonial life in the South.

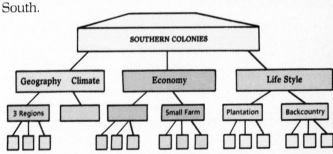

Geometric shapes connected with arrows work well for summarizing cause-and-effect relationships, while numbered boxes help youngsters sequence events. The diagram below combines both of these devices. An alternative graphic organizer for placing events in sequential order is the time line.

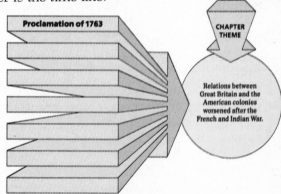

Active Learning, Enjoyable Teaching

As you can see, graphic organizers actively engage learners; children have to process information to complete them. Most youngsters enjoy fitting ideas into "pictures." Further, the use of graphic devices is a real plus for youngsters with language difficulties because they call into play nonverbal, visual faculties.

Graphic organizers offer you plusses, too. As you circulate among children working with them, you can acquire insight about each child's thinking process and offer assistance as needed. What's more, these learning devices can stimulate discussion, enhance motivation, and increase interest in social studies, making the subject even more fun to teach.

Dr. James F. Baumann is an authority on instructional design options, including teaching techniques that use graphic organizers to help students assume greater responsibility for their learning. Professor and Head of the Department of Reading Education, College of Education, The University of Georgia, Athens, Georgia, Dr. Baumann is the reading-language arts series consultant for PEOPLE IN TIME AND PLACE.

PEOPLE IN TIME AND PLACE
helps to sharpen thinking skills.

- **Graphic organizers** in the chapter review section of the student text, on review masters, and in the optional activities section of the teacher edition help students visualize their thinking

- **Lesson review questions** engage students in recalling, analyzing, inferring, synthesizing, evaluating, and hypothesizing

- **Thinking skills check** questions at the end of the lesson provide opportunities for practicing thinking skills

- **Thinking Critically** questions at the end of the chapter activate higher-level thinking

- **Understanding Source Material** questions engage students in thinking critically about print and nonprint sources of information

- **Skillbuilders** motivate students to learn, practice, and apply thinking skills

- **Thinking About Literature** questions in the teacher edition help students articulate the social studies-literature connection by having students relate literary excerpts to social studies content

- **Citizenship and American Values: You Decide** features enables students to evaluate alternatives, weigh evidence, and make decisions

- **Five Themes of Geography** questions in the teacher edition help students draw conclusions about the world around them

- **Highly appealing graphics with caption questions** in the student text and **Visual Thinking Skills** questions in the teacher edition get students to analyze visuals

Thinking Skills

are sharpened when students use graphic organizers to help visualize their thinking.

From Our Country, p. 269

SUMMARIZING THE CHAPTER

On a separate sheet of paper, draw the graphic organizer shown here. Copy the information from this graphic organizer to the one you have drawn. Fill in the blank boxes with important events from the chapter that support the chapter theme. Put the events in the correct sequence. The first box has been filled in for you. Be prepared to explain why you chose the events you did.

Proclamation of 1763

CHAPTER THEME

Relations between Great Britain and the American colonies worsened after the French and Indian War.

Graphic Organizer

To help the students recognize the different community workers whose help they depend on every day, draw the graphic organizer on the chalkboard. Have the students name as many community workers as they can. Add their responses to the board.

From Living in Communities T.E., p. 105

for more THINKING SKILLS look for
- **Thinking skills checks**
- **Citizenship and American Values: You Decide**

  and in the Teacher-to-Teacher Edition
- **Thinking Critically**
- **Visual Thinking Skill**

PEOPLE
in Time and Place

We bring it all together

Writing to Learn
Social Studies

A conversation with **Dr. Marian Davies Toth,** whose research on Writing to Learn and tireless efforts to bring improved writing instruction across the curriculum to **ALL** students have earned her national recognition as an educational leader and writing consultant.

> " Writing is a powerful tool for learning. . . . The social studies classroom provides a perfect time and place for exploring our world through an abundance of writing opportunities. "
> — Marian Davies Toth

Q: Traditionally we think of writing instruction as an English teacher's responsibility. What is the connection between writing and social studies?

A: Rather than teach writing, I suggest that social studies teachers **use** writing. Writing is a powerful tool for learning. It motivates thinking. The social studies classroom provides a perfect time and place for exploring our world through an abundance of writing opportunities. If writing is used in a nonthreatening way, the teacher and the students discover a dynamic strategy for personalizing learning and improving comprehension.

Q: Hasn't writing always been in the social studies curriculum?

A: True, we have always had "writing to show." Students read, memorize facts, and take a test to show their rote learning. There is a place for this kind of writing, but it is not the same as writing to learn. Here is the difference: Writing to learn is exploratory writing that helps students create their own "webs of learning."

Q: How does writing to learn work?

A: Let's look at it this way. Students gain fluency from writing frequently. Writing in social studies allows them to think abstractly. Writing forms a link between new material and known information. Compared to speaking, writing is a slow, deliberate process. As students write words and capture thoughts, they sustain their thinking over a period of time. The slower pace frees the mind to explore, relate, and connect. With writing, students shape their perceptions. This is why we see writing as a unique learning strategy.

Q: How may teachers best introduce writing to learn?

A: Writing to learn is an informal writing activity. A quick, effective way to make writing informal is to ask for students' opinions. Following a reading, give students opportunities to make choices and to write rapid answers to open-ended questions like these:

- What stood out for you?
- What surprised or impressed you?
- What did you learn that you did not know before?
- What would you have done if you had been in charge?
- What other decisions were possible?
- Does this event remind you of anything similar today?
- How will this information affect your own life?
- Why did these people make the decision they chose?

Here are some small exploratory writing activities from Dr. Marian Davies Toth that focus upon the Christopher Columbus story.

Free Write

Students write as fast as they can without worrying about spelling, punctuation, or grammar. The idea is to get words down quickly and make thinking visible. Students may use a Free Write as they respond to open-ended questions or a teacher-directed inquiry.

> *Wow! Christopher Columbus was such a brave man! Imagine sailing all alone to places uncharted in*

Question Generation

Students create their own questions and use those questions in a discussion with a partner or in a whole class discussion.

> ① *Why didn't Columbus take more ships and more supplies with him?*
>
> ② *I would like to know why Christopher Columbus was not afraid of falling off the end of the world as he knew it?*

The Journal Log

The journal log is a blank notebook or a separate section of a three-ring binder. It is a place for students to record their own ideas regarding the content in a social studies class. It takes from three to

Q: How does a writing activity like this help students learn social studies?

A: What I have observed is that students tend to become more independent learners. The questions encourage students to explore alternative interpretations of the historical story. Students see history in a different way — no longer simply as an account of what happened. When we imagine what might have happened if a different decision had been made, a subject has more relevance. We want students to have choices and freedom to express their own ideas in a non-intimidating environment. Another important consideration is this: We want to encourage students to contribute to their own learning.

Q: It's possible students will become more sensitive decision makers, too, don't you think?

A: Yes, that is true. Writing in itself is a decision-making activity when we allow students to choose topics and to decide what to include and what to exclude in the development of those topics.

Q: How do you grade "writing to learns"?

A: Usually teachers do not grade the writing to learns. They see this informal writing as an idea-generating activity. Writing to learn enhances personal learning and serves as a cognitive rehearsal for discussion. Also, it may become a beginning exploration for more demanding writing projects.

Q: What would you say are some of the most important benefits of writing to learn as a teaching strategy?

A: Research from cognitive psychology has taught us that all writing, even unfinished writing makes learning an active experience. Writing is thinking. Writing is learning. Writing is growing. I hope all social studies teachers will use it as a teaching strategy.

---

seven minutes of class time each day. Students write their spontaneous responses to a lesson, a lecture, or a class activity.

> *Today our class produced a Christopher Columbus play for the third grade. It was wonderful! I liked the sounds of the waves splashing and the realistic*

The "I Was There" Diary

Students imagine themselves to be a part of an historical event and record what happened by using the voice of a participant. In this way, students are better able to personalize history.

> *There I was standing on the hill with a wild turkey in one hand and a bow in the other when all of a sudden three ships*

Writing

helps personalize learning about people in time and place for ALL students.

From *Living in Families*, p. 124

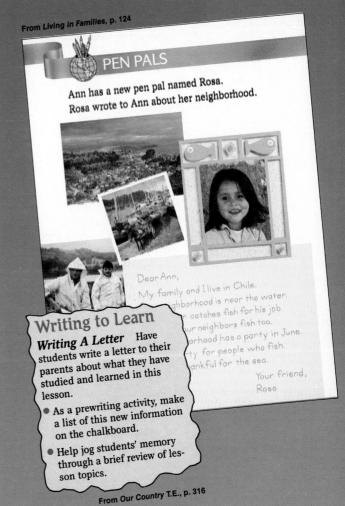

PEN PALS

Ann has a new pen pal named Rosa.
Rosa wrote to Ann about her neighborhood.

Dear Ann,
My family and I live in Chile.
...ghborhood is near the water.
...catches fish for his job.
...ur neighbors fish too.
...rhood has a party in June.
...ty for people who fish.
...nkful for the sea.

Your friend,
Rosa

Writing to Learn

Writing A Letter Have students write a letter to their parents about what they have studied and learned in this lesson.

● As a prewriting activity, make a list of this new information on the chalkboard.

● Help jog students' memory through a brief review of lesson topics.

From *Our Country* T.E., p. 316

for more WRITING look for

● **Writing skills checks**
● **Skillbuilder**

and in the Teacher-to-Teacher Edition

● **Curriculum Connection**
● **Multidisciplinary Activity**

PE●PLE
in Time and Place

We bring it all together

Social Studies and LITERATURE: Powerful Partners

Incorporating appropriate selections of top-quality literature right into the social studies text can shed light on content and motivate students to a greater understanding and appreciation of literature.

Dr. Ben Smith, Dr. Jesse Palmer, and Dr. John C. Davis

As Carlos reached the end of the selection about New Amsterdam's leader, he raised his voice for emphasis.

> *'This New World is a mess!' Peter cried in distress. 'These animals need gates and fences. Take these birds to a cage!' Peter shouted in rage. 'Oh, good Dutchmen, let's come to our senses.'*

Lively discussion followed. "Wow, I thought only *our* world was a mess," said Angela.

"Even three hundred years ago there was too much traffic — but too many animals instead of cars!" Carlos exclaimed. "No wonder they needed laws then, too!"

Through a selection from Arnold Lobel's *On the Day Peter Stuyvesant Sailed into Town,* these children have entered life in New Amsterdam, mid-1600s. The adjacent lively writing in their social studies textbook provides historical background and details, such as how Stuyvesant's bossiness led to the creation of the town's first government.

Literature Supports History as a Well-Told Story

Excerpts from top-quality literature *about* historical periods, such as Lobel's book, help students to identify with the emotions of others, to step into the shoes of people in time and place. Likewise, when literary excerpts *of* historical periods — such as quotes from **diaries** of pioneer women, **speeches** like Patrick Henry's, **letters** from Abagail Adams — are woven right into the text, it's as if people who actually lived in the past have stepped into your classroom to give students eyewitness views of events.

Literature Illuminates the Human Dimension of Social Studies

Relevant excerpts and selections, representing a wide range of literary genres and periods, encourage students to appreciate the diversity of humankind — the ordinary and the extraordinary, children and adults, representing many different cultures. Tales from the *Arabian Nights* and *The Anansi Tales,* for example, help provide multicultural perspectives. Literary works like *The Little Prince* provide students with an appreciation for the richness of geographic diversity.

Other Ways Social Studies and Literature Work Together

Just as literature stimulates interest in social studies content, prior knowledge of social studies content — of people, time, and place — increases students' understanding and appreciation of historical fiction, poetry, drama, myths, legends, fables, biography, and so on. For example, knowing about the history and geography of colonial New Amsterdam before reading *On the Day Peter Stuyvesant Sailed into Town* enabled the children to take greater delight, to be more actively engaged in reading and understanding the story.

Relating these two subjects can also encourage students to think critically. For instance, students will make comparisons, distinguish fact from fiction, and draw conclusions when they contrast an excerpt of a literary work — like Longfellow's "Paul Revere's Ride" — with historical accounts from their textbook.

In these and other ways, literary selections work for all grade levels, generating high interest in the fascinating world of people in time and place through the partnership of social studies and literature.

Dr. Ben A. Smith is Assistant Professor of Social Studies Education at Kansas State University, Manhattan, Kansas. Dr. John C. Davis is Professor of Elementary Education, University of Southern Mississippi, Hattiesburg, Mississippi. Dr. Jesse Palmer is Assistant Professor of Curriculum and Instruction, University of Southern Mississippi, Hattiesburg, Mississippi. Drs. Smith, Davis, and Palmer, all former classroom teachers, have collaborated on journal articles about the social studies-children's literature connection. They serve as the literature consultants for PEOPLE IN TIME AND PLACE.

PEOPLE IN TIME AND PLACE incorporates classic and contemporary literature to shed light on social studies content.

- **Short excerpts** from diaries, essays, poems, speeches, and other literary works, woven right into the text, provide quotes by and about historical people, places, and events

- **Read-Alouds** in Grades 1 and 2 and **Literature Selections** in Grades 3 through 7 provide longer literary excerpts that spark students' interest in learning about social studies and literature

- **Thinking About Literature** questions in the teacher edition help students articulate the social studies-literature connection by involving students in relating literary excerpts to social studies content

- **Annotated Bibliographies** in the teacher edition provide convenient references to literature for students and teachers

- **Multidisciplinary Activity** features and **Curriculum Connection** activities in the teacher edition provide a wide variety of ideas for involving students in extending the social studies-literature connection

Literature
illuminates the story of people in time and place for ALL students.

From World Cultures, p. 281

LITERATURE SELECTION

FROM: **The Anansi Tales**

By: Peggy Appiah
Setting: African Forest

Anansi, the spider, sometimes called Kwaku (Uncle) Anansi, is the trickster hero of the Ashanti peoples of Africa. His Adventures were passed down orally in the form of folktales.

In the story "How Wisdom Was Spread Throughout the World," Anansi, sometimes spelled Ananse, was the only wise creature in the world. Being greedy, he wished to keep all this wisdom to himself. He ...

Ananse's son, watching from behind a tree, advised his father to tie the pot to his back to free his hands.

Ananse was furious. Here his small son was teaching him a lesson — a lesson which he realized was only too true. Shaking with anger and exhaustion he lifted the pot, meaning to take it off and chastise (scold) his son. His hands were slippery with sweat and the great pot was heavy. It slipped through his fingers and crashed to the ground.

The pot burst open and its contents ... far and wide. There was ... wind swept ...

LITERATURE Read-Aloud

FROM **Stone Soup**
BY MARCIA BROWN

Three hungry soldiers went to a poor village. The people would not share their food. The soldiers decided to make stone soup. They started with a pot and some water.

"And now, if you please, three round, smooth stones."

Those were easy enough to find. The peasants' eyes grew round as they watched

From Living in Families, p. 130

for more LITERATURE look for
- Literature excerpts woven into the text

and in the Teacher-to-Teacher Edition

- Thinking About Literature
- Annotated Bibliography
- Curriculum Connection

PE⊕PLE
in Time and Place

We bring it all together

Cooperative Learning & Social Studies: A Natural Combination

Here's how you can begin putting it to work in your social studies classroom

Research, as well as classroom experience, shows that cooperative learning is right for the job!

What is cooperative learning?

Cooperative learning is a technique through which small groups of two to six students of different levels of ability work together to learn or to review concepts. As a teaching technique, cooperative learning is uniquely effective when the learning tasks are open-ended and require problem solving and decision making. But if you've never used cooperative learning, beginning with simpler, more specific assignments gives you and your students a chance to grow in comfort level, familiarity, and skill.

How might you lay the foundation for a simple first-time cooperative learning lesson?

First, you might present a social studies lesson, using teacher-directed instruction. Next, you would lead a discussion of a social skill (perhaps the importance of one person talking at a time), letting students know that practicing this skill will be one of the objectives of the cooperative learning activity. With the social skill objective in place, you would then set the academic objective (perhaps that each group will demonstrate understanding of the content by answering one or more lesson review questions). Although you introduce the social skill and academic objectives separately, the groups work on both simultaneously.

How does the group work get started?

Once this foundation for the cooperative learning activity is completed, students join teacher– or student–selected groups, of two to six students. Having different levels of ability in each group facilitates learning and positive interdependence. Once the groups are selected, each group member is assigned an individual objective to help the group achieve its goal. That objective may relate to a specific part of the group's learning task (each member will be assigned a different question and share with the group his or her answer to that question),

or it may relate to the entire task (each group member will answer and share his or her answers to all the group's questions). In either case, all the members of a group participate to help their group achieve both its individual and group objectives.

You might then write on the chalkboard the heading "Remember to talk about" key vocabulary and list under it words, names, places and events to help guide the cooperative learning groups' work. No special furniture is needed, but group members should be able to see their work and hear each other when they talk quietly.

What is your role while the groups are working cooperatively?

As each group works together, you should circulate among the groups, recognizing when the social objective is being met (only one person is talking at a time) and facilitating the progress of a group toward mastery of the academic objective (demonstrate understanding of the content by answering the review questions). When a group needs your help, it can signal you by using two cups — one blue and one red — that have been taped together, bottom to bottom. When the blue cup is up, the group is proceeding independently; when the red cup is up, your help is needed.

What happens when the group work is completed?

Cooperative learning group work usually culminates in class discussion; each group shares its work and tells how well it used the social skill that was selected before the group work began. Each student usually demonstrates his or her individual learning as well. The vehicle might be a quiz in which each student answers one or more review questions. A bonus (perhaps having no written homework) given to the groups in which every member reaches a preset score (perhaps 80%) on the quiz reinforces positive interdependence.

What are the benefits of cooperative learning in the social studies classroom?

While cooperative learning is now enthusiastically used in all areas of the curriculum, it's a natural in social studies, where working interdependently teaches many social participation skills necessary for full and informed citizenship. Cooperative learning further supports citizenship by increasing retention of social studies information, promoting critical thinking, and increasing the self-esteem of ALL students.

Once you and your students gain facility in using cooperative learning, you will find that it lends itself to cross-curriculum activities, such as making a diorama (art) or reenacting a play (language arts). Cooperative learning also facilitates multidisciplinary activities, where the learning groups each explore a different content area tie-in simultaneously. Using cooperative learning in conjunction with cross-curriculum or multidisciplinary activities helps increase student motivation, while maximizing teaching time spent on social studies.

PEOPLE IN TIME AND PLACE puts cooperative learning to work in your classroom.

• **Cooperative Learning** activities enable all students to practice social participation skills, think critically, experience positive interdependence, and grow in self-esteem

• A wide variety of **How To** projects and activities in the teacher edition allow you to vary your teaching approaches while sparking student motivation and increasing student retention

• **Multidisciplinary Activity** features in the teacher edition help you maximize teaching time spent on social studies through a rich menu of cooperative learning options that actively engage students in making connections between social studies and other curriculum areas

Cooperative Learning

increases interpersonal skills and self-esteem when ALL students work together to share discoveries.

From *Comparing Communities*, p. 317

UNIT **4** REVIEW

COOPERATIVE LEARNING

In this unit you learned about the past and present in several cities. In this activity you will work with four other classmates to make an exciting board game about the past and present in your own community. The object of the game will be to reach the square marked FUTURE by answering questions correctly.

REMEMBER TO:
• Give your ideas.
• Listen to other's ideas.
• Plan your work with the group.
• Present your project.
• Discuss how your group worked.

PROJECT

• With your group, choose a name for the board game.
• Two people should make question-and-answer cards about the past and present in your community. One side of an index card should have a question. The other side should have an answer. Below the answer, write *1, 2,* or *3* for the number of moves around the game board a correct answer is worth.
• Two people should make a game board of heavy posterboard or cardboard with colored squares drawn around the board. They should label the squares with names of special places in your community.
• One person should make game pieces that can be moved along the game board.

PRESENTATION AND REVIEW

• One person will explain your game.

Cooperative Learning

Plan a Community Divide the class into groups. Tell each group to pretend that they are going to form a new community. Ask them to decide the type of community they want and the kinds of things they will have in their community. Have each group report its decisions to the class.

From *Living in Communities* T.E., p. 51

for more COOPERATIVE LEARNING look for

• **Curriculum tie-ins**

and in the Teacher-to-Teacher Edition

• **Curriculum Connection**
• **How To**
• **Multidisciplinary Activity**

PE PLE
in Time and Place

We bring it all together

LEARNING by DOING:
Activities for Social Studies

For motivation, concept development, variety, and vitality — think social studies activities!

"Look sharp, sailor," says Captain Alex. "Do you see anything? We must be near now!"

"No, sir," answers Sailor Chris. "Not a thing. Maybe we've gone too far. Maybe we should turn back before it's too late."

"Nonsense," responds the captain. "I know we're near."

"Wait, Captain," breaks in First Mate Jesse. "Look over there. Land! Land ho!"

The captain seemed sure, though the sailors may have had their doubts — perhaps a typical situation in fifteenth- or sixteenth-century voyages of exploration. But in this case the explorers are twentieth-century elementary school children taking part in a role-playing activity.

Why are activities now playing such a vital role in social studies education?

For years, educators have acknowledged that social studies is one of the most important and relevant subjects taught in any classroom. Social studies is, after all, the study of people. Yet many of today's students reject the study of social studies as being too boring. What can be done to bring out the human interest in social studies? There is no single answer, of course. But one action that can help is to include a wide range of "hands-on/minds-on" activities in social studies instruction.

Activities provide the motivation and the direct experience essential to the development of concepts.

Compare, for instance, the prospect of memorizing state and country shapes with the prospect of participating in a classroom quiz show. Both teaching vehicles cover the same objective, but which promotes more student interest and understanding?

. . . What about learning latitude and longitude? Compare learning these concepts from a lecture with learning them through an activity that turns the entire classroom into a latitude and longitude game board!

. . . Consider the differences between reading about a historical debate and actively participating in one right in the classroom.

Activities bring vitality and variety to social studies.

Activities can be used to introduce, reinforce, or reteach concepts. They offer exciting alternative approaches and refreshing changes of pace. Activities can accommodate the learning styles of **ALL** students.

Multidisciplinary activities bring subject areas together.

There is no better way to help students see connections between social studies and other subjects they are learning than by doing activities that bring social studies together with math, language arts, science, art, and so forth. At the same time, such activities work toward our ultimate goal — helping students become active and informed citizens.

PEOPLE IN TIME AND PLACE gets students actively involved in "hands-on/minds-on" social studies.

- **Think About What You Know** activities help students connect prior knowledge with new learning

- **Curriculum tie-ins** help students integrate what they learn in social studies with what they learn in other subjects

- **Cooperative Learning** activities foster positive interdependence

- **Putting It All Together** chapter review activities, including graphic organizers, encourage thinking critically

- **Teacher-to-Teacher Edition** activities complement individual teaching and learning styles

  - **Meeting Individual Needs** activities provide alternative ways of helping students learn difficult concepts

  - **Motivation** activities help to tap prior knowledge

  - **Vocabulary** activities help to prepare students for reading

  - **Reteaching the Main Objective** activities offer alternatives for enhancing student understanding

  - **Current Events** activities increase student interest in history-in-the-making

- **Multidisciplinary Activity** features bring basal subjects together, enhancing understanding

- **How To** conduct projects and activities offer teachers easy-to-follow guidelines

- **Optional Activities** involve students in role-playing, writing to learn, working with maps, interviewing, making curriculum connections, and skillbuilding

Activities

bring alive the story of people in time and place with "hands-on/ minds-on" experiences for ALL students.

From *Living in Families*, p. 185

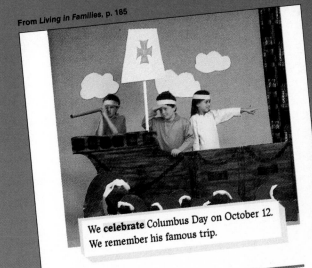

We **celebrate** Columbus Day on October 12. We remember his famous trip.

Lesson 1 ———— Review ————

Role-Playing

- Have the students pretend to be Christopher Columbus and his crew. Prepare a large piece of cardboard for a boat and make a flag.
- Have the students discuss how the crew prepared the ship for the trip. Have them role-play loading the ship.
- Then have the students imagine how it felt to leave the port, to sail on calm seas, to sail on rough seas, to be desperate to find land, and to find land.

From *Living in Families* T.E., p. 184

for more ACTIVITIES look for
- **Curriculum tie-ins**

  and in the Teacher-to-Teacher Edition

- **Meeting Individual Needs**
- **How To**
- **Multidisciplinary Activity**

PE PLE
in Time and Place

We bring it all together

Susan Grassmyer, Gr. 1

Janet Hogan, Gr. 1

Hazel Tseng Hsieh, Gr. 1

Charleen Kaaen, Gr. 1

Margaret Ricciardi, Gr. 1

Susan Barnes, Gr. 2

Gail Finger, Gr. 6/7

Linda Lucas, Gr. 6/7

Carol Gemmell, Gr. 6/7

Pamela Argo, Gr. 6/7

Eileen Lewis, Gr. 6/7

Teacher Tips for Successful Pacing

Making the most of time spent teaching social studies

Teacher-to-Teacher Edition Authors

PEOPLE IN TIME AND PLACE *proudly presents the teachers from across our nation who have been instrumental in bringing together everything you need to teach social studies to ALL students.*

We acknowledge the enthusiasm, conviction, and commitment they have displayed while participating in every stage of the development of this program, from critiquing every page of student text to authoring the Teacher-to-Teacher Edition.

We asked our Teacher-to-Teacher Edition authors to respond to the perennial question we are asked by elementary teachers: **Given everything that I have to teach, how can I realistically pace social studies instruction?**

We have collected their answers, based on insights gained from years of teaching experience. In summary, their suggestions fall into three categories: Be selective; Be flexible; Be good to yourself. We are pleased to share them.

Be selective.

One recurring recommendation is to be selective about the material that you teach. "A good starting point is your district's curriculum guide. Once you know what must be taught, you can look toward the textbook as one instructional tool at your disposal for meeting local goals and the needs of your students."

As you plan to use the textbook, don't feel that you have to "drag your students through the book, page by page, cover to cover," advises Susan Grassmyer.

Rather, use the textbook as "a resource that offers a smorgasbord of content and teaching ideas," adds Aldona Skrypa.

In deciding **what** to teach from the textbook, **with what emphasis,** and **when,** you may capitalize on timeliness to increase student interest. One way to do this is to "tie into the calendar," coordinating content with holidays, as Joyce Kemp does when she teaches patriotism in conjunction with Presidents' Day, or when she teaches the textbook material about American Indians' lifestyles, around Thanksgiving Day.

Another way to capitalize on timeliness is to use what's happening on the local, national, and international scene as a springboard into the text. Thus, in presidential election years, Marianne Geiger emphasizes chapters dealing with significant presidential elections.

Finally, although **you** are the professional decision maker, consider letting students participate in the content selection process by having them scan the table of contents at the start of the year. Don Smail suggests surveying students to find out what they're most interested in learning and then using that information as you prioritize content.

Susan Colford, Gr. 6/7

Sheila Allen, Gr. 6/7

Edward Graivier, Gr. 6/7

Lisa Johnson, Gr. 6/7

Don Smail, Gr. 6/7

Sharon Shelley, Gr. 6/7

Rhonda Allen, Gr. 2

Joyce Kemp, Gr. 2

Hortense Ward, Gr. 2

Mary Bosser Joyce, Gr. 3

Suzanne Peirsel, Gr. 3

Alfred Velasquez, Gr. 3

Be flexible.

One common thread in the suggestions about flexibility is "Don't feel that you are locked into presenting all social studies content in the same way." "Whatever you do, make sure you have a lot of student involvement," is the other.

Helping students become strategic readers in content-area materials is the key to flexibility for many teachers like Lisa Johnson, who feels that students' ability to read and acquire knowledge independently "opens the potential for a variety of instructional approaches."

One shared-learning alternative approach is cooperative learning. Rather than have the entire class reading the same lesson, let students take "group responsibility" for learning and sharing information, explains Mary Taylor, who believes it is important for students "to play an active role in the teaching/learning process." In this way, too, students who are more successful strategic readers can help those who are less successful.

Other alternative approaches include the use of "hands-on/minds-on" activities. Teachers like Beverley Wong Woo and Aldona Skrypa strongly advocate the use of unit multidisciplinary activities as a "time efficient" way to "tie into other subjects," while giving students an opportunity to use higher level thinking skills, such as synthesizing.

For other reading variations, students can learn the information from selected lessons or chapters by reading "just for pleasure," skimming, scanning, note-taking, or outlining.

Vardreane Elliot, Gr. 3

Beverley Wong Woo, Gr. 3

Aldona Skrypa, Gr. 4

Be good to yourself.

Being "the jack-of-all-trades of the educational field," as Ed Graivier terms it, can make elementary teachers feel insecure about their expertise in social studies and other subject areas. Acknowledging that pressure, as well as the pressure that comes from feeling overwhelmed by the amount of material to be taught in the time allotted, our teacher authors offer this advice: "Be good to yourself."

"Be selective . . . relax and enjoy what you are teaching," says Eileen Lewis. "No one can do everything."

"Use community-parent resources. Invite guest speakers from different ethnic backgrounds. Bring in hands-on materials. Make social studies come alive in your classroom. Let your students enjoy what they are learning and let yourself enjoy teaching it!" Beverley Wong Woo advises.

"Have fun," says Alfred Velasquez. "By keeping track of what worked and what didn't, you'll have a head start on next year."

"Most important of all, teach from the heart," says Susan Grassmyer.

The final word is Marianne Geiger's. After hearing all the recommendations about "not covering the textbook," about "skipping around," about "picking and choosing," Marianne was concerned that first-year teachers might be getting the wrong message as they struggle for the first time with an entire primary curriculum. Here's her be-good-to-yourself advice: "Don't worry. You can save your social studies creativity for the second year of teaching. For the first year, you can trust Silver Burdett & Ginn. You can feel good about 'plowing ahead' in the student text and teacher edition."

Gloria Ebbe, Gr. 4

Carolyn Hopp, Gr. 4

Joseph McGrath, Gr. 6/7

Mary Taylor, Gr. 5

Mary Jo Paniello, Gr. 5

Marianne Geiger, Gr. 5

Joan Atkinson, Gr. 5

Margaret Love, Gr. 4

Teacher-to-Teacher Edition

1 STARTING THE LESSON

■ Identifies the main (★ starred) objective and other objectives

(Optional activities for ★ Reteaching the Main Objective are found at the end of the lesson.)

■ Provides a variety of before-reading activities that involves ALL students in

• activating prior knowledge
• studying vocabulary
• establishing a reading purpose

LESSON 3   PAGES 310–316

The New Government Begins

Objectives

★1. **Analyze** the problems the new government faced and how it coped with them.

2. **Identify** the following people and places: *John Adams, Abigail Adams, Washington, D.C.,* and *New York City.*

1 STARTING THE LESSON

Motivation Activity
■ Before students learn about the specifics of our Bill of Rights, have them imagine what their life would be like without it.
■ Ask them to imagine gathering to talk to friends outside the school, but being in danger of being fined.
■ Question students as to whether they have ever complained about homework or a school policy. Tell them that without the Bill of Rights they might be arrested for such comments.

Think About What You Know
■ Assign the THINK ABOUT WHAT YOU KNOW activity on p. 310.
■ George Bush; answers should include the national debt, concerns over the environment, drugs, or world peace.

Study the Vocabulary
■ Have students create their own word-search puzzle from the new vocabulary terms on this page. Definitions or clues should be given to help find the words in the puzzle.
■ Then have students exchange papers and solve each other's puzzles.

310

LESSON 3

The New Government

THINK ABOUT WHAT YOU KNOW
Who is the President of the United States? What are some problems that the President is trying to solve today?

STUDY THE VOCABULARY
inauguration   Cabinet
Bill of Rights   political party

FOCUS YOUR READING
How did the new government begin its work?

A. The Great Experiment Begins

On receiving the news of his election to the Presidency, George Washington climbed into his coach and left for New York City, the temporary capital of the United States, where his **inauguration** would be held. An inauguration is a ceremony to put someone into a government office. With him rode the hopes of the American people. As Washington's coach moved from one town to the next, crowds cheered their new President.

Finally on April 30, 1789, George Washington stood before thousands of fellow citizens in New York City. Placing his hand on a Bible, he promised to "preserve, protect, and defend the Constitution of the United States."

Soon after, Congress met and quickly acted to keep a promise. James Madison of Virginia wrote a number of amendments to the Constitution to protect the rights of the people. In 1791, ten of these amendments were ratified and added to the Constitution. They are known as the **Bill of Rights**. These rights were much the same as those listed in the different state constitutions.

George Washington is being rowed across New York Bay to prepare for his inauguration in New York City. Ships welcome him with a roar of cannons.
▶ What are the sailors on the left doing?

National Gallery of Art, Washington, D.C. Gift of Edgar William and Bernice Chrysler Garbisch

Making Comparisons

● Students may want to look in an encyclopedia to find out about how the President of the United States is guarded today. During George Washington's term, he took a three-month trip to visit the South. Very few people accompanied him, and he slept in inns along the way.
● Have students compare and contrast the presidency today to the presidency during Washington's time.
● Write the following headings on the chalkboard: *Alike* and *Different.* In a vertical column, write *Today* and *Yesterday.*
● Have students work together to complete the chart.

Optional Activities

Optional Activities

Here you will find an exciting menu of optional activities for all lessons, including:

• **Graphic Organizers**
• **For Your Information**
• **Skillbuilder Review**
• **Cooperative Learning**

A Teacher Edition Written *for* Teachers *by* Teachers

Uniquely *practical* and *professional,* built on years of classroom experience. Everything you need to teach social studies easily and effectively, right at your fingertips . . . starting with a 3-step basic lesson plan and lesson-extending optional activities.

WASHINGTON'S FIRST CABINET

Office	Official	Duties
Secretary of State	Thomas Jefferson	To conduct the relations of the United States with other nations
Secretary of the Treasury	Alexander Hamilton	To handle the government's finances
Secretary of War	Henry Knox	To take charge of all military matters
Attorney General	Edmund Randolph	To act as chief legal adviser to the executive branch
Postmaster General	Samuel Osgood	To run the post office and mail service

The office of Postmaster General did not become a Cabinet department until 1829.

► Which cabinet position do you think is the most important one?

The Bill of Rights protects such important personal freedoms as freedom of speech, freedom of worship, and freedom of the press.

Congress also created several departments to help the President. The State Department deals with foreign countries. The Treasury Department collects taxes, pays bills, and takes care of the government's money. The War Department was in charge of the country's defense.

The head of each department was called a *secretary.* President Washington often called upon these secretaries for advice. When the President met with his advisers, the group was called the **Cabinet.**

B. Disagreements Lead to Political Parties

President Washington chose Thomas Jefferson to head the State Department. He chose Alexander Hamilton to be the first secretary of the treasury. Jefferson and Hamilton were two of the ablest people ever to serve in government. But they disagreed on almost everything. At times, President Washington felt as though he were driving a coach with horses pulling in opposite directions.

Hamilton wanted to encourage manufacturing to grow. He hoped the United States would soon have many large cities. He also favored an even stronger central government than the one that the new Constitution created.

Jefferson agreed that the country needed some manufacturing and trade. However, Jefferson did not want to see large cities grow. He wanted the United States to remain a nation of small farmers. As for the government itself, Jefferson wanted to keep it as small as possible.

The many disagreements between Hamilton and Jefferson led to the birth of **political parties.** A political party is a group of people who hold certain beliefs about how the government should be run and what it should do. These people join together to elect people who share their beliefs. In the 1790s, those Americans who favored Hamilton and his ideas were called *Federalists.* Supporters of Thomas Jefferson called themselves *Democratic-Republicans.*

311

---

② DEVELOPING THE LESSON

Read and Think

Sections A and B

In order for students to comprehend the beginning of the Bill of Rights and the beginning of political parties, ask these questions:

1. **What types of freedoms are protected in the Bill of Rights?**
   (Freedom of speech, freedom of worship, and freedom of the press *pp. 310-311*)

2. **What were some of the beliefs held by Jefferson and Hamilton?**
   (Hamilton wanted to encourage manufacturing, the growth of large cities, and a strong central government; Jefferson did not want to see the growth of large cities, and favored small government and a nation of small farmers. *p. 311*)

Thinking Critically **How, do you think, would our lives be different without the freedom of speech?** (Analyze)
(Answers may include that we would have to be careful about what we said, we could be punished for saying certain things, and we would feel less free. *p. 311*)

— Answers to Caption Questions —
p. 310 ► Saluting or waving
p. 311 ► Answers should reflect independent thinking.

Identifying Areas of Responsibility
● Assist students in remembering the responsibilities of each of the departments created to help the President of the United States.
● Create a *Concentration*-style game on index cards, writing the name of each of the departments on one set of cards, and their responsibilities on another set.
● Number the cards on the back and tape them, in random order, to the chalkboard, number-side up.
● As students call two numbers, turn over the corresponding cards, looking for a match. Return any unmatched guesses to their original position.

Curriculum Connection
Art Have students make a bulletin-board display of the President's Cabinet.
● Have students find and display the names of the departments in the Cabinet today. (State, Treasury, Justice, Defense, Interior, Agriculture, Commerce, Labor, Education, Health and Human Services, Housing and Urban Development, Transportation, and Energy departments.)
● Have students find and identify newspaper pictures of each cabinet member.
● Then have them design pictures to illustrate each cabinet member's job, or symbols for each department.

311

Optional Activities

---

② DEVELOPING THE LESSON

■ **Read and Think** questions, keyed to textbook sections, aid student comprehension through

• reading

• discussing

• thinking critically

■ Other lesson development features (shown on page 29) involve **ALL** students in

• reading and thinking about literature

• understanding difficult concepts by meeting their individual needs

• sharpening visual thinking skills

• building geography literacy

• **Writing to Learn**

• **Current Events**

• **Curriculum Connection**

• **Reteaching Main Objective**

...and more

Optional Activities

3 **CLOSING THE LESSON**

- ■ Provides answers to textbook questions to help you check students' comprehension

  - • Review questions
    (Annotations on the student text page indicates the thinking skill called for: recall, analyze, infer, synthesize, evaluate, hypothesize)

  - • Skills check questions

  - • Lesson focus question

- ■ Suggestions for additional practice help meet the needs of **ALL** students

  - • Lesson review master

  - • Workbook

---

3 **CLOSING THE LESSON**

Lesson 3 Review

Answers to Think and Write
A. The Bill of Rights, ratified in 1791, is a set of ten amendments to our Constitution designed to protect the rights of the people.
B. Many disagreements between Jefferson and Hamilton led to the birth of political parties. Those who favored Hamilton's views became Federalists, and supporters of Jefferson were called Democratic-Republicans.
C. The new government faced the problems of debt from the war, the Whiskey Rebellion (resulting from farmers' anger about taxes), and trouble with British seizure of American ships.
D. A decision John Adams faced was whether or not to avoid war with Britain because our country was not ready.
E. Maryland and Virginia each gave up some land for the District of Columbia.

Answer to Skills Check
Answers should reflect independent thinking.

Focus Your Reading
Ask the lesson focus question found at the beginning of the lesson: **How did the new government begin its work?**
(Congress met soon after Washington's inauguration. It ratified the Bill of Rights and created the State, War, and Treasury Departments to help the President. The new government had to deal with debt and angry farmers in the Whiskey Rebellion. There was trouble with British seizure of United States ships, but Washington and Adams avoided war.)

Additional Practice
You may wish to assign the ancillary materials listed below.
Understanding the Lesson p. 92
Workbook p. 83

┌─────────────────────────────────────┐
│ **Answers to Caption Questions** │
│ **p. 316** ▶ No room had been completely fin- │
│ ished, there was no firewood, the main │
│ stairway was unfinished, and there was no │
│ water. │
└─────────────────────────────────────┘

316

James Hoban won $500 in a design contest for a plan for the President's house. His plan was used in building the White House.
▶ Name some new-house problems Mrs. Adams had.

Abigail Adams

The White House The President's Palace, later called the White House, was the first building ready for use. President Adams and his family were the first to live in it. When the Adamses arrived, not a single room had been completely finished. The plaster walls were still damp. There were fireplaces in each room to take the chill off the house, but no arrangement had been made to supply the house with firewood. The main stairway to the second floor was not finished. The President's wife, Abigail Adams, even used one of the unfinished rooms for hanging the family wash to dry. Servants carried water from a distance of five city blocks.

Still, Abigail Adams had a sense of history. She knew how far the young republic had already come. Like the new nation itself, the President's Palace was unfinished. Its rough edges would need smoothing out. In time the new house, like the new nation, would become great. "This House is built for ages to come," Abigail Adams wrote to her sister. And so it was.

LESSON 3 REVIEW

THINK AND WRITE
A. What is the Bill of Rights? (Recall)
B. How did political parties begin in the United States? (Synthesize)
C. What were some problems that the new government faced? (Analyze)
D. What was one major decision that John Adams made as President? (Infer)
E. How was the District of Columbia created? (Recall)

316

SKILLS CHECK
WRITING SKILL
Read the section on the Bill of Rights on pages 310–311. Select one of the rights listed. Write a paragraph telling why you think that right is important.

Optional Activities
Review Master, p. 92

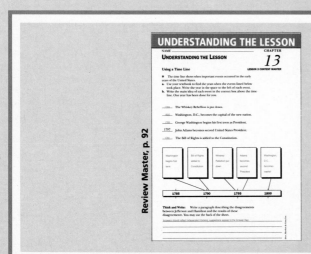

Writing to Learn
Writing A Letter Have students write a letter to their parents about what they have studied and learned in this lesson.
● As a prewriting activity, make a list of this new information on the chalkboard.
● Help jog students' memory through a brief review of lesson topics.

Optional Activities

Here you will find:

- • Reduced lesson review master

Developing the Lesson Features

involve ALL students in...

reading and thinking about literature

 Thinking About Literature

Use the information below to help students better understand the literature selection found on p. 266.

Selection Summary

The British soldiers were marching to Lexington and Concord to destroy the minutemen's supplies and to capture Sam Adams and John Hancock. These two leaders of the Sons of Liberty were troublemakers for the British. Paul Revere and William Dawes galloped on horseback, ahead of the British, warning the colonist that "The British are coming!"

Guided Reading

1. Where and when did "Paul Revere's Ride" take place?
   (Massachusetts, 1775)

2. What signal was Revere expecting?
   (Two lights in the church belfry)

3. What, do you think, was the author's attitude toward Paul Revere?
   (Answers may include that he was a hero.)

Literature-Social Studies Connection

1. From what you have learned in this lesson, why, do you think, did Henry Longfellow write that "the fate of a nation was riding that night"?
   (Answers may include that if the colonists had not been warned, General Gage's plan to destroy their supplies might have been successful, and the revolution might not have happened.)

VISUAL THINKING SKILL

Using a Photograph

■ Tell students that the four men shown on p. 298 were important delegates to the Constitutional Convention.

■ Ask students to decide which of the four they would like to interview the most. Students should then write five questions they would most like to ask that person.

sharpening visual thinking skills

GEOGRAPHY THEMES

 Location

■ Direct students' attention to the map on p. 296 and have them work in pairs to do the following activity. Have one student in each pair name a territory, state, or body of water shown on the map. The other student should then orally describe its relative location. For example, if the first student names Virginia, that student's partner should respond: "north of North Carolina, south of Maryland, west of the Atlantic Ocean, and east of the Ohio River." Students should alternate between naming and describing.

building geography literacy

understanding difficult concepts by meeting their individual needs

Meeting Individual Needs

Concept: Understanding a Love of Freedom

It may be hard for students to comprehend why and how someone could feel strongly enough about freedom to risk their lives. Have students do the following activities to aid in this understanding.

◆ **EASY** Tell students to pretend they have the opportunity to have a "free day" at school to do whatever they wish, within reason.

Ask them to list what things they might be willing to give up in exchange for this freedom. Then ask, What if you were told that you could not move to where you wanted or you had to feed soldiers in your home?

Relate this to colonists who were willing to give up their lives to have the freedom we now enjoy.

Discuss the concept of sacrifice. Together, list those things (discussed in the lesson) the British did to anger the colonists enough to make them want to sacrifice their lives for freedom.

◀▶ **AVERAGE** Write two to three sentences from Patrick Henry's famous speech. These may include: "Is life so dear, or peace so sweet, as to be purchased at the price of chains and slavery?" and "I know not what course others may take; but as for me, give me liberty, or give me death!"

Have students rewrite these sentences in their own words, and discuss them aloud. Give gold "freedom stars" for every word out of his speech that students look up in the dictionary.

◀▮▶ **CHALLENGING** Have students do some "think like a Patriot" exercises and write their own speech to the Virginia House of Burgesses. What stirring remarks would they make to inspire their listeners to take up arms?

Multidisciplinary Activity

A Trip Across America

From Sea to Shining Sea!
Planning an imaginary cross-country trip will give students a good chance to "see" the United States. Have students start any place they wish on the east or the west coast and chart a journey to any place on the opposite coast. Ask students what kinds of geographical features they might come across, such as mountains, mesas, plains, valleys, rivers, and deltas.

SOCIAL STUDIES

Geography Have students trace a map of the United States that shows state boundaries and major geographic features.

■ Then have students draw at least one possible route across the entire country. They may also wish to hypothesize about which route might be easiest to travel, and which might be the most difficult.

History When students have finished plotting their journeys across the country, direct them to the stories of other Americans who made the same journeys.

■ Students could research the Lewis and Clark expedition, the Santa Fe Trail, the Oregon Trail, the trails blazed by the Mountain Men, and those used by the gold seekers in the 1850.

■ Ask students how our journey today would be different from the journeys listed above.

Economics As students study the journeys of their forebearers, ask them to consider the motivation. Ask students why they think the settlers made these journeys. In many cases, such as the Gold Rush, economics was the prime motivation. Have students list the reasons why they think various historical journeys were made. While discussing economics, students may wish to think about the cost of a transcontinental journey.

■ Have students contemplate the cost of a journey today versus the cost of a journey 100 to 150 years ago.

Global Awareness After the students have completed their imaginary journeys have them look at a physical map of the world and ask them to compare the major geographic features of the United States with the major geographic features of other countries around the world. Ask students to choose one country that interests them and answer the following comparison questions:

1. Does the country have mountains and rivers similar to those of the United States? How are our geographic features similar and how are they different?

MATHEMATICS

■ Using a road map of the United States, have students figure the mileage for each of their various journeys.

Have them estimate how may miles they could travel in a day, in a week, or even a month. You may wish to have students compare the mileage covered by following the road to that of going straight "as the crow flies."

LANGUAGE ARTS

■ After students have chosen their routes across the country, have them write a rationale for their choices. They should include some information about the physical features and attractions of their journey and should explain their reasons for selecting that specific route.

SCIENCE

■ Transportation has certainly improved over the last few hundred years. Ask students to answer the following questions:

1. What role has technology played in improving our transportation systems?

2. Have all the changes been for the better?

3. What are the advantages and disadvantages of each form of transportation? Did the horse have any advantage over the airplane? Does the airplane have any disadvantages?

ART

■ Draw students' attention to the various physical features of the United States by focusing their attention on the physical features they will pass on their journey.

■ Have students create visuals of each of these features and arrange them on a bulletin board. Students may also wish to make travel posters about some of the places to which their imaginary journeys will take them.

LITERATURE

■ Have students read about past journeys in order to appreciate the nature of the journey they have planned. *Oregon Trail*, by Francis Parkman Airmont, © 1964, ISBN 0-8049-0037), tells the story of a journey in the 1840 while Peter Jenkin's *Walk Across America* (Morrow © 1979, ISBN 0-688-03427-6) provides a more contemporary version.

U1-C

U1-D

Multidisciplinary Activity features provide an exciting way to bring subject area integration into your classroom.

For more resources, look for

• **Resource Center that identifies supplementary materials to be used with each lesson**

• **Annotated Bibliography of books, audiovisual materials, and computer software**

More ways to help you teach social studies easily and effectively

How To

Study Current Events

INSTRUCTIONS FOR THE TEACHER:

Why Should Current Events be Used in the Social Studies Classroom? It is difficult to walk into the middle of a movie and fully understand everything that is going on. It is also hard to pick up a novel in the middle and completely comprehend the story. In a very real way, our students are placed in a similar situation. They find themselves in a world that is an ongoing drama — a drama that is often not easy to understand. The goal of the Social Studies class is to provide students with the information they need to become thinking, caring, participating citizens. The introduction of current events is an important step in this process.

Unit 7 discusses the United States in a changing world. The previous chapters have established the students' knowledge base. Now the students can put that base to use, applying it to their world and its problems. When placed in this context, the study of current events helps students understand the relevance of social studies and provides them with valuable information about their world and their role in that world.

Obtaining Material A great number of events are continually happening in the world. Students need some structure when attempting to tackle the extensive subject of current events.

Selecting a Current-Events Topic First, help students focus their attention on one subject. Ask each student to select a topic for study that interests him or her, but make sure that the topic is broad enough to meet the students needs for this lesson.

After the student has picked a general topic, it may be necessary to narrow it down. Students that are interested in government elections or politics may select a topic such as "Politics in America." Since that topic is extremely broad, it will be necessary to help the student focus on a smaller portion of the related information. By narrowing the focus of their topic, students will find research data more manageable.

Researching the Topic Have students research their topics. Information on current events can be found in a wide variety of places. Students may wish to obtain information from one or more of the following sources:

— News Broadcasts (radio and television)
— Television specials
— Newspapers and magazines
— Primary Sources such as guest speakers

Have students take notes on their research. They may be able to obtain copies of any written articles that they use, but they will probably need to take notes while monitoring radio or television broadcasts.

Using the Material Resource materials can be used in a variety of ways. Students may wish to organize their information and present it to the class in the form of an oral report. Other students may wish to make a scrapbook and a written report. Materials could be gathered for a round-table discussion or for a class debate. Some students may wish to create an ongoing journal, keeping abreast of the situation as it changes. Other students may wish to create a bulletin board displaying their research.

ACTIVITY FOR THE STUDENTS:

Creating a Current-Events Fair Tell students that the class is going to spend the next week of class creating a current-events fair. This will be a chance for students to complete research about something going on in the world and then share that research with the class in display form. Each student will be given a station within the fair to create a display that showcases an issue.

Have the students turn in a list of topics they are interested in studying. After the topic has been approved, ask them to create a list of places they intend to check for information on their topic. Students need to research their topic and prepare information that would explain what is going on to a person who is not fully informed. This may be done in a variety of ways. The students may wish to share information through artwork, or with an audio tape, written information, graphic organizers, maps, or any combination of the above. They may also wish to create a current-events notebook or time line delineating information about their issue. They can provide background information on the topic as well as a personal guess as to what will happen next. Finally, all this information needs to be organized and presented in a display that can be set up within the amount of size allowed by the room. Have all the displays set up at the same time and allow time for students to visit each display and learn about the issues that their fellow classmates have researched.

Follow-Up Upon completion of the unit, the class may wish to hypothesize about the future. Ask the class to discuss and decide "Which of the materials we have been discussing will be included in history books of the future?"; "Which of these events will our children be studying?" and "What we will we tell them about this period of time?" Have the students discuss their feelings in a class discussion or in small groups.

How To projects provide valuable information for teachers and students to do a wide variety of activities to enhance learning.

- **Pacing Guide**
- **Bulletin Board Idea and related student activity**
- **Reduced reproductions of chapter review masters, vocabulary masters, place geography masters, test masters, and Teacher Edition of the Workbook**

CONTENT SUMMARY

Grade 1

Living in Families
Increases students' understanding of their family, school, and neighborhood, while developing citizenship, map and globe skills, and an increased awareness of children in other countries.

Grade 2

Living in Communities
Broadens students' knowledge of communities, past and present, and of ways people live in a variety of communities in our country and in other countries, while increasing their map and globe skills.

Grade 3

Comparing Communities
Deepens students' understanding of different kinds of communities by focusing on the geography, history, economy, and government of communities in our country and in other countries.

Grade 4

Comparing Regions
Encourages students to do an in-depth study of the geography, culture, and economy of regions in the United States and to compare these regions with other regions in the world.

Grade 5

Our Country
Promotes citizenship and builds students' understanding of United States history, presented chronologically, by interweaving social, cultural, economic, and geography strands within a well-told story.

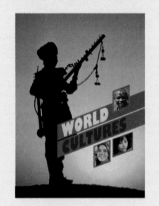

Grade 6 / 7

World Cultures
Engages students in the story of the development of civilization, presenting the geography, economy, government, and culture of the world's peoples, from the earliest times to the present.

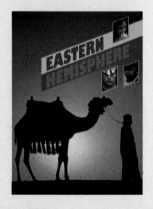

Grade 6 / 7

Eastern Hemisphere
Focuses students' attention on the geography, history, economy, government, and culture of regions within the Eastern Hemisphere.

Grade 6 / 7

Western Hemisphere
Provides students with a knowledge base about the geography, history, government, economy, and culture of other countries within our hemisphere.

TEACHER SUPPORT SYSTEM

Our Gifts to You. Your Gifts to Them.

Everything you need to lead ALL students to new heights of creativity and understanding.

► Review Masters

► Test Masters

► Workbook Teacher Edition

► Outline Maps

► Wall Maps

► Transparencies

► SILVER WINGS WORKSHOP
a multisensory, multimedia package
- Workshop Guide
- Workshop Prop
- Audio Cassette
- Activity Cards
- Poster
- Trade Book

Yours *FREE!* when you adopt **PEOPLE IN TIME AND PLACE**
from **SILVER BURDETT GINN**

PROGRAM COMPONENTS

Student Texts, 1-7

Student Workbooks, 1-7

Teacher-to-Teacher Editions, 1-7

Teacher Support Systems, 1-7

- ► Review Masters
- ► Test Masters
- ► Workbook Teacher Editions
- ► Outline Maps
- ► Wall Maps
- ► Transparencies
- ► SILVER WINGS WORKSHOPS - multimedia, multisensory packages
  - • Workshop Props
  - • Workshop Guides
  - • Audio Cassettes
  - • Activity Cards
  - • Posters
  - • Trade Books

Complete Poster Book Packages, K-2

- ► Poster Books
- ► Poster Book Teacher Manuals
- ► Poster Book Review Masters
- ► Poster Book Test Masters

Activity Kits, K-2

Videos, 1-7

Social Studies Libraries, 1-7

PE●PLE
in Time and Place

SILVER BURDETT GINN

Simon & Schuster   A Paramount Communications Company

ISBN 0-382-16892-5

04-92-203 (A137)

For information c
1 (800) 848-950

PEOPLE in Time and Place

LIVING IN FAMILIES

AUTHORS

Susan H. Grassmyer
Teacher, Shongum School
Randolph, NJ

Janet M. Hogan
Teacher, East School
New Canaan, CT

Hazel Tseng Hsieh
Teacher, Mohansic School
Yorktown Heights, NY

Charleen M. Kaaen
Teacher, Edison Elementary School
Walla Walla, WA

Margaret Ricciardi
Teacher, Woodland School
Convent Station, NJ

SERIES CONSULTANTS

Dr. James F. Baumann
Professor and Head of the Department of Reading Education
College of Education
The University of Georgia
Athens, GA

Dr. Theodore Kaltsounis
Professor of Social Studies Education
University of Washington
Seattle, WA

LITERATURE CONSULTANTS

Dr. Ben A. Smith
Assistant Professor of Social Studies Education
Kansas State University
Manhattan, KS

Dr. Jesse Palmer
Assistant Professor, Department of Curriculum and Instruction
University of Southern Mississippi
Hattiesburg, MS

Dr. John C. Davis
Professor of Elementary Education
University of Southern Mississippi
Hattiesburg, MS

SILVER BURDETT GINN

MORRISTOWN, NJ • NEEDHAM, MA

Atlanta, GA • Dallas, TX • Deerfield, IL • Menlo Park, CA

TEACHER EDITION

PUPIL EDITION AUTHORS

Dr. W. Frank Ainsley
Professor of Geography
University of North Carolina
Wilmington, NC

Dr. Herbert J. Bass
Professor of History
Temple University
Philadelphia, PA

Dr. Kenneth S. Cooper
Professor of History, Emeritus
George Peabody College for Teachers
Vanderbilt University
Nashville, TN

Dr. Gary S. Elbow
Professor of Geography
Texas Tech University
Lubbock, TX

Roy Erickson
Program Specialist, K–12
Social Studies and Multicultural Education
San Juan Unified School District
Carmichael, CA

Dr. Daniel B. Fleming
Professor of Social Studies Education
Virginia Polytechnic Institute and State University
Blacksburg, VA

Dr. Gerald Michael Greenfield
Professor and Director, Center for International Studies
University of Wisconsin
Parkside
Kenosha, WI

Dr. Linda Greenow
Assistant Professor of Geography
SUNY — The College at New Paltz,
New York, NY

Dr. William W. Joyce
Professor of Education
Michigan State University
East Lansing, MI

Dr. Gail S. Ludwig
Geographer-in-Residence
National Geographic Society
Geography Education Program
Washington, D.C.

Dr. Michael B. Petrovich
Professor Emeritus of History
University of Wisconsin
Madison, WI

Dr. Arthur D. Roberts
Professor of Education, University of Connecticut,
Storrs, CT

Dr. Christine L. Roberts
Professor of Education, University of Connecticut,
Storrs, CT

Parke Rouse, Jr.
Virginia Historian and
Retired Executive Director
of the Jamestown-Yorktown Foundation
Williamsburg, VA

Dr. Paul C. Slayton, Jr.
Distinguished Professor of Education
Mary Washington College
Fredericksburg, VA

Dr. Edgar A. Toppin
Professor of History and Dean of the Graduate School
Virginia State University
Petersburg, VA

ACKNOWLEDGEMENTS

Excerpt from *Columbus* by Ingri & Edgar Parin
D'Aulaire, copyright © 1955 by Doubleday, a division
of Bantam, Doubleday, Dell Publishing Group, Inc.
Used by permission of the publisher.

Excerpt and illustrations from *Make Way for
Ducklings* by Robert McCloskey. Copyright 1941,
renewed © 1969 by Robert McCloskey. All rights
reserved. Reprinted by permission of Viking Penguin,
a division of Penguin Books USA, Inc.

"Wake Up!" by Eva Grant, from *Poetry Place
Anthology*. Copyright © 1983 by Scholastic, Inc.
Reprinted by permission of Scholastic, Inc.

From *Stone Soup* by Marcia Brown. Reprinted with
permission of Charles Scribner's Sons, an imprint of
Macmillan Publishing Company. Copyright 1947
Marcia Brown; copyright renewed © 1975 Marcia
Brown.

CONTENTS

The Granger Collection

CHARTS AND TIME LINES

GRAPHS AND TABLES

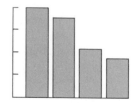

SPECIAL FEATURES

LITERATURE

PEN PALS

CITIZENSHIP AND AMERICAN VALUES

SKILLBUILDERS

Highlight

Skills are an integral part of any Social Studies program. Knowing where skills are introduced, practiced, and tested will enable you to incorporate the skills into your Social Studies lessons. To make the task easier for you, this **Teacher-to-Teacher Edition** includes a *Skill Trace Bar*. This bar, which appears only in the **Teacher-to-Teacher Edition**, tells you where key skills are introduced, practiced and tested in **PEOPLE IN TIME AND PLACE**. The bar will always appear in the marginalia where a skill is first introduced. A sample of a *Skill Trace Bar* is shown at the right. Listed below are all the skills that are traced at this grade level.

SKILL TRACE:	Understanding Sequence	
INTRODUCE PE, p. 56	**PRACTICE** TE, p. 83 WB, p. 19 RMB, p. 15	**TEST** Unit 2 Test, TMB

MAP AND GLOBE SKILLS

SKILL	INTRODUCE	PRACTICE	TEST
Understanding the Globe	**PE** p. 24	**PE** p. 25; **TE** p. U1-C; **WB** pp. 28–29	Unit 1 Test, **TMB**
Understanding the Legend (Key)	**PE** p. 44	**TE** p. 44; **WB** p. 10; **RMB** p. 17	Unit 2 Test, **TMB**
Understanding Bar Graphs	**PE** p. 80	**PE** p. 81; **TE** p. 79; **RMB** p. 26	Unit 5 Test, **TMB**
Understanding Pictographs	**PE** p. 98	**TE** p. 98; **WB** p. 18; **RMB** p. 31	Unit 4 Test, **TMB**
Understanding Directions	**PE** p. 120	**PE** p. 127; **TE** p. 120; **RMB** p. 37	Unit 5 Test, **TMB**
Understanding Tables	**PE** p. 142	**PE** p. 143; **TE** p. 141; **RMB** p. 42	Unit 5 Test, **TMB**
Understanding Continents and Oceans	**PE** p. 150	**PE** p. 153; **TE** p. 152; **WB** pp. 28–29	Unit 6 Test, **TMB**

SKILLBUILDER LESSONS

SKILL	INTRODUCE	PRACTICE	TEST
Understanding Traffic Lights	**PE** p. 30	**PE** p. 31; **TE** p. 47	Unit 1 Test, **TMB**
Understanding Sequence	**PE** p. 56	**TE** p. 83; **WB** p. 19; **RMB** p. 15	Unit 2 Test, **TMB**
Classifying and Categorizing Words	**PE** p. 88	**PE** p. 89; **TE** p. 110; **RMB** p. 21	Unit 3 Test, **TMB**
Following Written Directions	**PE** p. 114	**PE** p. 115; **TE** p. 120; **WB** p. 21	Unit 4 Test, **TMB**
Understanding Main Ideas	**PE** p. 146	**TE** p. 147, 157; **RMB** p. 18	Unit 5 Test, **TMB**
Identifying Landforms	**PE** p. 178	**PE** p. 179; **TE** p. 195, U6-E	Unit 6 Test, **TMB**
Understanding Time Lines	**PE** p. 204	**PE** p. 205; **TE** pp. 204–205	Unit 7 Test, **TMB**

KEY

PE — Pupil Edition   **TE** — Teacher Edition   **WB** — Workbook   **RMB** — Review Master Booklet   **TMB** — Test Master Booklet

UNIT ACTIVITIES

Highlight

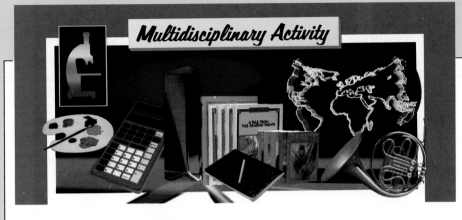
Multidisciplinary Activity

Multidisciplinary Activities provide an exciting way to integrate Social Studies content into other curriculum areas. This special feature is found in every unit interleaf section. Below is a list of the *Multidisciplinary Activities* in this book.

How To Activities

How To activities provide not only student projects but also valuable information that helps the teacher prepare for and execute the projects. *How To* activities can be found in every unit interleaf. Below is a list of the *How To* activities in this book.

Unit 1 Resource Center

School
(pp. 2–27)

Unit Theme: School is an active environment for children to learn in. Many workers are needed to fulfill the needs of the students while they are at school.

UNIT RESOURCES
Unit 1 Test

LESSON 1 How Do We Get to School?
(pp. 4–7)
Theme: Students use different modes of transportation to travel to school.

LESSON RESOURCES
Workbook, p. 3
Review Master Booklet
   Previewing Lesson Vocabulary, p. 3
   Understanding the Lesson, p. 4

SOCIAL STUDIES LIBRARY: *Fox at School*

LESSON 2 Who Are the People at School?
(pp. 8–11)
Theme: Many people use their special training and tools to make a school operate smoothly.

LESSON RESOURCES
Workbook, p. 4
Review Master Booklet
   Understanding the Lesson, p. 5

SOCIAL STUDIES LIBRARY: *Fox at School*

LESSON 3 Why Do Schools Have Rules?
(pp. 12–15)
Theme: Schools have rules to keep the students safe and to help them work and play together.

LESSON RESOURCES
Workbook, p. 5
Review Master Booklet
   Previewing Lesson Vocabulary, p. 6
   Understanding the Lesson, p. 7

LESSON 4 How Are Children Alike and Different?
(pp. 18–21)
Theme: Each student is unique. However, students can find ways that they are alike and different.

LESSON RESOURCES
Workbook, p. 6
Review Master Booklet
   Previewing Lesson Vocabulary, p. 8
   Understanding the Lesson, p. 9

SOCIAL STUDIES LIBRARY: *The Balancing Girl*
Happy Birthday, Ronald Morgan!

LESSON 5 What Do We Learn in School?
(pp. 22–27)
Theme: Students participate in a wide range of activities while at school. School is also a place to develop friendships.

LESSON RESOURCES
Workbook, p. 7
Review Master Booklet
   Previewing Lesson Vocabulary, p. 10
   Understanding the Lesson, p. 11

PACING GUIDE

September	October	November	December	January	February	March	April	May
UNIT	UNIT	UNITS	UNIT	UNIT	UNIT	UNITS	UNIT	UNIT
1	2	2–3	3	4	5	5–6	6	7

Annotated Bibliography

Books for Teachers

Hill, Susan. *Books Alive! Using Literature in the Classroom.* Portsmouth, NH: Heinemann Educational Books, 1986. ISBN 0-435-08513-1. Four approaches to using literature with students are presented: responding to text, focusing on a particular author, focusing on the story, and experiencing the "great books."

Lima, Carolyn W. *A to Zoo: Subject Access to Children's Picture Books,* 3rd ed., New York: R.R. Bowker, 1989. ISBN 0-835-22599-2. This book categorizes children's picture books by subject, author, illustrator, and title and gives bibliographic information about each book.

Books for Read Aloud

Allard, Harry and James Marshall. *Miss Nelson Is Missing.* Boston: Houghton Mifflin Co., 1977. ISBN 0-395-25296-2. The kids in room 207 take advantage of their nice teacher until she disappears and they must face a nasty substitute.

Arnold, Caroline. *Where Do You Go to School?* New York: Franklin Watts, 1982. ISBN 0-531-04442-4. This book discusses types of schools, the different types of jobs at schools, and what people do at school.

Cohen, Miriam. *When Will I Read?* New York: Greenwillow Books, 1977. ISBN 0-688-80073-4. A boy learns that there is more to reading than just books.

Cohen, Miriam. *Will I Have a Friend?* New York: Macmillan Publishing Co., 1967. ISBN 0-027-22790-1. The text deals with school friendship.

Crews, Donald. *School Bus.* New York: Greenwillow Books., 1984. ISBN 0-690-00277-7. School buses are followed as they take children to and from school.

Hoban, Tana. *I Read Signs.* New York: Greenwillow Books, 1983. ISBN 0-688-02317-7. This book introduces signs and symbols frequently seen in a child's environment.

Oxenbury, Helen. *First Day of School.* New York: Dial Books for Young Readers, 1983. ISBN 0-803-70012-1. A little girl is anxious about her first day of school.

Filmstrips and Videos

A Kid's Guide to Manners. Long Branch, NJ: Kimbo Educational. 2 filmstrips, 2 cassettes, and a guide (LT1069). These filmstrips teach in a humorous way that manners are necessary for safety and order.

How to Have Fun Safely. Mahwah, NJ: Troll Associates. 12-minute video (VH030). Teaches being responsible and considerate while playing in parks and playgrounds.

School Manners. Mahwah, NJ: Troll Associates. 8-minute video (VS019). Rex meets a classroom of rude children and is determined to teach them manners.

Bulletin Board Idea

Student Activity
Give the students paper doll shapes 5″ high to decorate as themselves. Have the students make other dolls for the workers in the school. Attach the dolls to the bulletin board. Have the students dictate a list of school rules to add to the bulletin board.

Alike and Different

How are components of our world alike and how are they different?

In Unit 1 the students will be introduced to the concept of similarities and differences by learning how children are alike and different in physical appearance and in what they like to do. The students will practice what they have learned by telling how they and other children are alike and different. The following activities encourage the students to expand their knowledge by comparing a variety of items, including recordings of music, measuring tools, and drawings.

SOCIAL STUDIES

Economics Have the students compare various denominations of United States currency. Show the class a $1, a $5, a $10, and a $20 dollar bill. Ask them to describe the bills. Discuss with the students how people use money. Then ask the students how the bills are alike and how they are different. For example, they are all made of paper, but they show different numbers.

Show the students a half dollar, a quarter, a dime, a nickel, and a penny. Again, ask them to describe what they see. Ask the students how the coins are alike and how they are different. Then have the students explain how the bills and coins are alike and different.

Geography Review the information presented about the globe in this unit. Show the students a globe and ask them to identify it. The students should say that a globe is a model of the earth. Then ask the students what a globe shows. The students should reply that a globe shows water and land.

■ Have the students look closely at the globe. Point out several land masses and ask the students to tell how they are alike and different. (Answers will vary but may include that they are alike in color but different in size.)

■ Show the students the United States on the globe. Tell the students that our country is made up of different parts called states. Select several states that contain large bodies of wa-ter. Ask the students to explain how the states selected are alike and different.

Global Awareness Show the students small flags or pictures of flags from different nations. You may wish to look in an encyclopedia or almanac for pictures of flags. Tell the students that a flag is one thing that identifies a country. Then ask these questions.

1. Where have you seen flags flying?

2. What does the flag in the school-yard stand for?

■ Have the students explain how the flags presented are the same and how they are different.

MATHEMATICS

■ Show the students measuring tools, such as a metric ruler and a scale. Ask the students to identify the objects or to supply the correct names for them. Explain to the students what each tool is used for. Ask these questions to help the students explain how the objects are alike and different.

1. **What do the ruler and scale both do?**

2. **Which tool would you use to find out how wide the classroom door is?**

3. **Which tool would you use to find out how heavy a package of crayons is?**

MUSIC

■ Obtain recordings of three different kinds of music, such as an organ prelude, a drum solo, and a popular song. Play these for students and discuss how the recordings are alike and how they are different. Ask the following questions.

1. **In which pieces did you hear instruments?** (You may need to tell or remind students that the voice is an instrument.)

2. **In which piece did you hear a tune?**

3. **In which piece did you hear words?**

SCIENCE

■ Have the students find two leaves each. Ask them to think about how the leaves are alike and different.

■ Ask volunteers to help you make groups of leaves by giving you one of the leaves that they found. Put the leaves where everyone can see them. Discuss how you can group, or classify, the leaves by the ways that they are alike and different. For example, you could make one pile of broken leaves and one pile of unbroken leaves.

■ Hold up the leaves one at a time and have students tell which group each leaf belongs in.

ART

■ Tell the students to draw pictures of the schoolyard. Have four students at a time present their drawings to the class. Then discuss how the drawings are alike and how they are different. Encourage the students to think about the artwork by asking questions such as:

1. **How are the drawings alike in the colors used? How are they different in the colors used?**

2. **How are the sizes of the schoolyard alike in these drawings? How are the sizes different?**

3. **What has each artist drawn as the most important part of the schoolyard in his or her drawing?**

Make a
TV Viewer

INSTRUCTIONS FOR THE TEACHER:

Focus   The students will be learning about the school environment in this unit. They will need to organize information about teachers, administrators, and other people in the school, as well as about the rules that are in place in the school. The schedule, or daily routine, also helps the students anticipate and organize information about the school day.

For students at this age, it is essential that material be presented in a concrete manner. This activity utilizes illustrations to represent the students' activities during the school day.

Lesson 5 shows many of the activities taught in school during a typical day. Use this lesson as a base for your classroom discussion as you prepare for the activity. Explain to the students that they will be making a TV viewer and a set of pictures that will become the TV show. The show will depict the students' activities during the school day.

Warm-up Activity   Ask the students to name all the school activities that they participate in. List all their answers on the chalkboard. Mathematics, reading, social studies, and music are possible answers.

The students will need to illustrate each of these activities. To help them prepare, pantomime something the students would do while participating in each activity. Have the students name the activity you are showing. For example, for reading you may hold up a book and pretend to read. If you wish, have the students pantomime other ways to show the same activity.

Explain to the students that each subject area will become part of their TV show, since they will be describing a typical day.

ACTIVITY FOR THE STUDENTS:

Procedure   Divide the class into groups of three or four students. Each group will be responsible for illustrating a school subject or an activity that occurs during the school day, such as recess. Either assign topics or have each group select a topic. Ask each group to plan how it is going to illustrate its topic. Remind any group having difficulty of the pantomime ideas that were done for that activity.

Cut butcher paper into 10″ × 12″ pieces. The width of the paper should be less than the height of a cardboard tube from a roll of paper towels. Have each group use a piece of the paper and crayons or markers to illustrate its topic. Collect all the pictures and sequence them according to the daily schedule. Have one group make a picture that introduces the show. Have another group make a picture that gives credit for the drawings to the class.

Making the TV Viewer You will need two cardboard tubes from rolls of paper towels and a cardboard box whose bottom has a height close to that of the cardboard tubes. Turn the box so that the bottom faces you and cut a hole in the bottom. Make the hole slightly smaller than 10″ × 12″. This will be the TV screen. With the screen facing you, cut a hole approximately 2½″ × 15″ in the top of the box. The long side of the hole should correspond to the length of the TV screen. The cardboard tubes will be dropped into place on either end of the hole. Have the students paint and decorate the TV viewer.

Preparing the Show Prepare the TV show by putting the pictures in chronological order from *right* to *left*. The pictures corresponding to beginning of the day should start at the right. Have the students help you tape the pictures together in one long strip. Add a blank section of paper on each end. Tape the left edge of the last section on the left to one tube. Roll the pictures around the tube. Tape the right edge of the first section to the other tube. Place the tubes and the scroll into the hole in the TV viewer. Center the first picture in the screen.

For the show, have the students gather around the viewer. Rotate the cardboard tube to show the pictures. As each group see its picture, have one member from the group describe the activity for the class.

Follow-up Discussion Have the students summarize the events of their TV program. To check the students' understanding of the sequence of events, rewind the scroll and point to several scenes, one at a time. Have the students explain whether each event took place before or after an event you name. If necessary, find the second event on the roll to explain to the students the relationship between it and the first and third events.

Extension Throughout the year, have the students make other shows for the TV viewer. Reinforce the students' sequencing skills by having them make short shows that illustrate how a task is completed. The students can also make a show about their community. Have them explain the special places in the community and the community workers who help them. The students may wish to make a show about the different occasions people celebrate and the ways these occasions are celebrated.

For a yearlong project, have the students summarize their activities at the end of each month by making a few pictures. Include a sheet that names each month within the school year. Assemble the completed work and show it at the end of the year.

For convenient storage you may wish to rewind each scroll and use a rubber band to hold the two tubes together. Add a label to the top of one of the tubes for easy recognition. Store all scrolls in a box near the TV viewer so that the students may view them during their free time.

Workbook Pages

HOW DO WE GET TO SCHOOL?

Reading a Picture

✳ We can get to school in many ways. Color the pictures that show ways to get to school.

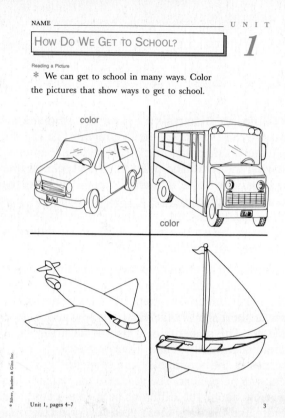

color

color

PEOPLE IN YOUR SCHOOL

Identifying

✳ Look at the pictures.

teacher   principal

nurse   librarian

✳ Find the word that names each picture.
Write the word under the picture.

teacher	nurse
librarian	principal

SCHOOLS HAVE RULES

Matching

✳ The pictures show people following rules.
Draw a line from the correct rule to each picture.

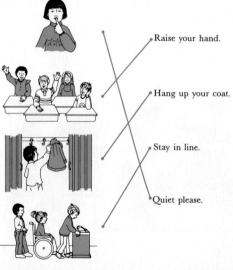

Raise your hand.

Hang up your coat.

Stay in line.

Quiet please.

ALIKE AND DIFFERENT

Observing

✳ Look at the pictures. Find the things that are alike. Color them red.

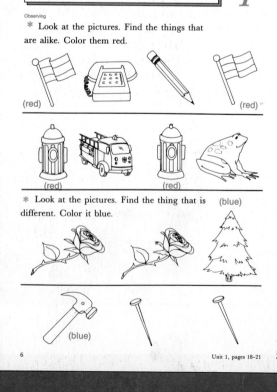

(red)   (red)

(red)   (red)

✳ Look at the pictures. Find the thing that is different. Color it blue.

(blue)

(blue)

NAME _____

UNIT
1

WHAT DO WE LEARN IN SCHOOL?

Reading a Picture

✳ Circle the pictures that show things you learn at school.

© Silver, Burdett & Ginn Inc.

Unit 1, pages 22–27

7

TEACHER NOTES

UNIT 1

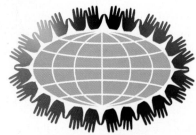

MULTICULTURAL PERSPECTIVES

Learning Around the World

(pages 18–27)

Prepare for this lesson by gathering the following items.

- Pictures from books and magazines as well as postcards and posters that show children from around the world in different learning situations
- Examples of different alphabets used around the world
- The posters, "1, 2, 3, Go!" and "What Time Is It?" from the K–2 portion of the Silver Burdett & Ginn Mathematics Program

Show the students the pictures of children learning around the world. You may wish to include the picture of the schoolchildren in Lesotho, Africa, on the poster "What Time Is It?" Point out on the globe the different places that are represented in the pictures.

Then explain to the children that no matter how different or alike we are as people, we all can learn.

Show the different alphabets to the students. Explain that everyone does not learn the same alphabet that is learned in the United States. Some people learn to read an entirely different set of symbols.

Use the poster "1, 2, 3, Go!" to show how number names are written in other languages. Ask the students if they know how to count in any other languages.

Have the children compare and contrast their school experiences to what they observe in the pictures.

2

Class Discussion

- Have the students look at the picture on pp. 2–3. Help them to read the sign on the bulletin board behind the children in the picture.
- Discuss with the students what they expect school to be like and some of the things they are looking forward to learning.

The United Nations *(pages 16–17)*

Prior to the class discussion, gather the following photographs of the United Nations (UN) headquarters in New York City.

- A picture showing the UN buildings
- A picture of the member countries' flags flying in front of the headquarters
- A picture showing the General Assembly in session
- A picture of the flag of the United Nations

Discuss with the students some of the problems that may result when countries disagree. A war may be fought. Then, people can be injured or killed and buildings and land are destroyed.

Explain to the students that the United Nations is an organization that was designed to help countries resolve problems. Over 150 countries belong to the United Nations. The goals of the organization are to have peace in the world and to respect the people who live in the world.

Show the students the photographs of the United Nations headquarters. Explain that there is a flag for each member country. Then explain that the United Nations flag has a map of the world and olive branches, which represent peace.

Ask the students to describe when someone helped to resolve a problem that they were having with someone. Explain that the United Nations works to play that role for countries.

Garrett A. Morgan (1877-1963)

(pages 30–31)

In 1923, Garrett A. Morgan, an African American, patented a version of the traffic light. He sold the rights to his invention to the General Electric Company for $40,000. Although today's traffic light looks different than Mr. Morgan's version, his version did contain red, yellow, and green lights.

Ask the students to imagine what would happen in a busy intersection without a traffic light. Have them draw such a scene. Discuss the pictures with the students.

For your information, Morgan's first invention was a belt fastener for a sewing machine (1901). In 1914, he won a prize for his invention of a breathing helmet and smoke protector. He demonstrated the use of this device in a rescue operation at the scene of an explosion at the Cleveland (Ohio) Waterworks.

Optional Activities

How Do We Get to School?

Objectives

★ 1. **Name** examples of ways students travel to school.

2. **Identify** the people who help students travel safely to school.

3. **Name** safety rules for pedestrians and car and bus passengers.

1 STARTING THE LESSON

Motivation/ Prior Knowledge

■ Ask the students to think about the different ways people travel.

■ List the students' answers on the chalkboard.

■ Have the class use the list to identify the ways of travel that bring students to school.

Study the Vocabulary

NEW WORDS	DISCUSSION WORDS	ORAL VOCABULARY
school	bus driver crossing guard	safety rules

■ Ask the students where they are now; then have them identify the people who go to school.

■ Ask the students to think of people who help them get to school. List the people on the chalkboard.

■ Ask the students how the people help them and how the people keep them safe when traveling to school.

4

Optional Activities

Lesson 1

How Do We Get to School?

Pam is excited.

It is her first day of **school**.

Pam is in first grade.

4

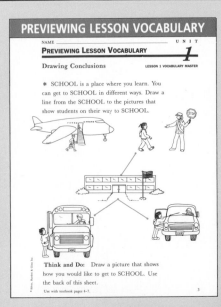

PREVIEWING LESSON VOCABULARY

NAME _____ UNIT **1**

PREVIEWING LESSON VOCABULARY

Drawing Conclusions LESSON 1 VOCABULARY MASTER

★ SCHOOL is a place where you learn. You can get to SCHOOL in different ways. Draw a line from the SCHOOL to the pictures that show students on their way to SCHOOL.

Think and Do: Draw a picture that shows how you would like to get to SCHOOL. Use the back of this sheet.

Use with textbook pages 4–7.

Review Master Booklet, p. 3

...m rides on the school bus.
...r. Lee is the bus driver.
...e makes sure everyone is safe.
...ne children sit in their seats.

Read and Discuss
Text pages 4–7

To identify the ways students travel to school and the people who help them, ask the students these questions after they have read pp. 4–7.

1. **What is Mr. Lee's job?**
   (Bus driver *p. 5*)

2. **How does Jill get to school?**
   (Her mother drives her. *p. 6*)

3. **Who helps students cross the street?**
   (The crossing guard *p. 7*)

   Thinking Critically **How would you come to school if you could choose a way? Why?** (Evaluate)
   (Accept all reasonable answers. *pp. 4–7*)

VISUAL THINKING SKILL

Analyzing the Photographs

■ Ask the students to look at the photographs on pp. 4–5. Then ask the following question.
How are you and Pam the same when getting ready for school?
(Answers may include getting lunch, packing a backpack, riding a bus.)

5

Cooperative Learning

Making a Mural Have the class list some ways students get to school. Divide the class into groups of three or four and give each group a job.

● One group should draw on a large piece of mural paper the school, the roads, and the walkways that lead to the school. Each member should be responsible for completing a section of the mural.

● Using construction paper, one group should make crossing guards and people walking to school. Another group should make cars and buses. Each group member must complete a figure or vehicle.

● One member of each group should help glue the pieces in place.

● Each group should evaluate how well its members worked together. The class should evaluate how well the mural shows the different ways to get to school.

Optional Activities

Meeting Individual Needs

Concept:
Safety Rules

Safety rules for pedestrians and passengers are essential for students to know as they travel to and from school. Review with the students the safety rules below.

Walk on the sidewalk.

Cross the street with a guard.

Do not push while getting on or off a bus.

Sit down while the bus is moving.

The activities below will reinforce the safety rules for the whole class.

◆**EASY** Ask each student to make a hand puppet of someone who helps students travel to school safely.

Ask each one to display his or her puppet and to explain how the real person keeps students safe.

◀▶**AVERAGE** Have each student make a poster of students following a safety rule and dictate the rule for the poster.

The posters should be presented to the class and the rules should be identified by the class.

◀▮▶**CHALLENGING** Cut holes for a head and arms in a brown paper bag to make a vest for each student.

Ask the students to decorate their vests to look like a crossing guard's vest. Have the students make, from paper, the hand-held equipment, too. The students should wear their vests while they explain the safety rules the guard has people follow.

VISUAL THINKING SKILL

Interpreting the Photographs

■Ask the students to look at the photographs on pp. 6–7 and answer the following question.

What safety rules are the boys following?

(They are walking on the sidewalk. They are following the directions of the crossing guard. *pp. 6–7*)

6

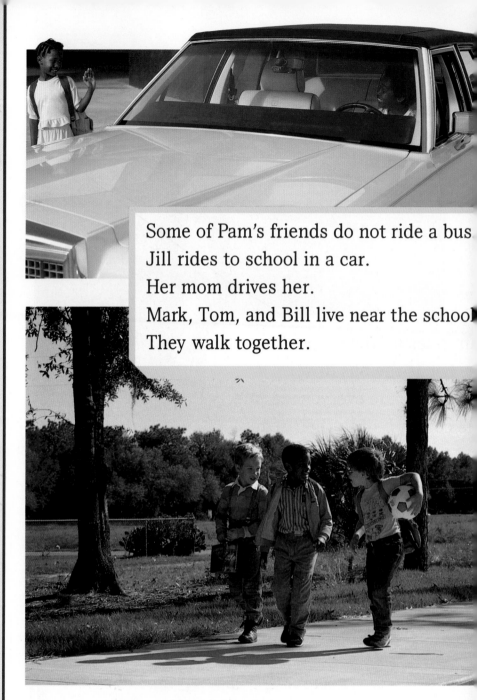

Some of Pam's friends do not ride a bus.
Jill rides to school in a car.
Her mom drives her.
Mark, Tom, and Bill live near the school.
They walk together.

Optional Activities

Curriculum Connection

Mathematics Help the students make a class pictograph showing how they travel to school. Have each student draw a picture on a 9″ × 9″ sheet of paper showing how he or she travels to school. Make a label for each type of travel used.

● Create the pictograph on the floor or on a bulletin board by aligning the pictures with the correct labels.

● Ask the students to count the number of pictures in each group and then compare the numbers.

The crossing guard tells them when to cross the street.
She helps children get to school too.

esson 1 — Review

Read and Think

1. Name some ways to get to school. (Recall)

2. Who helps you get to school? (Evaluate)

Skills Check

Look at the picture on page 7.
How does the crossing guard help the children?

7

Answers to Read and Think

1. Riding in a school bus or car and walking are some of the ways to get to school.

2. Answers may include parent, brother or sister, crossing guard, bus driver, friend.

Answer to Skills Check

The crossing guard signals the students to cross the street.

Answer to Lesson Title Question

Ask the lesson title question, found at the beginning of the lesson:
How do we get to school?
(There are different ways to get to school. Students can walk to school or ride in a bus or a car.)

Additional Practice

You may wish to assign the ancillary materials listed below.
Understanding the Lesson p. 4
Workbook p. 3

Reteaching Main Objective

⭐ *Name examples of ways students can travel to school.*

● Have the students cut out, mount, and label pictures of forms of travel that children might use to get to school.

Writing to Learn

Transportation and Safety Have the students draw pictures of a form of travel that they do *not* use to get to school. The picture should show a safety rule.

(The white star that appears before the objective refers to the starred objective found at the beginning of the lesson. The first objective is always the lesson's main objective.)

Review Master Booklet, p. 4

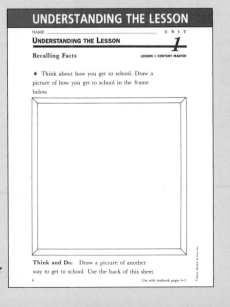

UNDERSTANDING THE LESSON

NAME _____
UNDERSTANDING THE LESSON   U N I T **1**

Recalling Facts   LESSON 1 CONTENT MASTER

✳ Think about how you get to school. Draw a picture of how you get to school in the frame below.

Think and Do: Draw a picture of another way to get to school. Use the back of this sheet.

4   Use with textbook pages 4–7.

Optional Activities

7

Who Are the People at School?

Objectives

★1. **Identify** some of the workers in a school.

2. **Name** the kind of work each worker does and the equipment needed for the job.

3. **Tell** how schools rely on workers to complete their jobs.

1 STARTING THE LESSON

Motivation/ Prior Knowledge

■ Tell the students that some people have special jobs. Ask the students to name these workers.

1. Whom would you go to see if you were sick? (The doctor)

2. Whom would you go to see to learn to play the piano? (Piano teacher)

■ Tell the students that today they will learn about the workers in school.

Study the Vocabulary

DISCUSSION WORDS	ORAL VOCABULARY
teacher	*library*
principal	*office*
librarian	*classroom*
nurse	
cafeteria worker	

■ Make two columns on the chalkboard. In the first column list the Discussion Words shown above. In the second column, in a different order, write the names of the people who hold those jobs in your school.

■ Have students come to the chalkboard to connect each job to the correct name.

Who Are the People at School?

This is a first-grade class.
Pam is part of the class.
The class learns together.
Mrs. Johnson is the teacher.
She helps the class learn.

Optional Activities

School Tour and Floor Plan

● Take the class on a tour of the school. Introduce the class to the school workers by name and by position. Ask the students to name the tools that they see in each special room.

● Draw a floor plan of your school. Label each room and the worker who works there.

● Have the students draw pictures of the tools found in the different rooms. Attach the pictures to the floor plan. Display the floor plan.

The class walked around the school.

The class met Mr. Diaz.

He is the principal.

The principal is the head of the school.

PRINCIPAL'S OFFICE

9

Read and Discuss
Text pages 8–11

Write *office*, *nurse's office*, *classroom*, *cafeteria*, and *library* on the chalkboard. Ask the students to name the kind of worker in each room. To further develop the lesson, ask the students these questions about pp. 8–11.

1. **Who is the head of the school?**
   (The principal, Mr. Diaz *p. 8*)

2. **Who helps the class choose books in the library?**
   (The librarian, Mr. Jones *p. 10*)

3. **Whom does the school nurse help?**
   (Sick people and those who are hurt *p. 10*)

Thinking Critically Why do people need to do different jobs in a school? (Evaluate)

(Answers may include that there is a great deal of work to be done in a school and that some jobs require special training. *pp. 8–11*)

Thinking Critically If you could have one of the jobs at your school, which one would you pick? Why? (Evaluate)

(Accept all answers that have explanations. *pp.8–11*)

Curriculum Connection

Language   Have the students copy the following poem from the chalkboard.

We need the workers in our school.
They help us every day.
They teach us how to work and play
In a safe and happy way.

● Each student should then draw a picture of a favorite school worker and deliver the poem and the picture to that person.

I'm Thinking. . .

● Ask the students to guess the identity of different school workers from the clues that you give them.

I'm thinking of someone who works in the library and helps students choose books. Who is it? (The librarian)

I'm thinking of the person who is the head of the school. Who is it? (The principal)

● Have the students give clues about other workers.

9

Concept:
Jobs and Tools

Jobs are specialized and require different tools. The activities that follow will help the whole class relate the jobs in the school to the tools the jobs require.

◆ **EASY** Have each student draw a picture showing a school worker.

Have the student draw the worker first.

Then have the student draw, around the person, the tools that the worker uses.

Have the students present their pictures to the class and explain how the workers use the tools.

◀▶ **AVERAGE** Each student will attach squares of heavy paper to a coat hanger to make a mobile. Each square will represent one worker. At least three workers should be represented.

On one side of each square, the student will draw and label a school worker. On the other side, the student will draw the tools that his or her worker uses.

Tie each square to a mobile.

Display the mobiles in the classroom.

◀▮▶ **CHALLENGING** Have each student select a school worker.

Give each student construction paper, scissors, glue, and crayons.

Have each student make, from paper, the tools that his or her worker uses.

Have the student write a paragraph about the worker and the tools needed to do his or her job.

VISUAL THINKING SKILL

Comparing the Photographs

■ Have the students examine the photographs on pp. 10–11. Then ask them this question.
Which workers are wearing uniforms?
(Cafeteria workers, nurse *pp. 10–11*)

Mr. Jones is the librarian.
He works in the school library.
He helps the class choose books.
Sometimes Mr. Jones reads to the class.

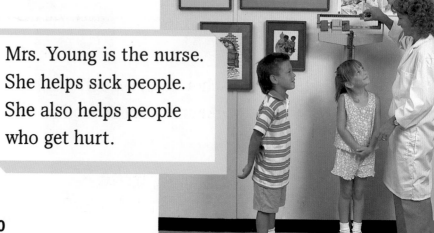

Mrs. Young is the nurse.
She helps sick people.
She also helps people who get hurt.

10

Optional Activities

Writing to Learn

Writing About a School Worker   Have each student write about the job performed by a school worker.

● Copy the four sentence parts on the chalkboard.

The school nurse helps

The principal helps

The librarian helps

The teacher helps

● Each student should write an ending for at least one worker.

These people work in the school too. Can you tell what they do?

Review

Read and Think

1. What does a teacher do in school? (Recall)

2. Who are the workers in your school? (Synthesize)

Skills Check

Look at the top picture on page 10.
What does Mr. Jones use to do his job?

11

3 CLOSING THE LESSON

Lesson 2 Review

Answers to Read and Think

1. The teacher helps the class learn.

2. Answers will vary but should include the principal, the teacher, the nurse, and the librarian.

Answer to Skills Check
Mr. Jones uses books.

Answer to Lesson Title Question

Ask the lesson title question, found at the beginning of the lesson: **Who are the people at school?**
(Teachers, the principal, the nurse, the librarian, and the cafeteria workers are some of the people at school.)

Additional Practice

You may wish to assign the ancillary materials listed below.
Understanding the Lesson p. 5
Workbook p. 4

Reteaching Main Objective

⭐ *Identify some of the workers in a school.*

● Create a panel interview by having students portray a teacher, a nurse, a principal, a librarian, and a cafeteria worker. Students should wear name tags indicating their jobs.

● The real classroom teacher should question each panel member about the type of job he or she does and the supplies needed to do his or her job.

(The white star that appears before the objective refers to the starred objective found at the beginning of the lesson. The first objective is always the lesson's main objective.)

Review Master Booklet, p. 5

UNDERSTANDING THE LESSON

NAME _____   U N I T

UNDERSTANDING THE LESSON   **1**

Recalling Facts   LESSON 2 CONTENT MASTER

✱ Circle the pictures that answer the questions about workers in your school.

1. Who would you visit if you were sick?

2. Where would you go to get a book?

3. Who would teach you to read?

Think and Do: Write the name of your teacher. Use the back of this sheet.
Use with textbook pages 8–11.   5

Optional Activities

11

Why Do Schools Have Rules?

Objectives

★ 1. **Explain** the purpose of rules and describe when rules are needed.

2. **Name** rules that help students work and play together.

3. **Learn** fire drill rules.

1 STARTING THE LESSON

Motivation/ Prior Knowledge

■ Take out a game board that the students will recognize. Ask for two volunteers to play the game with you.

■ Do not follow the rules during your turn. Have the students explain the rules to you.

■ Have the class identify how rules help people play together.

Study the Vocabulary

NEW WORDS	DISCUSSION WORDS	ORAL VOCABULARY
rules	fire drill fairly safe	obey follow

■ Write on the chalkboard the six words listed above and review the meaning of each word. Have the students use the words to complete the sentences below.

A _____ lets people practice leaving a building without talking. (fire drill)

It is not _____ to run in the hallway. (safe)

_____ help people work together. (Rules)

People _____ or _____ rules when they play games together. (obey, follow)

People use rules to be sure that they are playing a game _____ . (fairly)

12

Lesson 3

Why Do Schools Have Rules?

FIRE DRILL RULES
1. Make a single line.
2. Walk to nearest exit.
3. No talking.

Ding! Ding! Ding!
It was a fire drill.
Rules told the class what to do.
The class quickly got in a line.
No one talked.
The class went outside.

12

Optional Activities

PREVIEWING LESSON VOCABULARY

NAME _____

PREVIEWING LESSON VOCABULARY   UNIT **1**

Using a New Word   LESSON 3 VOCABULARY MASTER

✱ A RULE keeps people safe. Write the word RULE next to any sentence that is a RULE.

1. Stay in your seat on the school bus.   __rule__

2. I like to go to school. _____

3. Do not cross the street alone.   __rule__

✱ Circle the names of people who help you follow RULES in school.

(teacher)   painter   firefighter

baker   (principal)   (librarian)

Think and Do: Draw a picture of a friend following a RULE. Use the back of this sheet.

6   Use with textbook pages 12–17.

Review Master Booklet, p. 6

Schools have many rules.

Rules help keep everyone safe.

Some rules tell children what to do.

13

Read and Discuss
Text pages 12–15

Help the students recognize the rules that are in use by naming specific rules in school and the places that have them. Then ask these questions about pp. 12–15.

1. **What did the class do during the fire drill?**
   (It got in line without talking and left the building. *p. 12*)

2. **How do schools keep the students safe?**
   (They have rules. Some rules tell the students what to do. *p. 13*)

   Thinking Critically How do rules help you while you are working and playing with friends? (Evaluate)
   (Answers may include that rules help people organize their games and work. *pp. 13–15*)

VISUAL THINKING SKILL

Comparing the Photographs

■ Have the students look at the pictures of the fire drill and the slide on pp. 12–13. Then ask this question.
   What rule are the students following in both pictures?
   (They are moving in an orderly line.)

Cooperative Learning

Role-Playing Have the students work in groups of three or four. Assign each group a playground rule. Each group should discuss what would happen if no one followed that rule and what happens when people do follow the rule.

● Each group will be role-playing the scene that would occur if the rule was not followed and then the scene that would occur if the rule was followed. Each group member must have a role. One member must be the narrator.

● Each group should practice once alone. The narrator should practice introducing the scenes. Then the groups should perform their situations for the rest of the class.

● Each group should evaluate how well it planned its presentation and how well it listened to other groups' presentations.

Optional Activities

Meeting Individual Needs

Concept:
Following Rules

Following rules on the playground keeps the students safe. The three activities listed below will help the students identify the playground rules they follow.

◆ **EASY** Have each student use a sheet of drawing paper to draw two playground scenes concerning one playground rule.

On one side of the paper, have the student draw a picture of a playground rule being followed properly. On the other side, have the student draw a picture depicting the same rule not being followed.

Ask the student to explain the pictures to the class and tell why the rule is needed.

◀▶ **AVERAGE** Have a group of three or four students work together to make a playground safety book. The students should each draw a picture of a safety rule in use. Below the picture, the student should write or dictate the rule and how it keeps students safe.

Have the students make a cover for their book and bind the pages together.

◀▮▶ **CHALLENGING** Have a small group of students draw a sequence of pictures about a playground situation to be shown on a cardboard viewer. (See pages U1-E and U1-F for assembly instructions.)

The first frame should show the students using a playground rule. The second frame should show the same students not following the rule. The third frame should show the students solving the problem. The last frame should show the students using the rule again.

VISUAL THINKING SKILL

Interpreting the Photograph

■ Have the students look at the picture on p. 14.
What rule are the students following?
(Raise your hand to give an answer.)

14

Some rules are for a class.
Rules help the children work in the room.

14

Optional Activities

Curriculum Connection

Health and Safety Have each student state his or her full name and address. Practice with the students until each one attains the skill.

● Invite a firefighter to visit your class.

● Have the officer review fire safety rules at school and at home. Have the officer explain how to call for help in case of a fire.

● Have the students practice the procedure for reporting a fire. Use play telephones if available.

Rules help children play together.
Children use rules to play fairly.

Lesson 3

Review

Read and Think

1. What do rules tell you? (Recall)

2. What are the rules in your school? (Synthesize)

Skills Check

Look at the picture on page 14.

How are rules helping the children?

15

Answers to Read and Think

1. Rules tell you what to do.

2. Answers will vary but should be correct for your school building.

Answer to Skills Check

The students will be able to hear each other's answers. They know to raise their hands to give an answer during this type of activity.

Answer to Lesson Title Question

Ask the lesson title question, found at the beginning of the lesson:

Why do schools have rules?

(Schools have rules to keep the students safe and to help them know what to do while learning and playing.)

Additional Practice

You may wish to assign the ancillary materials listed below.

Understanding the Lesson p. 7

Workbook p. 5

Writing to Learn

Places with Special Rules Have the students write about or draw a place where rules are in use. The students should say why the rules are needed there.

Reteaching Main Objective

⭐ ***Recognize the purpose of rules and when rules are needed.***

● Have each student draw a picture of a school rule being followed. The student should write or dictate the rule and why it is needed. A playground rule should not be chosen.

(The white star that appears before the objective refers to the starred objective found at the beginning of the lesson. The first objective is always the lesson's main objective.) **Review Master Booklet, p. 7**

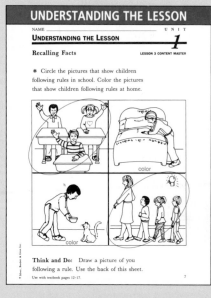

UNDERSTANDING THE LESSON

NAME _____

UNDERSTANDING THE LESSON

UNIT 1

Recalling Facts

LESSON 3 CONTENT MASTER

✳ Circle the pictures that show children following rules in school. Color the pictures that show children following rules at home.

color

color

color

Think and Do: Draw a picture of you following a rule. Use the back of this sheet.

Use with textbook pages 12-17.

7

Optional Activities

15

CITIZENSHIP AND AMERICAN VALUES

Objectives

1. **Identify** the reasons why we need rules.
2. **Name** the classroom rules and the problems they solve.

Guided Reading

To identify the need for rules in the classroom and the ways they help us, ask the students the following questions after they read pp. 16–17.

1. **Why are Peter and Jim angry?**
   (They both want to use the same markers. *p. 16*)
2. **How did the class solve this problem?**
   (They made rules about the markers. p. 17)

How Can Rules Help Us?

We have learned about rules.
Rules help the class work together.
Peter and Jim are angry.
They both want all the new markers.

16

Optional Activities

Current Events

● Invite an official from an organization or committee in the community to come in and speak to the class about an upcoming project in the community, such as the building of a new road or the restoration of a historical building. Have the speaker discuss the process with the students and have them identify the rules that must be followed in order for the project to be successful.

The class made some rules
about the markers.
The rules tell
how to use
the markers in
the classroom.

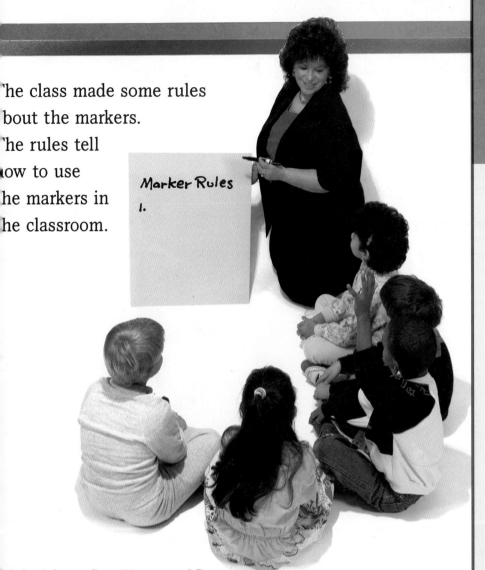

Marker Rules
1.

Thinking for Yourself

1. What marker rules do you think the class made?
2. What other rules might help the class?
3. What rules help your class?

17

Answers to Thinking for Yourself

1. Answers may include only being able to take one marker at a time, putting the markers back after you use them, waiting your turn to use them.

2. Answers may include sharing classroom materials, asking permission before borrowing someone else's things, not interrupting someone when they are speaking, and so on.

3. Rules should include the class rules listed on chalkboard at the beginning of the lesson plus any acceptable new rules the students suggest.

For Your Information

The First Continental Congress met in Philadelphia on September 5, 1774. There were 56 delegates in attendance to represent the colonies. This convention marked the beginning of a unified government in which rules were agreed upon and followed by all of the colonies.

The Second Continental Congress, which met the next year, would be responsible for creating the Declaration of Independence.

Optional Activities

How Are Children Alike and Different?

Objectives

★1. **Recognize** and respect others as individuals.

2. **Describe** how others are alike and different.

1 STARTING THE LESSON

Motivation/ Prior Knowledge

■ List four possible free-time activities, such as *playing a game, doing a puzzle, reading,* and *drawing,* on the chalkboard.

■ Name each choice and have the students raise their hands to vote for their favorite activity.

■ Tell the students that the different choices show us that people are not exactly the same.

Study the Vocabulary

NEW WORDS	DISCUSSION WORDS	ORAL VOCABULARY
alike different	special	unique

■ Seat the children in a circle and select one student to state why he or she is special. Have each student repeat his or her neighbor's statement and add his or her own statement. For example, "_____ is special because _____, and I am special because _____."

■ Complete the circle and then ask two students who are alike in some way to stand up. Have the other students guess how the standing students are alike.

■ Have the class identify other groups of students who are alike or different in some way.

How Are Children Alike and Different?

All About Us

Mrs. Johnson's class made a book.
It tells about the children.
This picture shows some of the children.
They are **alike** in some ways.
All the children are in first grade.

18

Optional Activities

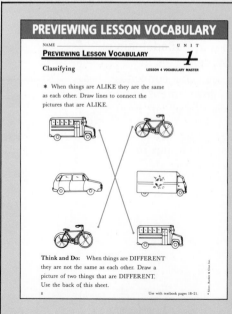

PREVIEWING LESSON VOCABULARY

NAME _____ UNIT **1**

PREVIEWING LESSON VOCABULARY

Classifying LESSON 4 VOCABULARY MASTER

✱ When things are ALIKE they are the same as each other. Draw lines to connect the pictures that are ALIKE.

Think and Do: When things are DIFFERENT they are not the same as each other. Draw a picture of two things that are DIFFERENT. Use the back of this sheet.

8 Use with textbook pages 18–21.

Review Master Booklet, p. 8

The children are **different** in some ways.
Different means not the same.
Some of the children have dark hair.
Some of the children have light hair.
In what other ways are they different?

by Mrs. Johnson's Class

19

Read and Discuss
Text pages 18–21

To heighten the students' awareness of alike and different, have the students review pp. 18–21, and ask them the following questions.

1. **How are all the students in Mrs. Johnson's class the same?**
   (They are all in first grade. *p.18*)

2. **In what ways are the students different?**
   (Hair color *p.19*)

3. **What class do all the students in Mrs. Johnson's class like?**
   (Music *p. 20*)

   Thinking Critically **What makes you special?** (Evaluate)
   (Encourage the students to explain why they feel that they have a certain talent. *p. 21*)

   Thinking Critically **Why is it important that people are not exactly the same?** (Analyze)
   (Encourage the students to think of ways that we learn from others and help others with our talents. For example, some students may teach athletic skills to others. Accept all reasonable answers. *pp. 18-21*)

Curriculum Connection

Mathematics Have the students, as a group, select four games that they like to play in school. Draw a chart with four columns and label each column for a game.

- Have each student write his or her name on an index card and decorate it. The student should attach the card to the chart below the label of the game that he or she likes to play.

- Have the students count the number of people who selected each game and compare preferences.

Making a Necklace

- Have the students draw each other's names from a hat. Each student should dictate why the named classmate is special. Have the student copy the message into the middle of a 5″ construction paper circle.

- Have the student decorate the space around the writing and the back of the circle. Then punch a hole in the circle and add a yarn necklace.

- Each student should present the necklace to the classmate and state why he or she is special.

Optional Activities

Meeting Individual Needs

Concept: Using Alike and Different

Each person is unique. Use the three activities below to help the students recognize how people are alike and different.

EASY Have each student think of a question about a food or an activity to ask ten classmates. For example, "Do you like swimming?" The question must be stated so that the answer will indicate like or dislike.

Have the student fold an 8½″ × 11″ piece of paper in half. The student should draw a happy face on one side of the paper for the "like" responses and a sad face on the other side for the "dislike" responses. The student should list the classmates' names under the appropriate response.

The student should share the results of his or her question with the class.

AVERAGE Have each student think about one friend. Ask the student to write two ways that he or she and the friend are alike and two ways that they are different.

CHALLENGING Have each student select a family member. Have the student label the sides of an 8½″ × 11″ piece of paper *Alike* and *Different*.

The student should draw pictures to show three ways that he or she and the family member are alike and pictures to show three ways that they are different.

VISUAL THINKING SKILL

Comparing the Photographs

- Have the students examine the photographs on p. 21. Then ask the following question.
  How are the activities that the students are shown doing on p. 21 the same?
  (Ballet and painting are artistic. Jump rope, soccer, and ballet are athletic. Reading and painting are quiet activities.)

Sometimes we like to do the same things

Here is another page from the book.
The children are alike and different in what they like to do.
They all like music class.

Some children like other things too.

Optional Activities

Writing to Learn

Comparing Objects Have each student draw a picture containing two objects.

- Under the picture, the student should write one way that the objects in the picture are alike and one way that they are different.

Sometimes we like to do different things.

Each of us is special.

Lesson 4

Review

Read and Think

1. What does <u>different</u> mean? (Recall)
2. How are you and other children alike? (Synthesize)

Skills Check

Look at the pictures on page 21.

How are the children different?

21

Lesson 4 Review

Answers to Read and Think

1. *Different* means not the same.

2. Answers might include that they are in the same class and that some of the students are the same age. Accept all correct answers.

Answer to Skills Check

Answers may include the following: Some of the students are boys; others are girls. Some of the students have long hair; others have short hair. The students are from different races. Accept all reasonable answers.

Answer to Lesson Title Question

Ask the lesson title question, found at the beginning of the lesson: **How are children alike and different?**

(Answers should include that they are alike and different in the way they look and in the things they like to do.)

Additional Practice

You may wish to assign the ancillary materials listed below.

Understanding the Lesson p. 9

Workbook p. 6

Reteaching Main Objective

⭐ *Recognize and respect others as individuals.*

● Have the students work in pairs to find out how they are alike and different. One student should keep track of how they are alike. The other student should record how they are different.

● The students should report to the class on their findings. Each student should state one reason why he or she thinks that his or her partner is special.

(The white star that appears before the objective refers to the starred objective found at the beginning of the lesson. The first objective is always the lesson's main objective.)

Review Master Booklet, p. 9

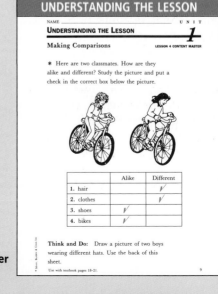

UNDERSTANDING THE LESSON

NAME _____ U N I T

UNDERSTANDING THE LESSON *1*

Making Comparisons LESSON 4 CONTENT MASTER

✱ Here are two classmates. How are they alike and different? Study the picture and put a check in the correct box below the picture.

	Alike	Different
1. hair		✓
2. clothes		✓
3. shoes	✓	
4. bikes	✓	

Think and Do: Draw a picture of two boys wearing different hats. Use the back of this sheet.

Use with textbook pages 18–21.

9

Optional Activities

21

What Do We Learn in School?

Objectives

★ **1. Name** the subject areas learned in school.

2. Identify the different ways that students work together in school.

3. Distinguish between water and land on a globe.

1 STARTING THE LESSON

Motivation/ Prior Knowledge

■ Write the schedule for the day on the chalkboard. Have the students identify the different subjects included in the schedule. Ask the students to give examples of the types of activities they do in each subject.

Study the Vocabulary

NEW WORDS	DISCUSSION WORDS
globe	*learn*
alone	*earth*
group	*model*

■ Ask a student to stand alone in front of the room. Then ask a group of students to stand in the front of the room. Explain that the students represent the terms *alone* and *group*.

■ List materials that the class uses in school. Ask the students to state whether people use the item alone, in a group, or both ways. For example, flash cards can be used alone and in a group.

■ Display a globe. Explain that the globe shows water and land and that we learn from the globe. Ask the students to think of ways the globe might be used.

Lesson 5

What Do We Learn in School?

Pam and her class are busy.
They learn many things in school.

Optional Activities

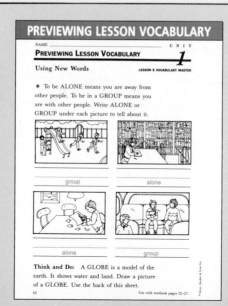

PREVIEWING LESSON VOCABULARY

NAME _____   UNIT **1**

PREVIEWING LESSON VOCABULARY

Using New Words   LESSON 5 VOCABULARY MASTER

✱ To be ALONE means you are away from other people. To be in a GROUP means you are with other people. Write ALONE or GROUP under each picture to tell about it.

_____ group   _____ alone

_____ alone   _____ group

Think and Do: A GLOBE is a model of the earth. It shows water and land. Draw a picture of a GLOBE. Use the back of this sheet.

10   Use with textbook pages 22–27.

Review Master Booklet, p. 10

They read and write stories.
They learn about numbers.

Read and Discuss
Text pages 22–25

To help the students reflect on the variety of activities in school, ask them to review pages 22–25. Then ask the following questions.

1. **Why is Pam busy at school?**
   (She is reading and writing stories, learning about numbers, and learning about the globe. *pp. 22–25*)

2. **What is a globe?**
   (A model of the earth *p. 24*)

   Thinking Critically **What activities do you do in school that Pam does not tell about?** (Analyze)
   (Answers might include go to the gym, learn about music, and practice handwriting. *pp. 22–25*)

Writing a Class Story

● Have the class dictate a story about a typical day at school. Have the students describe the day according to the schedule for the selected day. Write the story on large chart paper so that the students can refer to the story as they are adding to it.

● Divide the story into small sections. Give each student a section of the story to copy and illustrate. Gather the pages and assemble them in book form.

Reading a Calendar

● Display a calendar in the classroom. Help the students to name the days of the week and the current month.

● Have the students use the terms *before* and *after* to describe the sequence of days in a week. Then have the students describe activities that occur on different days. Indicate these special events on the calendar.

● Throughout the school year, help the students to identify and to sequence the months of the year. Encourage the students to sequence holidays during the school year as well.

Optional Activities

Analyzing the Photographs

■ Have the students examine the picture of the globe on page 24. Then ask the following questions.

How can you tell that a globe is a model of the earth?

(The globe has the same shape but is smaller.)

Most of the globe is blue. What does that tell us about the earth?

(It tells us that most of the earth is covered with water.)

SKILL TRACE:	Understanding the Globe	
INTRODUCE	**PRACTICE**	**TEST**
PE, p. 24	PE, p. 25	Unit 1 Test,
	TE, p. U1–C	TMB
	WB, pp. 28–29	

The class learns about the **globe** too.
The globe is a model of the earth.
The globe shows water and land.
Water is blue on this globe.

24

For Your Information

● The photograph of the earth shows North America and South America. The photograph was taken by a satellite at an altitude of 22,300 miles. The western coasts of the United States, Mexico, and Central America are clearly visible. Clouds are present over the eastern coasts of the United States, the Great Lakes, and most of South America.

Curriculum Connection

Science Use a flashlight and a classroom globe to explain how the earth has day and night. Rotate the classroom globe one time and explain that the earth rotates one time each day.

● Tell the students that the flashlight is like the sun. Shine the light on North America. Help the students understand that this would be daytime in North America.

● Turn North America away from the light. Explain that this would be nighttime in North America.

The class learns about new places at school.
The children find the places on the globe.

25

Meeting Individual Needs
Concept:
Alone vs. Group

People work and play under a variety of situations. Sometimes we work with others. Sometimes we work alone. Help the students recognize different working and playing conditions by assigning one of the activities listed below.

◆ **EASY** Have the students cut out from magazines pictures of people alone and in groups. Have the students paste the pictures on a sheet of paper. All the "group" pictures should be on one side; the "alone" pictures should be on the other side. The students should label one side *group* and the other side *alone*.

Have the students present their pictures to the class.

◀▶ **AVERAGE** Have each student choose his or her favorite activity to do alone at school and his or her favorite activity to do in a group.

Have the student draw a picture of each activity. The student should write a sentence describing each picture.

◀▮▶ **CHALLENGING** Have each student pick an activity that can be done alone or in a group. Have the student illustrate the activity being done alone and in a group. The illustrations should be on opposite sides of the paper.

The students should write a sentence using the word *group* or *alone* to describe each situation.

Graphic Organizer

To help the students link the ideas presented in this lesson, draw the graphic organizer on the chalkboard and ask the students to name entries for each category. Possible entries are shown here.

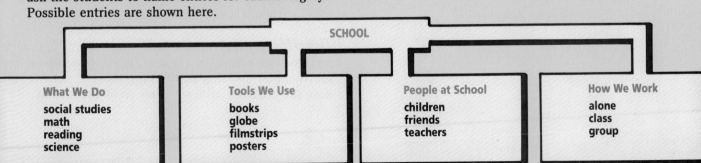

SCHOOL

What We Do	Tools We Use	People at School	How We Work
social studies	books	children	alone
math	globe	friends	class
reading	filmstrips	teachers	group
science	posters		

Optional Activities

25

Read and Discuss
Text pages 26–27

Have the children review the social concepts discussed on pp. 26–27 by answering the following questions.

1. **Sometimes Pam works alone. How else does she work in school?**
   (In a group *p. 26*)

2. **What does Pam do at school with her friends?**
   (She works and plays with them. *p. 27*)

   Thinking Critically What kinds of activities can Pam do in a group?
   (Analyze)
   (Answers may include play outside and do art projects. *pp. 22–27*)

VISUAL THINKING SKILL

Interpreting the Photograph

■ Have the students look at the photograph on p. 27. Then ask this question. **How can you tell that the students are friends?**
(Their arms are around each other, and they look happy.)

Sometimes Pam works **alone**.
Sometimes she is part of a **group**.

26

Optional Activities

Group Games
● To emphasize the concept of group, have the class play kickball or follow the leader. Discuss with the students what would happen if someone tried to play the games alone.

Writing to Learn
Drawing the Globe   Have the students draw a picture of a globe. They should show land and water on the globe. Have the students label the picture *Globe* and write a sentence about it.

Describing an Activity   Ask the students to draw a picture of an activity or a type of activity (read aloud time, for example) that they really enjoy doing at school. Then have the students write why they enjoy the activity.

Pam has friends at school.
She works and plays with them.
Pam has fun in school.

Lesson 5
Review

Read and Think

1. What does Pam do in school? (Recall)
2. How is Pam's school like your school? (Synthesize)

Skills Check

Think about what you learn in school.
List the things you do in one day.

27

Lesson 5 Review

Answers to Read and Think
1. Pam reads, writes, learns about numbers, uses the globe, and works alone or in groups.
2. Answers should reflect a comparison of the subjects taught and the manner in which work is completed.

Answer to Skills Check
Answers may include reading, math, science, social studies, gym, and music.

Answer to Lesson Title Question

Ask the lesson title question, found at the beginning of the lesson: **What do we learn in school?**
(Students learn how to read, how to write, how to compute mathematics, and how to use the globe in school. They also learn to work alone and in groups.)

Additional Practice

You may wish to assign the ancillary material listed below.
Understanding the Lesson p. 11
Workbook p. 7

Reteaching Main Objective

⭐ *Name the subject areas learned in school.*

- List on the chalkboard objects that you use to teach different subjects. Make a second list in a different order that shows the subjects' names.
- Have the students match the objects to each subject.

(The white star that appears before the objective refers to the starred objective found at the beginning of the lesson. The first objective is always the lesson's main objective.)

Review Master
Booklet, p. 11

UNDERSTANDING THE LESSON

NAME _____ UNIT 1
UNDERSTANDING THE LESSON
Drawing Conclusions   LESSON 5 CONTENT MASTER

✱ What do you learn at school? Draw lines from the teacher to the things you learn at school.

Globe

Think and Do: Draw a picture of a group of your school friends. Use the back of this sheet.
Use with textbook pages 22–27.   11

27

Using the New Words

The vocabulary terms in this review were introduced in the unit. Some students may have difficulty distinguishing between similar concepts. Discuss the meaning of each word in relation to the pictures before having the students match the words to the pictures.

Suggested Answers

1. G
2. A
3. D
4. B
5. E
6. C
7. F

Accept other responses if students can explain their choice.

A. Using the New Words

Find the picture that best matches each word.

1. school _____
2. alike _____
3. group _____
4. different _____
5. globe _____
6. alone _____
7. rule _____

A.

B.

C.

D.

E.

F.

G.

28

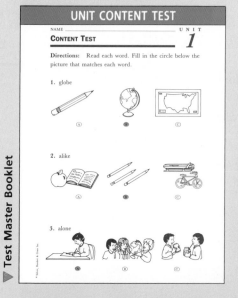

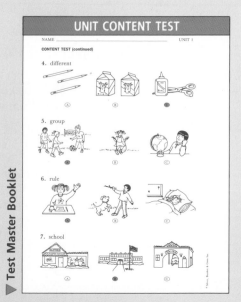

B. Remembering What You Read

Answer these questions about the unit.

1. What does Pam's class do in school?

2. What do rules tell people?

3. Look at the pictures below.

   What other things can you do alone?

   What other things can you do in a group?

C. Summarizing the Unit

Make a puppet of a worker in your school.

Tell the class about your worker.

Why did you choose this worker?

How are the workers in your school alike?

29

Remembering What You Read

Answer these questions about the unit.

1. The class learns together. The students read and write stories. They learn about numbers, and they learn about the globe.

2. Rules tell people what to do.

3. Accept all reasonable answers. Reading and jumping rope are two possible answers for activities done alone. Kickball and singing are possible answers for activities done in a group.

Summarizing the Unit

Review with the students some of the workers in the school, such as the librarian, the nurse, teachers, and the principal.

Have the students each make a puppet from a sock or a paper lunch bag. Have them use felt, construction paper, buttons, and yarn to decorate the puppet.

Have the students discuss their puppet with the class. They should tell the class how their worker helps the students in the school.

UNIT CONTENT TEST

NAME _____ UNIT 1

CONTENT TEST (continued)

Directions: Read each sentence. Fill in the circle below the picture that matches the sentence.

8. I help children who are sick.

   Ⓐ   Ⓑ   ●

9. I help children cross the street.

   Ⓐ   Ⓑ   Ⓒ

10. I help children choose books.

   Ⓐ   Ⓑ   Ⓒ

▶ Test Master Booklet

UNIT SKILLS TEST

NAME _____ UNIT 1

SKILLS TEST

Directions: Look at the traffic light. Write the correct color of each light on the lines next to the traffic light. Use the colors in the word box.

Sample   red

1.   yellow

2.   green

| green | red | yellow |

Directions: Read each rule below. Write the correct color next to the rule. Use the colors in the word box.

3. BE CAREFUL   yellow

4. GO   green

5. STOP   red

▶ Test Master Booklet

Objectives

1. **Read** the signals on a traffic light.
2. **State** the traffic rules associated with each color of a traffic light.

Why Do I Need This Skill?

To help the students recognize the need to have and follow traffic lights, ask the follow questions.

1. **Where are traffic lights found?**
   (Answers should include at street intersections.)

2. **How, do you think, do people decide where to place traffic lights?**
   (Answers should include at places where many people and vehicles need to go in different directions.)

Learning the Skill

To help the students recognize and understand the functioning of a traffic light, ask them the following questions.

1. **What are the three colors on a traffic light?**
   (Red, yellow, and green)

2. **Where is each color found on the traffic light?**
   (Red—top; yellow—middle; green—bottom)

3. **What does each color mean?**
   (Red—stop; yellow—be careful; green—go)

SKILL TRACE:	Understanding Traffic Lights	
INTRODUCE PE, p. 30	**PRACTICE** PE, p. 31 TE, p. 47	**TEST** Unit 1 Test, TMB

 ## Why Do I Need This Skill?

Streets can be busy places.
Traffic lights help you use streets safely.

 ## Learning the Skill

There are three colors in a traffic light.
There is a rule for each color.

A red light means stop.

A yellow light means be careful.

A green light means go.

Optional Activities

Curriculum Connection

Art   Have the students use an 8½" × 11" piece of yellow paper and three 2½" diameter white circles to make a model of a traffic light.

● Have the students color one circle red, one circle yellow, and one circle green. Then have them outline the edge of the circle in black.

● Have the students write the rule for each color in the correct circle. Use the terms *Go, Stop,* and *Be careful.* Have the students paste the circles in a vertical column in the correct order to represent the traffic light.

 ## Practicing the Skill

Look at the three traffic lights in the box.
There is a letter under each light.
Find the letter that matches each rule.

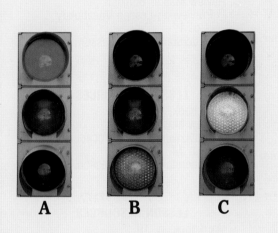

A   B   C

1. Go. _____

2. Stop. _____

3. Be careful. _____

Applying the Skill

Look at the traffic light in the picture.
Can the person cross the street now?

31

Practicing the Skill

Have the students find the letter that matches each rule.

1. B

2. A

3. C

For students having difficulty with this concept, you may wish to assign the Reteaching activity.

Applying the Skill

Have the students look at the traffic light in the picture. Since the light is green, the person can cross the street.

Reteaching Activity

Have the students review the three traffic light rules as a class.

Have the students line up in a cleared space. Have them play Red Light, Green Light. After the first game, allow a student to call the commands.

Add a yellow-light command to the game. Have the students slow down whenever they hear this command.

Optional Activities

Unit 2 Resource Center

CITIZENSHIP AND AMERICAN VALUES VIDEO LIBRARY: *Celebrate with Me*

Family
(pp. 32–53)

Unit Theme: Families are special groups of people who love each other and work and play together.

UNIT RESOURCES

Unit 2 Test

SOCIAL STUDIES LIBRARY: *Dear Daddy*
Georgia Music
The Wednesday Surprise

LESSON 1 What Is a Family?
(pp. 34–37)

Theme: A family is a special group of people who love and help each other.

LESSON RESOURCES

Workbook, p. 8
Review Master Booklet
  Previewing Lesson Vocabulary,
  p. 12
Understanding the Lesson, p. 13

LESSON 2 How Do Families Change?
(pp. 38–41)

Theme: Families experience change when they add or lose members and when they move.

LESSON RESOURCES

Workbook, p. 9
Review Master Booklet
  Previewing Lesson Vocabulary,
  p. 14
Understanding the Lesson, p. 15

LESSON 3 What Is a Map?
(pp. 42–45)

Theme: A map is a special kind of drawing that contains a map key so that people can understand and use the map.

LESSON RESOURCES

Workbook, p. 10
Review Master Booklet
  Previewing Lesson Vocabulary,
  p. 16
Understanding the Lesson, p. 17

SOCIAL STUDIES LIBRARY: *Jamaica Tag-Along*
The Wednesday Surprise

LESSON 4 What Do Family Members Do Together?
(pp. 46–49)

Theme: Family members choose the ways that they work and play together.

LESSON RESOURCES

Workbook, p. 11
Review Master Booklet
  Understanding the Lesson, p. 18

LESSON 5 What Were Families like Long Ago?
(pp. 50–53)

Theme: Family that lived on farms long ago worked together to meet their needs. Their social activities were done with family members and neighbors.

LESSON RESOURCES

Workbook, p. 12
Review Master Booklet
  Previewing Lesson Vocabulary,
  p. 19
Understanding the Lesson, p. 20

PACING GUIDE

September UNIT	October UNIT	November UNITS	December UNIT	January UNIT	February UNIT	March UNITS	April UNIT	May UNIT
1	2	2–3	3	4	5	5–6	6	7

Annotated Bibliography

Books for Teachers

Lipson, Eden Ross. *The New York Times Parent's Guide to the Best Books for Children.* New York: Times Books, 1988. ISBN 0-812-91688-3. A comprehensive reference book for parents as well as teachers. Books are categorized as follows: wordless, picture books, storybooks, early reading, middle reading, and young adult. Each title is accompanied by a description.

McElmeel, Sharron L. *My Bag of Book Tricks.* Englewood, CO: Teachers Ideas Press, 1979. ISBN 0-872-87722-1. This book categorizes books by themes and gives suggestions for literature-related activities to do with children.

Books for Read Aloud

Blaine, Marge. *The Terrible Thing That Happened at Our House.* New York: Parents Magazine Press, 1975. ISBN 0-819-30781-5. A young child tells the story of the changes that occurred at his house when his mother went back to work.

DePaola, Tomie. *Now One Foot, Now the Other.* New York: Putnam, 1981. ISBN 0-399-20774-0. A boy teaches his grandfather how to walk again after he has a stroke.

Levinson, Riki. *I Go with My Family to Grandma's.* New York: Dutton, 1986. ISBN 0-525-44261-8. Five cousins and their families gather at grandma's house in Brooklyn.

Wilhelm, Hans. *A New Home, a New Friend.* New York: Random House, 1985. ISBN 0-394-97226-0. A boy is anxious about moving to a new house until he becomes friendly with a big dog.

Williams, Vera B. *A Chair for My Mother.* New York: Greenwillow Books, 1982. ISBN 0-688-00914-X. Because all of their furniture was lost in a fire, a child, her waitress mother, and her grandmother save dimes to buy a chair.

Filmstrips and Videos

Farm Family in Autumn. Chicago: Britannica Films and Video. 15-minute video (2654). The whole farm family is depicted during harvest time.

Farm Family in Spring. Chicago: Britannica Films and Video. 15-minute video (2557). Springtime is busy on the farm. Adults and children are shown involved in various activities.

Learning to Read Maps. Chicago: Britannica Films and Video. 12-minute video (3673). A clown helps young children learn how maps are useful.

Computer Software

Lollipop Dragon's World of Maps and Globes. Apple II. Chicago: Society of Visual Education.

Bulletin Board Idea

FAMILIES ARE SPECIAL

caring   working   helping   sharing

Student Activity

Have the students each make a paper chain. The first name of each family member should be written on a separate link. The family name should also be written on one of the links. Have the students form circles with their links. Each family will be represented by a separate circle.

Then have the students draw pictures to illustrate caring, sharing, helping, and working in families.

Working Together in Families

How do people work together in families?

In Unit 2 the students will learn that family members work together in many ways. They will learn about some of the ways that members of farm families worked together long ago. The following activities are designed to reinforce students' awareness of how families work together.

SOCIAL STUDIES

Geography Have the students think about the places in their community that they visit every week. Ask the students the following questions to help them remember these places.

1. Do you usually go straight home after school?

2. What do you do on Saturdays and Sundays? Do you go to visit special places?

■ Make two columns on the chalkboard. Label the first column *Where We Go* and the second column *Who Helps Us Get There*. In the first column, list some of the places that the students visit. Ask the students whether other members of their family help them get to these places. List these family members in the second column.

■ Then discuss with the students how the members of a family work together to get one another to the places they need to be. For example, a father may drive a mother to a commuter train, or an older sister may walk her brother to school.

Economics Discuss with the students how families earn money to buy what they need and want. Tell the students that families earn money in many different ways. In some families, both parents may earn money by working outside the home. Have the students interview a parent or an older sibling about his or her job. The students may ask these questions.

1. What job do you have now, or what job would you like to have?

2. Have you had different jobs?

Sociology Explore how individual families work within larger groups. Have the students think about different groups their family participates in. They may be religious groups, sports groups, community groups, or social concerns groups. Have each student draw a picture of his or her family participating in one of these groups. Have the students explain their picture to the class.

LANGUAGE ARTS

■ Tell the students to pretend that they are the mother or father in a family. The other family members include a ten-year-old girl, a seven-year-old boy, a six-month-old boy, two dogs, and one cat.

■ Then tell students to imagine how carefully this family must work together every morning in order to get the children to school, the baby to day care, and the parents to work. Discuss who would feed the baby, who would walk and feed the animals, and who would take care of other responsibilities.

■ Assign volunteers a role in this family. Include the dogs and the cat.

Have the actors show in words and in pantomime how the family works together every morning, from the time that the alarm goes off to the time that the last person leaves the house.

LITERATURE

■ Read Chapter 1 of *Pippi Longstocking* to the class. *Pippi Longstocking* was written by Astrid Lindgreen (New York: Harmony Raine, 1980, ISBN 0-899-67013-X) and tells the story of a ten-year-old girl who lives with a horse and a monkey in a large house called Villa Villekulla. Pippi has many adventures with her friends Tommy and Annika, who live in a more conventional family. Discuss Pippi's "family" with the students asking questions such as these.

1. **What do you think are the best and worst things about Pippi's life?**
2. **How is Pippi like other children?**
3. **How is she different?**

ART

■ Discuss how families can work together to prepare meals and to clean up after meals. Ask the students if they have jobs to do at dinner time. Then ask them what kinds of foods they prepare for themselves. Students may say that they prepare simple dishes, such as cold cereal with milk or peanut butter sandwiches.

■ Have the students draw pictures of food that they prepare themselves. Have the students present their pictures to the class. Display the pictures.

Make a Mobile

INSTRUCTIONS FOR THE TEACHER:

Focus In this unit the students will learn that family structures vary. Family structures vary in relation to family size, the members who make up the family, and the family members who live at home. In some cases the students may be living with people to whom they are not related. For this activity, have the students consider the people they are living with as their family.

Review the concept of family as presented in Lesson 1, "What Is a Family?" and in lesson 4, "What Do Family Members Do Together?". *Family* is defined as "a special group of people who love and help each other." Family members also plan how they will work and play together.

Tell the students that this activity asks them to think about their family members. They will be making mobiles about their families.

Warm-up Activity Remind the students that every person is special. Have the students begin by each naming something that he or she likes to do. Playing sports and reading a book are two possible answers. List the students' answers on the chalkboard.

Ask the students to continue this activity by listing the names of the people in their families. Ask the students if they can name other activities that people in their families enjoy. Add these activities to the list on the chalkboard.

Ask each student to name two people in his or her family and something that makes each of them special. Tell the students that they will name something special about the rest of their family members when they make a mobile.

Ask the students what they might draw to show that someone likes to swim. A swimming pool is one possible answer. Have the students name possible drawings for some of the activities listed on the chalkboard.

ACTIVITY FOR THE STUDENTS:

Procedure Assemble the following materials for your class to complete the activity: one coat hanger per student, one 6″-length of sentence strip paper per student, construction paper, markers, crayons, scissors, 4″ pieces of yarn, and glue for the class.

Making the Mobile Distribute one sentence strip to each student. Have each one write his or her last name on the sentence strip. Tape the sentence strip across the top of the coat hanger. This will identify the family represented on each mobile.

Distribute the construction paper, crayons, markers, scissors, yarn, and glue. Ask the students to illustrate the members of their families. Have the students write their family members' names below the illustrations. Help the students spell the names correctly. On another sheet of paper, the students should draw something to show how each family member is special. The ideas generated during the Warm-up Activity should help here.

Once the drawings are complete, have the students cut out the picture for each family member and the drawing to show how that person is special. Have the students glue these pictures back to back and glue one end of a piece of yarn to the paper. Once the glue has dried, have the students tie their pictures onto the hangers.

Follow-up Activity Ask the students to describe their family members by showing their mobiles to the class. Have them explain each of the illustrations selected to describe their family members.

Extension You may wish to have the students make other mobiles throughout the year. They may make mobiles to show their basic needs. They may also make mobiles to show workers making goods or providing services. Your students may also wish to make mobiles that show the different states they have visited and what they saw while they were there.

Workbook Pages

NAME _____

MEMBERS OF A FAMILY

Observing

✳ Everyone is a member of a family. Can you find the four members of this family? Circle them.

8

Unit 2, pages 34–37

© Silver, Burdett & Ginn Inc.

NAME _____

HOW THINGS CHANGE

Following Directions

✳ When something changes, it does not stay the same. Draw a line from each picture in Column A to a picture in Column B to show the change.

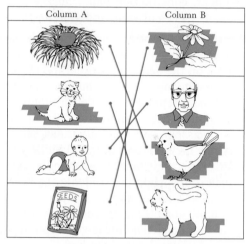

© Silver, Burdett & Ginn Inc.

Unit 2, pages 38–41

9

NAME _____

USING A MAP

Understanding Direction Words, Using a Map Key

✳ Look at the map of a department store. The key shows the departments in the store. Use the key to answer the questions.

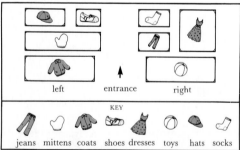

left   entrance   right

KEY

jeans mittens coats shoes dresses toys hats socks

1. What is the symbol for the department that is nearest the coat department? _____

2. Which department is the farthest away from the hat department? _____
   toys

3. Which department is to the left of the shoe department? _____
   hats

10

Unit 2, pages 42–45

© Silver, Burdett & Ginn Inc.

NAME _____

THINGS FAMILIES DO TOGETHER

Identifying

✳ Color each picture that shows what families do together.

color

color

© Silver, Burdett & Ginn Inc.

Unit 2, pages 46–49

11

U2-G

Workbook Pages

NAME _____

UNIT
2

TODAY AND LONG AGO

Reading a Picture

❋ People and things look different now from the way they did long ago. Write "long ago" under each picture that shows something from a long time ago. Write "today" under each picture that shows something you may see today.

today

long ago

long ago

today

12

Unit 2, pages 50–53

© Silver, Burdett & Ginn Inc.

TEACHER NOTES

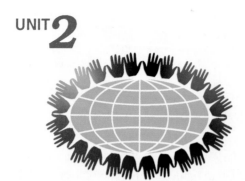

UNIT 2

MULTICULTURAL PERSPECTIVES

Family Favorites (*pages 34–37*)
Discuss with the students types of special family celebrations. Encourage the students to consider yearly celebrations, such as birthdays, religious celebrations, and cultural experiences. Ask the students to bring in photographs of a special family celebration.

Have a show-and-tell session with the class. Have each student describe his or her photograph. Have the students mention the following points when describing the celebration.

- The size of the celebration
- Family members who were present
- Distances (if any) that people traveled to attend the celebration
- Any special traditional clothes worn
- Any special foods eaten

Have each student write or dictate a few sentences about the celebration he or she described. Make a bulletin board with the pictures and stories.

If some students are not able to bring in a photograph, have them draw a picture of an event and describe it to the class.

Explain to the students that families have traditions that are based on their heritage. In some communities, many families have similar cultural backgrounds. In other communities, the families have different cultural backgrounds.

Unit 2 FAMILY

New Words

family

change

house
street
grass

map

map key

farm

32

Optional Activities

Making Paper Dolls

- In advance of the lesson, make patterns of generic paper dolls in adult and child sizes.

- Begin the lesson by having the students look at the picture on pp. 32–33. Tell them this family is outside its home. Have them identify who the different members of the family might be.

- Have each student use the paper doll patterns to trace a paper doll for each member of his or her family.

Welcoming New Family Members
(pages 38–41)

Ask the students how a family may gain new members. Students may mention one of the following.

- Wedding
- Birth of a new child
- Adoption

Families often gather to celebrate a new member joining a family. Ask the students if they have attended or participated in christenings, baptisms, brists, engagement parties, or weddings. Have the students describe the events. Conclude the discussion with the point that there are many different ways to welcome new family members.

Family Fun *(pages 46–49)*

Mirandy and Brother Wind by Patricia McKissack (New York: Knopf, 1988) is the story of two young teenagers who participate in a local cakewalk competition.

Prepare the class for the story by reading the Author's Note to the students. Ask them if they have seen pictures of their grandparents or even great-grandparents when they were younger. Ask them if the people in the pictures seem to be dressed differently than people dress now. Finally, ask the students whether the people shown were living in the United States or other countries when the pictures were taken.

Read the story aloud to the students and show the pictures. *Note:* This story is written in dialect. You may choose to improvise and read it without the dialect.

After you have finished the story, review it and have the students identify the family relationships of the people in the story to Mirandy.

Probe the students' understanding of the story by asking them about the following.

- The setting
- When the story takes place
- The cakewalk

Conclude the classroom discussion with the thought that even though the setting and time may be different for this family-community event, people enjoy a fun evening.

Provide markers, crayons, yarn, tissue paper, and construction paper for the students to use to decorate their dolls.

Have the students glue the dolls so that each family is holding hands in a row. Make a tag to label each family Display the dolls around the room.

Optional Activities

What Is a Family?

Objectives

★ **1. Define** *family* as a special group of people.

2. Recognize that families differ in size and structure.

1 STARTING THE LESSON

Motivation/ Prior Knowledge

■ Have the students think about the different people in their families. Ask the students to name the roles of the people in their families—mother, father, and so on. Make a list of family roles on the chalkboard.

■ Call out 2, 3, 4, 5, 6, and so on. Have the students raise their hands when they hear the correct number of members for their family. Tell the students that families are not all the same size.

Study the Vocabulary

NEW WORDS	DISCUSSION WORDS	ORAL VOCABULARY
family	*member*	*mother* *father* *sister* *brother* *parent* *grandparent*

■ Have each student draw a picture of his or her family. Have each student show the picture to the class and introduce each family member. For example, the student might say, "This is my brother, Tom." Have the students use the vocabulary terms in their introductions.

34

What Is a Family?

A **family** is a special group of people. Everyone is a member of a family.

34

Optional Activities

PREVIEWING LESSON VOCABULARY

NAME _____

PREVIEWING LESSON VOCABULARY UNIT **2**

Using a New Word LESSON 1 VOCABULARY MASTER

✱ A FAMILY is a special group of people.
Write the names of two people in your family.

1. _____ 2. _____

✱ Everyone is a MEMBER of a family. Draw
a picture below of a MEMBER of your family.

Think and Do: Draw a picture that shows
something you do with your FAMILY. Use the
back of this sheet.

12 Use with textbook pages 34–37.

Review Master Booklet, p. 12

Families are different in some ways. Families are different sizes. Sometimes the whole family does not live together.

DEVELOPING THE LESSON

Read and Discuss
Text pages 34–37

Have the students read pp. 34–37. Help the students use the definition of family by asking them these questions.

1. **How do we describe a family?**
   (A special group of people *p. 34*)

2. **How can family members help each other?**
   (Play with challenging toys, learn new skills *p. 36*)

   Thinking Critically How can family members show that they love one another? (Evaluate)
   (A kiss or a pat on the shoulder are two possibilities. Accept all reasonable answers. *pp. 36–37*)

VISUAL THINKING SKILL

Comparing the Photographs

■ Help the students identify various family structures by having them compare the photographs on pp. 34–35.
How are the family structures shown in the three photographs different?
(Different number of members and different members present *pp. 34–35*)

Graphic Organizer

To help the students develop their definition of *family*, put this graphic organizer outline on the chalkboard. Complete the organizer with the students' answers. Some examples are included.

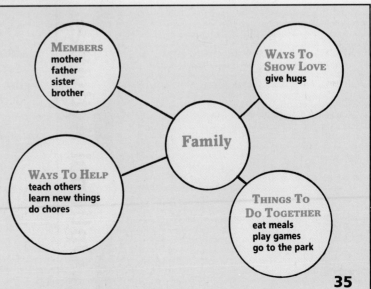

MEMBERS
mother
father
sister
brother

WAYS TO SHOW LOVE
give hugs

Family

WAYS TO HELP
teach others
learn new things
do chores

THINGS TO DO TOGETHER
eat meals
play games
go to the park

Optional Activities

Meeting Individual Needs

Concept:
Family Structure

The students must recognize that family structures vary. Assign one of these activities to help develop this concept.

◆ **EASY** Have the students draw pictures of two different families and then explain how the families are different (one parent, more members, and so on).

◀▶ **AVERAGE** Have each student cut out pictures of four families from magazines. Have the student mount the pictures on drawing paper and label the members of each family. Then ask the student to write two sentences that compare two of the families.

◀▮▶ **CHALLENGING** Have each student list the family members in two imaginary families and write a story about them.

VISUAL THINKING SKILL

Comparing the Photographs

■ Have the students look at the photographs on p. 36. Then ask the following question.
How is the first grader's job different in each picture?
(Top—helping brother; bottom—learning from brother)

Family members help each other.
Tom is helping Tim with the train.
Nina is learning to ride a bike.

36

Optional Activities

Writing to Learn

Helping in Families Ask the students to list three ways that they can help people in their families. Mount the list on a piece of drawing paper and have the students decorate it. Have the students take their lists home.

Family members show they love
each other in many ways.
A hug is one way to show love.

sson 1

Review

Read and Think

1. How are families different?

2. How do you help your family?

Skills Check

Write a story about a special day you had
with your family.

 CLOSING
THE LESSON

Lesson 1 Review

Answers to Read and Think

1. Families are different in size and in
   structure.

2. Answers may include making the bed
   or setting the table. Accept all reasonable answers.

Answer to Skills Check

Stories will vary, but must involve family
members.

Answer to Lesson Title Question

Ask the lesson title question, found at the
beginning of the lesson: **What is a family?**
(A family is a special group of people who
love and help each other.)

Additional Practice

You may wish to assign the ancillary mate-
rials listed below.
Understanding the Lesson p. 13
Workbook p. 8

Reteaching Main Objective

⭐ *Define* family *as a special group of people.*

● Have each student make a book about his or her family.
Each page of the book should show a picture of one
family member and say why that person is special.
Assemble the pages into a book for the student.

Review Master
Booklet, p. 13

UNDERSTANDING THE LESSON

NAME _____

UNDERSTANDING THE LESSON

UNIT
2

Recalling Facts

LESSON 1 CONTENT MASTER

✱ Families are alike in some ways. They are
different in other ways. Draw lines to join the
families that have the same number of
members.

Think and Do: Draw a picture of your
family. Use the back of this sheet.

Use with textbook pages 34-37.   13

Optional Activities

How Do Families Change?

Objectives

★**1. Define** *change*.

2. Identify the feelings that can be caused by change.

3. Name events that can cause change in a family.

1 STARTING THE LESSON

Motivation/ Prior Knowledge

■ Play two versions of Simon Says with the students. In the first game, give only one command and then keep repeating it. Ask the students what they notice about the game.

■ Then play the game again, using different commands. Ask the students how this game is different.

■ Tell the students that the second version has many changes in it. The commands do not stay the same.

Study the Vocabulary

NEW WORDS	DISCUSSION WORDS	ORAL VOCABULARY
change	happy sad moved	scared excited upset

■ Tell the students that events can make us feel different ways. List *happy*, *sad*, *excited*, *upset*, and *scared* on the chalkboard. Have the students give examples of when they might experience these feelings.

■ Have the students identify any of the experiences that are changes.

38

How Do Families Change?

Dan's family had a **change**. A change is when something does not stay the same. Dan has a new baby sister. His family is bigger now.

38

Optional Activities

PREVIEWING LESSON VOCABULARY

NAME _____

PREVIEWING LESSON VOCABULARY   UNIT **2**

Comparing and Contrasting   LESSON 2 VOCABULARY MASTER

✳ CHANGE means something does not stay the same. Look at the pictures below. If a picture shows CHANGE for a family, write CHANGE on the line next to it.

____change____

_____

_____

____change____

Think and Do: Draw a picture that shows a CHANGE your family has had. Use the back of this sheet.

14   Use with textbook pages 38–41.

Review Master Booklet, p. 14

Dan told the class about his new sister.
Then the class talked about other changes.
Some changes make people happy.
Some changes make people sad.

Read and Discuss
Text pages 38–41

To help the students understand that there are changes in families and that changes create different emotions, have them read pp. 38–41 and answer these questions.

1. **What change happened in Dan's family?**
   (A sister was born. *p. 38*)

2. **What changes happened to the families shown on pp. 40–41?**
   (Family moved, *p. 40*, brother went away to school, *p. 40*, grandfather moved in, *p. 41*)

   Thinking Critically Name a change that can make you feel happy and sad. (Evaluate)
   (Accept supported answers. Moving can make people feel happy and sad.)

VISUAL THINKING SKILL

Analyzing the Photographs

■ Ask the students to look at the pictures on pp. 38–39. Then ask the following question.
How do you think Dan feels about the change in his family? How can you tell?
(He is happy. He is smiling in both pictures and holding the baby in one.)

Curriculum Connection

Science Have the students observe how plants change as they grow.

Give each student a small clear plastic cup, some potting soil, and some marigold seeds. Have the students plant the seeds and water them.

Set up an observation chart near the plants. Record the growth changes daily.

Summarize the changes with the students once the flowers are full grown.

Feelings Change

● Help the students recognize experiences when they have felt different emotions. Ask the students to draw a picture of an event that made them sad. Then have the students draw a picture of an event that made them feel better.

● Have the students label their pictures Sad and Happy.

Optional Activities

39

Meeting Individual Needs

Concept:
Feelings and Change

Changes can cause students to have many different feelings. It is important for students to identify and discuss their feelings. They must also learn to handle their emotions. Assign one of the activities below to help the students understand their feelings.

◆**EASY** Have the students draw two pictures of faces showing different feelings. Have the students tell what they do to express their emotions.

◀▶**AVERAGE** Have the students cut out pictures of at least four people from magazines. The people's faces should show different emotions. Mount the pictures on drawing paper. Have the students tell what may have happened to each person to show that emotion.

◀▮▶**CHALLENGING** Have each student dictate two synonyms for *happy* and two synonyms for *sad*. Put the words on different sides of a sheet of drawing paper. Have the student draw a picture of a family feeling happy on one side of the paper and a picture of a family feeling sad on the other side. Display the pictures and discuss the synonyms.

VISUAL THINKING SKILL

Analyzing the Photographs

■ Have the students look at the changes in the photographs on pp. 40–41. Then ask each student to draw a picture of one of those changes happening to his or her family.

Meg's family moved to a new house. It was a change for her family. Meg likes her new house.

There was a change in Len's family. His brother went away to school. Len misses his brother.

40

Optional Activities

Writing to Learn

Growth and Changes Help the students recognize the changes that have occurred during their growth. Have them complete the sentence below and illustrate it. The students can do more than one example.

"When I was a baby, I could not _____ , but now I can!"

```
    #310   08-06-2009 9:04AM
Item(s) checked out to POLZIN, MARGARET.

TITLE: People in time and place
BARCODE: 25054006722167
DUE: 09-03-09

TITLE: The World around us
BARCODE: 25054006342578
DUE: 09-03-09

TITLE: The World around us
BARCODE: 25054006342560
DUE: 09-03-09

TITLE: The World around us
BARCODE: 25054006332736
DUE: 09-03-09

TITLE: Scott Foresman social studies
BARCODE: 25054007762600
DUE: 09-03-09
```

Jill's grandfather came to live with her family. She likes seeing him all the time.

Review

Read and Think

1. What is a change? (Recall)
2. Name one change your family has had.

(Synthesize)

Skills Check

Look at the top picture on page 40.
How can you tell this family moved?

41

Answers to Read and Think
1. A change is when something does not stay the same.
2. Accept all answers that are changes.

Answer to Skills Check
The family is unpacking boxes.

Answer to Lesson Title Question

Ask the lesson title question, found at the beginning of the lesson: **How do families change?**
(New members arrive, families move, and individual members move away.)

Additional Practice

You may wish to assign the ancillary materials listed below.
Understanding the Lesson p. 15
Workbook p. 9

Reteaching Main Objective

⭐ *Define* change.

● Have the students draw two pictures of the same family. The first picture should identify the family. The second picture should show a change happening to the family.

● The students should share with the class the change that the family has undergone.

Review Master
Booklet, p. 15

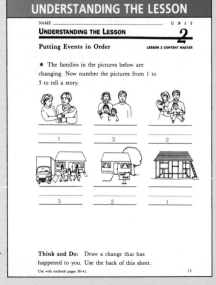

UNDERSTANDING THE LESSON

NAME _____
UNDERSTANDING THE LESSON   U N I T
                                              2
Putting Events in Order   LESSON 2 CONTENT MASTER

✱ The families in the pictures below are changing. Now number the pictures from 1 to 3 to tell a story.

1   3   2

3   2   1

Think and Do: Draw a change that has happened to you. Use the back of this sheet.
Use with textbook pages 38–41.   15

Optional Activities

41

What Is a Map?

Objectives

★1. **Define** the word *map* and **read** a map, using the map key.

2. **Discriminate** between right and left.

1 STARTING THE LESSON

Motivation/ Prior Knowledge

■ Have each student draw a large circle on a piece of drawing paper. Then ask each student to draw an *X*, a box, and a triangle near each other inside the circle.

■ Have the students compare their pictures. Ask if the items are in the same places in all the pictures.

■ Tell the students that in this lesson they will learn how to describe where items are placed.

Study the Vocabulary

NEW WORDS	DISCUSSION WORDS	ORAL VOCABULARY
map	right	symbol
map key	left	direction
	near	forward
	far	back
		floor plan

■ Write *left*, *right*, *forward*, and *back* on the chalkboard. Have the students stand near their seats. Give oral directions for the students to move forward, back, left, or right. Point to the correct word on the board as you give each direction.

■ Then have the students name items that are near and far from them.

Lesson 3

What Is a Map?

Dave and his family went to a shopping center. They went to the bank first. Then they went to the pet shop. The pet shop is near the bank.

42

PREVIEWING LESSON VOCABULARY

NAME _____   U N I T
PREVIEWING LESSON VOCABULARY   **2**

Following Directions   LESSON 3 VOCABULARY MASTER

✱ A MAP is a drawing that shows places. It uses pictures to show these places. A MAP KEY tells you what the pictures stand for. Look at the MAP of a school below. Look at the MAP KEY. Then follow the directions.

One classroom should be colored in.

MAP KEY
⬛Library   ☲☲Classroom   🍴Lunchroom   ⚽Gym

1. Put a circle around the library.

2. Put an X on the lunchroom.

3. Color a classroom.

Think and Do: Draw a picture of something in your classroom. Use the back of this sheet.

16   Use with textbook pages 42–45.

Review Master Booklet, p. 16

Next they went to the sports shop.

The sports shop is far from the bank.

Dave looked into the shoe store.

The sports shop is to the right of the shoe store.

The restaurant is to the left of the shoe store.

RIGHT

43

43

Read and Discuss
Text pages 42–45

To help the students differentiate between right and left and work with maps, ask the students the following questions.

1. **What are some of the words that tell us where things are?**
   (*Near, far, left, right pp. 42–43*)

2. **Look at the drawing of the shopping center. Pretend you are walking into the center. What is to the right of the entrance?**
   (*Clothing store or shop p. 43*)

   Thinking Critically If you were going to a zoo, what kinds of places would you look for in a map key?
   (Hypothesize)
   (Answers might include a monkey house, a seal pool, and a lion's den. Accept all reasonable answers. *pp. 44–45*)

GEOGRAPHY THEMES

Location

■ Have the students look at the shopping center shown on pp. 43–44. Ask the following question.
What stores are near the restaurant?
(Answers may include the pet shop, the bank and the shoe store.)

Cooperative Learning

Mapping an Island Ask the students to work in pairs to create a map of an imaginary island. They should begin by listing the places that they would like to have on the island such as a movie theater or a sports stadium. Then the students should decide on the shape of the island and which places to include on the island.

● The students should agree on the placement of the places on the map and evenly divide the drawing responsibilities. Then the students should draw the symbols for the map key.

● The students should decide on a name for the island. One person should write in the title. The partner should color the background of the map.

● The students should prepare to tell the class about their island. Each student should state two facts about the island when speaking to the class.

● Each pair should present its island to the class. The partners should evaluate how well they planned their island and used their time.

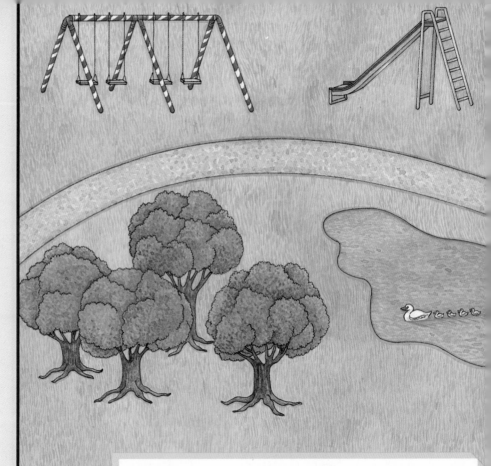

Dave and his family went to a park too.
This is a **map** of the park.
A map is a special kind of drawing.
Maps tell you where different places are.
A **map key** helps you understand the map.
Find the picture for table in the map key.
Now find the tables on the map.
How many tables are there in the park?

44

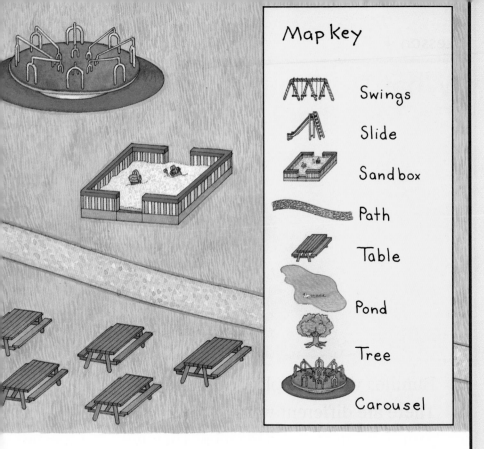

Map Key

Swings

Slide

Sandbox

Path

Table

Pond

Tree

Carousel

Lesson 3 — **Review** —

Read and Think

1. What does a map tell you? (Recall)

2. Tell where you would play in the park and why.
(Evaluate)

Skills Check

Look at the map on pages 44 and 45.

What is near the slide?

45

---

3 CLOSING THE LESSON

Lesson 3 Review

Answers to Read and Think

1. A map tells you where different places are.

2. Answers should relate to places shown on the map and include the reasons the students want to play there.

Answer to Skills Check

The swings, the carousel, and the pond are near the slide.

Answer to Lesson Title Question

Ask the lesson title question, found at the beginning of the lesson: **What is a map?** (A map is a special kind of drawing that helps you find different places. A map has a map key to help you understand the map.)

Additional Practice

You may wish to assign the ancillary materials listed below.
Understanding the Lesson p. 17
Workbook p. 10

Reteaching Main Objective

⭐ *Define the word* map *and read a map, using the* map key.

- Draw a simple map of a room. Include a map key. Position the items on the map so that they can be described in terms of being right or left of each other.

- Give each student a map and name a starting point. Tell the students to go to the right or left of objects on the map and identify where they land by reading the key.

Review Master Booklet, p. 17

UNDERSTANDING THE LESSON

NAME _____

UNDERSTANDING THE LESSON

U N I T
2

Using a Map   LESSON 3 CONTENT MASTER

✱ Look at the map of the park. Use the map key to answer the questions.

Map Key

🪑 bench   🌳 tree   ⬭ pond   🛝 slide

1. How many trees are in the park? ___6___

2. What is next to the pond? ___bench___

3. How many slides does the park have? ___1___

Think and Do: Draw a map of your school playground. Label it. Use the back of this sheet.

Use with textbook pages 42–45.   17

Optional Activities

45

What Do Family Members Do Together?

Objectives

★1. **Name** three activities that family members might choose to do together.

2. **Describe** possible activities of an English family.

3. **Locate** the United Kingdom on the world map.

1 STARTING THE LESSON

Motivation/ Prior Knowledge

■ Ask the students to think of something they did with a family member recently.

■ Have each student share his or her answer with a partner. Then ask several students to name the activity they thought of.

■ Tell the students that in this lesson they will learn about things that families can choose to do together.

Study the Vocabulary

DISCUSSION WORDS	ORAL VOCABULARY
choice	*responsibility*
help	
London	
work	
play	

■ On chart paper, write *Work* and *Play*. Ask the students to give examples of how their families work and play. Write their answers under the appropriate heading.

46

Lesson 4

What Do Family Members Do Together?

Families work and play together.
There are different ways to work and play.
Family members choose what they will do together.

46

Optional Activities

Curriculum Connection

Mathematics   Create word problems describing family situations for the children to solve. For example, "The Holton family has five members. Three members went to the park. How many members stayed home?"

Writing to Learn

Describing Family Activities   Have the students write about or illustrate one activity that they like to do with their families and one activity that they do not like to do.

Mark and his family help each other.
They work in the yard.
The family plays games too.
The family does many things together.

2 DEVELOPING THE LESSON

Read and Discuss
Text pages 46–49

Have the students read pp. 46–49 and answer the questions below to recognize the variety of activities families do.

1. **What are some things that families can do together?**
   (Work together, play together, help each other, and take trips together *pp. 46–49*)

2. **What kinds of activities do Mark's and George's families do together?**
   (Play together, work together, shop together *p. 47–48*)

   Thinking Critically What are your jobs at home, and how do they help your family? (Analyze)
   (Setting the table is a possible answer. Accept all reasonable answers that have an explanation. *pp. 46–49*)

VISUAL THINKING SKILL

Comparing the Visuals

■ Ask the students to look at the pictures and art work on pp. 46 and 47. Then ask:
   What kinds of activities are the families choosing to do together?
   (Origami, sledding, playing ball, going to the beach and garden work)

Host a Guest Speaker

● Invite someone who has lived in another country to speak to the class about family life in that country.

● Prior to the visit, you may wish to develop a list of American family activities. Then ask the visitor to compare the customs and activities of the other country with those on your list.

SKILLBUILDER REVIEW

Understanding Traffic Lights On pp. 30 and 31, the students learned how to read traffic lights. Remind the students that when they visit places with their families, they must read the traffic lights to be safe.

● Draw the outline of a traffic light and distribute copies to the students. Have the students color the lights correctly and name the rule associated with each color.

Optional Activities

Meeting Individual Needs

Concept:
Making Choices

Help the students understand the variety of work and relaxation activities available to families by assigning one of the activities described below.

◆ **EASY** Have the students work in pairs to create lists of play activities and work activities. Each list should have at least three entries. Have the students star the activities that they do with their families.

◀▶ **AVERAGE** Have the students work in pairs to make a "Busy Week" book. Have the students draw seven pictures of a family working and playing together. For each picture, have the students write a sentence following this pattern: "On _____ the _____ family does _____." Assemble the pages in weekday order and have the students design a cover.

◀▮▶ **CHALLENGING** Have each student find a picture from a magazine of family members doing a job around the house.

Have the student draw a picture of the family playing instead of working. Then have the student draw a picture to show what will happen if the family does not do the job.

GEOGRAPHY THEMES

Location

Have the students locate the United Kingdom, on the Atlas map on page 209. Tell the students that London is an important city in the United Kingdom.

PEN PALS

Mark and George are pen pals. They write to each other about their families.

Dear Mark,

It is fun to live in London.
My family and I have been busy.
We ride double decker buses.
We play football in the park.
We shop at the markets on the street.
I like to buy fresh bread for teatime.
Write back soon.

Your friend,
George

48

Optional Activities

For Your Information

● London is the capital city of the United Kingdom of Great Britain and Northern Ireland.

● London is an active city, but there are parks within it for residents and tourists. The photograph above shows the Clock Tower of the Houses of Parliament, which is located along the River Thames in the West End section of London.

● The English version of football, referred to in the letter, is equivalent to American soccer.

Sometimes families take trips.
Jan's family visits new places together.
Jan likes these special trips.

Goya and the Spirit of Enlightenment

Lesson 4 — Review

Read and Think

1. What does each family choose? (Recall)
2. What do you do with your family? (Analyze)

Skills Check

Look at the pictures on pages 46 and 47.
How are the families alike?

49

Answers to Read and Think
1. Each family chooses what its members will do together.
2. Answers will reflect the students' experiences with their families.

Answer to Skills Check
Answers may include that the families look happy and that the family members are together. All the families are small.

Answer to Lesson Title Question

Ask the lesson title question, found at the beginning of the lesson: **What do family members do together?**
(Family members work and play together. Chores around the house and playing games or taking trips are some of the activities that families do together.)

Additional Practice

You may wish to assign the ancillary materials listed below.
Understanding the Lesson p. 18
Workbook p. 11

Reteaching Main Objective

⭐ *Name three activities that family members might choose to do together.*

● List work and play activities on index cards. Have the students sort the cards into containers marked *Work* and *Play*. At the end of the activity, have the student name three family activities.

Review Master Booklet, p. 18

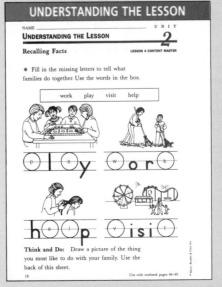

UNDERSTANDING THE LESSON

NAME _____
UNDERSTANDING THE LESSON

UNIT 2

Recalling Facts   LESSON 4 CONTENT MASTER

✻ Fill in the missing letters to tell what families do together. Use the words in the box.

| work | play | visit | help |

o l o y   w o r k

h o o p   v i s i o

Think and Do: Draw a picture of the thing you most like to do with your family. Use the back of this sheet.
18   Use with textbook pages 46–49.

Optional Activities

49

What Were Families like Long Ago?

Objectives

★1. **Compare** the daily life of a family on a farm of long ago with daily life today.

2. **Name** four jobs that were done on a farm long ago.

3. **Compare** the social opportunities on the farm of long ago with the social opportunities available today.

1 STARTING THE LESSON

Motivation/ Prior Knowledge

■ Ask the students to name the kinds of things one can see on a farm. List the items on the chalkboard.

■ Tell the students that today they are going to learn about life on a farm of long ago.

Study the Vocabulary

NEW WORD	DISCUSSION WORDS	ORAL VOCABULARY
farm	*long ago*	*chore*

■ Write the words *farm*, *long ago*, and *chore* on the chalkboard. Explain the meaning of each term. Then read aloud the sentences below and ask the students to use the words to fill in each blank.

People had to carry water to their homes _____ . (long ago)

There are many jobs to do on a _____ . (farm)

Making your bed might be a _____ that you do. (chore)

■ Have the students use the words in their own sentences.

50

Lesson 5

What Were Families like Long Ago?

My name is Anna.
My family and I live on a **farm**.
We care for animals and grow corn to sell.

Optional Activities

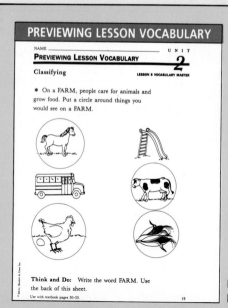

PREVIEWING LESSON VOCABULARY

NAME _____

PREVIEWING LESSON VOCABULARY

UNIT **2**

Classifying

LESSON 5 VOCABULARY MASTER

✳ On a FARM, people care for animals and grow food. Put a circle around things you would see on a FARM.

Think and Do: Write the word FARM. Use the back of this sheet.

Use with textbook pages 50–53.   19

Review Master Booklet, p. 19

My father and my brother work in the field.
My mother makes our clothes and cooks.
I help my mother.

51

Read and Discuss

Text pages 50–53

Have the students read pp. 50–53 and answer these questions about daily life on a farm of long ago.

1. **What jobs does each family member do on the farm?**
   (Everyone—care for animals; father and brother—fieldwork; Anna and mother—clothes and cooking *pp. 50–51*)

2. **What do Anna and her family do with their friends?**
   (Dance *p. 53*)

   Thinking Critically **How is the way we make and wash clothes today different from how it was done on farms of long ago?** (Analyze)
   Long ago, clothes were made and washed by hand. Today, people buy clothes and wash them in machines. *pp. 51–52*)

VISUAL THINKING SKILL

Analyzing the Drawing

■ Have the students look at the drawing on pp. 50–51, and ask them this question.
   What kinds of jobs do you think the family has to do on this farm?
   (Take care of the animals and the house, tend the garden and the fields)

Cooperative Learning

Summarizing Life Today Ask the students to work in groups of three. Each group should be assigned four or five letters of the alphabet.

● Have the students brainstorm in their groups to think of things that relate to life today that start with the letters of the alphabet that they have been assigned. For example, dogs, dryers, and dishwashers are examples for the letter D. One student should keep track of the ideas.

● Have the students draw or cut out pictures for each idea and mount them on a separate page for each letter. Have the group decide which pictures might have been present in families of long ago.

● Add word labels to each picture and assemble the pages in order. Add a cover page with the title "ABC's of the 1990s." Review the book with the class and have each group explain its pages.

● Have each group evaluate how well its members worked together.

Optional Activities

Meeting Individual Needs

Concept:
Making Comparisons

To help the students identify differences between situations, assign one of the activities below.

◆**EASY** Have the students work in pairs to draw two pictures of the same present day chore being done. Have the students include obvious differences in the pictures.

Have the students show the pictures to their classmates and ask them to identify the differences. The students should acknowledge correct answers.

◀▶**AVERAGE** Have the students name three appliances that people use today to do work around their homes. Write the words for the students and have the students use the words in a sentence. Then have the students illustrate their sentences.

Have the students present their pictures to the class. Ask the students to name ways the chores might have been done without the appliances.

◀▮▶**CHALLENGING** Have each student select one of the chores shown in the lesson and draw a picture of how the chore is currently done. Then have the student write how the chore was done long ago and how it is done today.

Analyzing the Drawing

■Ask the students to look at the picture on p. 52. Then ask this question.
How are the family members working together?
(Mother is washing, daughter is hanging clothes, son is bringing water. *p. 52*)

There are many jobs to do on our farm.
We work together to do some of the jobs.

52

Optional Activities

Curriculum Connection
Music Teach the students to sing "Old MacDonald Had a Farm." Once the students have learned the original version of the song, encourage the students to make up new verses to the song to describe life on a farm of long ago.

Writing to Learn
Writing a Diary Entry Have the students pretend to be Anna or her brother. Have the students describe their jobs on the farm for one day.

Friends come to our house too.
We all like to dance.
We have fun when our friends visit.

esson 5

Review

Read and Think

1. What kinds of jobs are there on a farm? (Recall)
2. What jobs do you do that are like Anna's? (Evaluate)

Skills Check

Look at the picture on pages 50 and 51.
How is Anna's house like your home?

53

3 CLOSING THE LESSON

Lesson 5 Review

Answers to Read and Think
1. Growing crops, caring for animals, and taking care of clothes are some of the jobs on a farm.
2. Answers will vary but must include jobs that compare to Anna's jobs.

Answers to Skills Check
Answers will vary but may include a reference to two stories, a chimney, or a porch.

Answer to Lesson Title Question
Ask the lesson title question, found at the beginning of the lesson: **What were families like long ago?**
(Families living on a farm had to provide their own food and clothing. They worked together to get the jobs on the farm done. They visited with friends and many enjoyed dancing.)

Additional Practice
You may wish to assign the ancillary materials listed below.
Understanding the Lesson p. 20
Workbook p. 12

Reteaching Main Objective
⭐ *Compare the daily life of a family on a farm long ago with daily life today.*
● Make a chart with the headings *Long Ago* and *Today*. Have the students compare the chores and socializing done long ago on a farm with today's equivalents. Record the students' responses in the chart.

Review Master
Booklet, p. 20

UNDERSTANDING THE LESSON

NAME _____ UNIT
UNDERSTANDING THE LESSON **2**

Drawing Conclusions   LESSON 5 CONTENT MASTER

✱ Circle the pictures that show what families were like long ago.

Think and Do: Draw a picture of a family from long ago doing something together. Use the back of this sheet.

20   Use with textbook pages 50–53.

Optional Activities

53

Using the New Words

The vocabulary terms in this review were introduced in the unit. Some students may have difficulty distinguishing between similar concepts. Discuss the meaning of each word in relation to the pictures before having the students match the words to the pictures.

Suggested Answers

1. E
2. B
3. C
4. A
5. D

Accept other responses if students can explain their choice.

A. Using the New Words

Find the picture that best matches each word.

1. farm _____
2. map _____
3. change _____
4. family _____
5. map key _____

A.

B.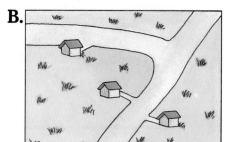

C.

D. MAP KEY

house

street

grass

E.

54

UNIT CONTENT TEST

NAME _____ UNIT 2

CONTENT TEST

Directions: Read each sentence. Fill in the circle below the picture that answers each question.

1. Which picture shows a family?

Ⓐ Ⓑ Ⓒ

2. Which picture shows a family member helping?

Ⓐ Ⓑ Ⓒ

3. Which picture shows a change in a family?

Ⓐ Ⓑ Ⓒ

▶ Test Master Booklet

UNIT CONTENT TEST

NAME _____ UNIT 2

CONTENT TEST (continued)

4. Which picture shows a family of long ago?

Ⓐ Ⓑ Ⓒ

5. Which picture shows a farm?

Ⓐ Ⓑ Ⓒ

6. Which picture shows a map key?

tree
swing
pond

Ⓐ Ⓑ Ⓒ

7. Which picture shows a family on a trip?

Ⓐ Ⓑ Ⓒ

▶ Test Master Booklet

54

B. Remembering What You Read

Answer these questions about the unit.

1. What is a family member?
2. What kinds of changes can families have?
3. How is your family different from Anna's family?

C. Summarizing the Unit

Look at the park map above.

1. What can families do in the park?
2. What would you do with your family?

55

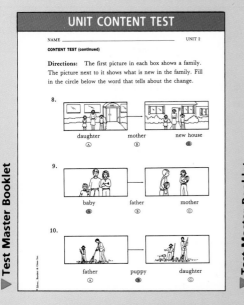

UNIT CONTENT TEST

NAME _____ UNIT 2

CONTENT TEST (continued)

Directions: The first picture in each box shows a family. The picture next to it shows what is new in the family. Fill in the circle below the word that tells about the change.

8.

daughter   mother   new house
Ⓐ   Ⓑ   Ⓒ

9.

baby   father   mother
Ⓐ   Ⓑ   Ⓒ

10.

father   puppy   daughter
Ⓐ   Ⓑ   Ⓒ

▶ Test Master Booklet

UNIT SKILLS TEST

NAME _____

SKILLS TEST

U N I T
2

Directions: The pictures below tell a story. To show what happened in order, write the correct word under each picture. Use the words in the box.

Then	Last	First	Next

Last   Next

Then   First

Circle the order word below:

5. map   family   (next)

▶ Test Master Booklet

Remembering What You Read

Answer these questions about the unit.

1. A family member is a person who is part of a family.
2. Families can get bigger or smaller. Families can move to new places to live.
3. Accept all reasonable answers. The students may compare the size of their family with the size of Anna's family. The students may also note differences in how the family performs it's daily chores.

Summarizing the Unit

Have the students utilize the map and the map key to answer the questions.

1. Families can ride in a boat, in a car, on the ferris wheel, or on the carousel. They can also get something to eat or buy a balloon.
2. Accept all answers that relate to activities that could be done in the park shown on p. 55.

55

SKILLBUILDER

Understanding Order

Objectives

1. **Sequence** a chain of four events.

2. **Recognize** *first, next, then,* and *last* as terms denoting sequence.

3. **Correlate** the terms *first, next, then,* and *last* to correct stages in a series of events.

Why Do I Need this Skill?

Recognizing the sequence or order of events helps people learn and process information. Help the student recognize the need for this skill by asking the following questions.

1. **How do you put your sneakers on?**
   (Answers should include opening the laces or the velcro, putting your foot in the sneaker, and tying the laces or closing the velcro.)

2. **What would happen if you closed the velcro or tied the laces before you put your foot in the sneakers?**
   (You would not be able to get your foot in the sneaker.)

3. **What are some other times when you need to do things in order?**
   (Accept all correct answers and list them on the chalkboard for later use.)

Learning the Skill

Write the four order words on the chalkboard. Have the students match each word to a picture on p. 56.

Have the students divide each of the activities that they named in part A into four steps. Have them attach an order word to each step.

SKILL TRACE:	Understanding Sequence	
INTRODUCE	**PRACTICE**	**TEST**
PE, p. 56	TE, p. 83	Unit 2 Test,
	WB, p. 19	TMB
	RMB, p. 15	

A Why Do I Need This Skill?

Everything happens in order.

Order helps us know how things happen.

Order helps us learn about new things.

B Learning the Skill

Some words tell us about order.

<u>First</u>, <u>next</u>, <u>then</u>, and <u>last</u> tell about order.

This story is in order.

<u>First</u> Mark ate dinner.

<u>Next</u> he wrote to his pen pal.

<u>Then</u> he read a story.

<u>Last</u> he went to bed.

Optional Activities

Writing to Learn

Sequencing the Morning's Activities Have the students describe four things they did this morning to prepare for school. Have the students begin each sentence with an order word. Have the students circle the order word in each sentence.

Practicing the Skill

an and her family went on a trip.
'ind the sentence for each picture.

. Next they packed the car.
. First they made their lunch.
. Last they ate the lunch.
. Then they went to the lake.

Applying the Skill

)raw four pictures in order.
Vrite the correct order word under each picture.

Reteaching Activity

Write yesterday's schedule on the chalkboard. Have the students select four activities from the schedule.

Have the students draw a picture and write a sentence containing an order word for each activity.

Have the students exchange pictures and sentences to sequence properly.

Optional Activities

Practicing the Skill

Have the students read the sentences and look at the pictures on p. 57.

From left to right, the correct sentences are the following.

2. First they made their lunch.

1. Next they packed the car.

4. Then they went to the lake.

3. Last they ate the lunch.

For students having difficulty with this concept, you may wish to assign the Reteaching activity at this time.

Applying the Skill

Have the students select a chain of events to illustrate. Below each picture, have the students write the correct sequence term.

Needs and Wants
(pp. 58–85)

Unit Theme: People must have food, clothing, and shelter to live. People can fulfill these needs in many ways.

UNIT RESOURCES
Unit 3 Test

LESSON *1* What Are Needs and Wants?
(pp. 60–63)

Theme: People must have their basic needs met to live. Wants are things that people would like to have.

LESSON RESOURCES
Workbook, p. 13
Review Master Booklet
  Previewing Lesson Vocabulary,
  pp. 21–22
Understanding the Lesson, p. 23

LESSON *2* What Kinds of Shelters Are There?
(pp. 66–69)

Theme: Shelters vary according to the climate they are in and the number of people that will live in them.

LESSON RESOURCES
Workbook, p. 14
Review Master Booklet
  Previewing Lesson Vocabulary,
  p. 24
Understanding the Lesson, p. 25

LESSON *3* Where Do We Get Food?
(pp. 76–81)

Theme: Farms and stores are people's main food sources.

LESSON RESOURCES
Workbook, p. 15
Review Master Booklet
  Previewing Lesson Vocabulary,
  p. 26
Understanding the Lesson, p. 27

LESSON *4* How Do We Get Clothing?
(pp. 82–85)

Theme: Clothing can be purchased in stores or made by hand.

LESSON RESOURCES
Workbook, p. 16
Review Master Booklet
  Understanding the Lesson, p. 28

PACING GUIDE

September	October	November	December	January	February	March	April	May
UNIT	UNIT	UNITS	UNIT	UNIT	UNIT	UNITS	UNIT	UNIT
1	2	2–3	3	4	5	5–6	6	7

Annotated Bibliography

Books for Teachers

Lipson, Eden Ross. *The New York Times Parent's Guide to the Best Books for Children.* New York: Times Books, 1988. ISBN 0-812-91688-3. A comprehensive reference book for parents as well as teachers. Books are categorized as follows: wordless, picture books, storybooks, early reading, middle reading, and young adult. Each title is accompanied by a description.

Polette, Nancy. *E Is for Everybody.* Metuchen, NJ: Scarecrow Press, 1976. ISBN 0-810-80966-4. This book presents information on reading aloud to children, includes 147 children's book titles that cover a broad range of topics, and gives ideas for activities that can be done with the books.

Trelease, Jim. *The Read Aloud Handbook,* 2nd ed. New York: Penguin Books, 1985. ISBN 0-140-46727-0. The author presents reasons why reading aloud to children is essential at all ages. In addition, he has compiled a list of good read-aloud books, complete with descriptions.

Books for Read Aloud

Hoban, Russell. *Bread and Jam for Frances.* New York: Harper & Row, 1964. ISBN 0-06-022359-6. Frances eats only bread and jam until one day she decides to expand her tastes.

Hoberman, Mary Ann. *A House Is a House for Me.* New York: Viking Press, 1978. ISBN 0-670-38016-4. This book lists in rhyme the houses of various animals and things.

Hutchins, Pat. *You'll Soon Grow into Them, Titch.* New York: Greenwillow Books, 1983. ISBN 0-688-01770-3. The tables turn at last for Titch who has always inherited an older sibling's clothes.

Kessler, Leonard. *Do You Have Any Carrots?* Champaign, IL: Garrard, 1979. ISBN 0-811-66074-5. Two little rabbits travel around the neighborhood looking for carrots and find out that their neighbors like to eat many different things.

 McCloskey, Robert. *Make Way for Ducklings.* New York: Viking Press, 1941. ISBN 0-670-45149-5. Mr. and Mrs. Mallard search for a home for their family in the Boston area.

Schaaf, Peter. *An Apartment House Close Up.* New York: Four Winds Press, 1980. ISBN 0-590-07670-1. This book is a photographic introduction to all aspects of an apartment house.

Spier, Peter. *Food Market.* New York: Doubleday, 1981. ISBN 0-385-15731-2. Pictorial book of what goes on at a market.

Bulletin Board Idea

NEEDS AND WANTS

FOOD	CLOTHING	SHELTER	WANTS
We eat food to stay healthy. Eggs, milk, lettuce, and tomatoes are some of the foods we can eat.	We wear clothes to protect ourselves. Hats, coats, and sweaters keep us warm.	A shelter is a place to live. Houses and apartments are examples of two kinds of shelters.	Puppies and kites are wants.

PICTURES

Student Activity

Have the students draw pictures for each category shown on the bulletin board. Have the students sort and hang the pictures on the bulletin board. If the pictures are hung with thumbtacks, they can be sorted many times.

You may wish to have the class dictate a summary about each need after each lesson is completed.

Clothing: One of Our Basic Needs

How do people meet their need for clothing?

In Unit 3 the students will learn that clothing is a necessity in people's lives. They will learn that people can meet this need by buying clothes in stores or by making them at home. In the following activities the students will learn more about clothing, both as a necessity item and as a luxury item.

SOCIAL STUDIES

History Explain to the students that when our country was very young, many families not only made their own clothing but they also sheared their own sheep, carded their own wool, spun the wool into yarn, and wove their own cloth. Describe these activities so that students can visualize the tasks involved in meeting the need for clothes.

■ Have each student make a poster showing the many tasks that you described. Tell the students to entitle their poster *Getting Clothes Long Ago.*

Economics Find pictures of contemporary children's clothing. You may wish to look in a library for back issues of the Sunday *New York Times,* which publishes a supplement on children's clothes each fall and spring, or simply bring in some colorful advertising brochures from local department stores. Show these pictures to the class.

■ Tell the students that sometimes people like to purchase more clothes than they need for survival. These extra clothes can be considered wants. Discuss this situation with the students by asking these questions.

1. Which clothes do you think are needs?

2. When would a new winter coat be a need? When would it be a want?

3. Which clothes are wants?

Sociology Have the students interview an older female relative or friend about how clothes for girls and women have changed during her lifetime. The students may wish to ask the following questions.

1. How were the clothes you wore to school and the clothes girls wear today alike? How are the clothes different?

2. How were the clothes you wore for swimming and the swim clothes today alike? How are they different?

3. Do you like the changes in girls' and women's clothes?

■ Have the students share the results of their interviews.

MATHEMATICS

Write the following information on the chalkboard under the heading *Ramon's Warmest Clothes*: *one overcoat, four pullover sweaters, two pairs of flannel pajamas.*

■ Have the students make a bar graph that tells how many overcoats, pullover sweaters, and pairs of flannel pajamas Ramon has. The students may wish to use the bar graph on p. 80 as a reference.

SCIENCE

■ Bring to class one long-sleeved sweater, one jacket or parka, one cotton or polyester shirt, and one T-shirt. Have the students put the clothes in order from the least warm to the warmest.

■ Ask the students to raise their hands when they know which item should be ranked first, second, and so on. Call on a student to say the correct item aloud and have a volunteer arrange the clothes in the proper order. You may wish to write the names of the items in the proper sequence on the chalkboard as the volunteer arranges them in sequence.

■ Ask the students to check the arrangement for errors. Have volunteers make any necessary corrections.

LANGUAGE ARTS

■ Ask the students to think about the kinds of clothing they wear for different activities. Brainstorm all the types of activities that students do. Some examples include going to school, playing outside, scouting, going to worship, sleeping, taking dance lessons, skiing, sledding, swimming, and horseback riding.

■ Invite the students to give an oral report describing all the different types of clothing they wear.

LITERATURE

Read to the students the story of "The Emperor's New Clothes" by Hans Christian Andersen. The tale appears in *The Complete Fairy Tales and Stories,* translated from the Danish by Erik Haugaard (New York: Doubleday & Co., Inc., 1974, ISBN 0-385-01901-7). Help the students interpret the story by asking these questions.

1. Do you think that the emperor was easily misled? Tell why.

2. Why, do you think, did the people pretend to see beautiful new clothes on the emperor?

3. Who is the hero of the story? Why?

Create a Classroom Store

INSTRUCTIONS FOR THE TEACHER:

Focus In this unit the student will learn that all people, in order to survive have basic needs that must be met. There are three basic needs: food, clothing, and shelter. The students will also learn that people have wants. Wants are items that people would like to have but do not need in order to survive.

This unit teaches the students to distinguish between needs and wants in Lesson 1, "What Are Needs and Wants?". It also explains to the students in Lesson 3, "Where Do We Get Food?" some of the places where people get food. Explain to the students that food is a basic need because people need food for good health. In the activity that follows, the students will deepen their understanding of food stores and the process of selecting food.

Warm-up Activity Write as column heads on the chalkboard the names of the four basic food groups: *Milk and Dairy, Fruits and Vegetables, Breads and Cereals,* and *Meats and Fish.* Ask the students to name foods that belong in each group. List their responses under the correct heading.

Review with the students examples of other basic needs. Then have the students give examples of things they want but do not require. Be sure the students understand the distinction between wants and needs before proceeding.

ACTIVITY FOR STUDENTS:

Procedure Ask the students to bring in empty food boxes and empty plastic food containers. Have the students bring in small plain boxes as well. Evaluate the labeled food boxes that the class has gathered. Cover the plain boxes with white paper and have the students make cartons of the types of foods that are missing from the basic food groups. For example, the students could label and color different vegetables on some boxes to represent frozen food. You might have the students cut out or color pictures of fresh fruit as well.

Divide the class into small groups and ask each group to make a sign for one of the four basic food groups. Be sure that the group names are listed on the chalkboard.

Creating the Classroom Store Clear a section of the classroom or have the students arrange their desks in rows to simulate rows in a classroom store. Hang the food-group signs above different sections. Have the students organize the packages in the appropriate aisles. Price each item accurately or on a scale from one to ten to allow the students to do math problems with the boxes.

Ask each student to make a shopping list that contains one item from each food group. Have the students alphabetize their lists.

Prepare other shopping lists for the students.

Ask them to find the total cost of the items on each list. If the students have completed the Skillbuilder at the end of this unit, you may wish to ask them to categorize the foods according to the different food groups.

Let the class members pretend to purchase items at the store. Give them counters to use as money. For students requiring an extra challenge, you may wish to provide a shopping list and insufficient funds for all the items on the list. Have the students decide which items they will purchase.

Follow-up Activity Invite another first-grade class to shop at your store. To prepare for this, have the students select items to be put on sale and create special advertising flyers.

Extension You may wish to show another type of shopping. Create a classroom clothing catalog. Have the students bring in magazine pictures or draw different items of clothing. Encourage the students to think of articles of clothing for all four seasons. Place each clothing item on its own page. Price each item. Make a catalog with the pictures.

Have the students create shopping lists to use with the catalog. Perhaps the students need to buy a shirt, shoes, and shorts. You may wish to have the students categorize the clothing items on their lists.

Workbook Pages

U N I T
3

NEEDS AND WANTS

Identifying

✳ Color the pictures that show something a person needs.

color   color

color

✳ Draw a picture of something you want.

Unit 3, pages 60–65   13

U N I T
3

DIFFERENT TYPES OF SHELTERS

Drawing Conclusions

✳ People live in many kinds of shelters. Draw and color a picture that shows a shelter of a family you know.

14   Unit 3, pages 66–75

U N I T
3

SHOPPING FOR FOOD

Making Choices

✳ Food is sold in different places. Circle the places where families get food.

Unit 3, pages 76–81   15

U N I T
3

HOW CLOTHES ARE MADE

Identifying

✳ Here are some clothes that Mrs. Jones sews.

_____
- - - - - - - - - - - - - - -
coat
_____
- - - - - - - - - - - - - - -
shirt
_____
- - - - - - - - - - - - - - -
dress
_____
- - - - - - - - - - - - - - -
skirt

✳ Write the correct word next to each picture.

skirt	shirt
coat	dress

16   Unit 3, pages 82–85

U3-G

TEACHER NOTES

MULTICULTURAL PERSPECTIVES

Clothing as a Need *(pages 61, 82–85)*
Explain to students that clothing is a need, but that the weather and climate of a location may alter the types of clothing that people wear.

Show the students pictures of a variety of styles of dress. You may include the following.
- Moslem women with covered heads
- Indian women in saris
- Pakistani men in turbans
- Arab men with long, white flowing clothing
- Africans and Hawaiians in brightly colored, loose-fitting clothes

Have the students look in books and magazines for different styles of dress. If you have students whose parents wear the traditional clothing of another country, ask the student to bring in pictures or samples of clothing items.

Once a variety of pictures has been accumulated, use a world map or globe to show where people wear each style of dress.

Make a class book about clothing. Mount the pictures on heavy construction paper or oak tag. Then add labels and descriptions for the pictures.

Eskimos *(pages 60–61, 66–69)*
Share with your students the information below about Eskimos. Ask the students to compare and contrast the Eskimos' former lifestyle with their lifestyle today. Then ask the students what kinds of changes they would have in their lives if they lived near the North Pole today.

Unit 3 · NEEDS AND WANTS

New Words

food

needs

clothing

shelter

apartment

wants

Pets

	Cat			
Cat				
Dog				
Fish				

bar graph

58

Optional Activities

Identifying Needs and Wants

- Have the students look at the title of the unit. Ask them to explain what they think the difference is between a need and a want. Conclude the discussion with the definition of a need as "something that one must have to live."

- Write a total of ten needs or wants, each on an index card. Include the needs of food, clothing, and shelter among the cards. You might write "a place to live," "clothes to wear," and "food to eat" to describe those needs and "new package of colored markers" to describe a want. Have the children identify whether each card describes a need or a want.

Optional Activities

● Then have the children look at the picture on pages 58–59. Ask them what needs they see being met in the picture. (The family has a place to live, clothes to wear, and food to eat.)

Eskimos live near the North Pole. Eskimos refer to themselves by different names that mean "people." The term *Eskimo* comes from a Native American word that means "eaters of raw meat."

Today, Eskimos live in houses in small towns or communities. They wear modern clothing and eat store-bought food.

In the area where some Eskimos live, the sun shines 24 hours a day for part of the summer and not at all for part of the winter. Although it does not snow a great deal, the snow stays on the ground from September until June because the temperature is so low.

Long ago, many Eskimos lived in tents during the summer and sod houses during the winter. Eskimos in some regions did live in snow houses during the winter, but other Eskimos built and lived in snow houses only as temporary homes.

During the winter, most Eskimos wore two layers of clothing made from caribou skin or sealskin. The inside layer of clothing had fur touching the skin and the outside layer had fur facing outside. The layer of clothing included a hooded coat, leggings, socks, boots, and mittens. During the summer, only one suit of clothing was worn.

The Eskimos ate mostly raw meat because they did not have a great deal of fuel for fires. If they cooked over an oil lamp, it took a long time for the meat to cook. The Eskimos ate caribou and seal meat. Soup was made with seal blood and hot water.

International Foods (*pages 76–81*)
Many communities now have stores that sell foods from around the world. Name some stores that sell this type of food in your area. Ask the students if they have any favorite foods from other countries.

You may wish to make some simple recipes from other countries with the class and have the students taste the foods. This may encourage them to try different types of food on their own.

59

What Are Needs and Wants?

Objectives

★1. **Differentiate** between needs and wants.

2. **List** examples of people's needs and wants.

3. **Name** the three basic needs that all people have.

1 STARTING THE LESSON

Motivation/ Prior Knowledge

■ Show the students a gift-wrapped package. Ask the students to suggest what might be in the package and list their ideas on the chalkboard.

■ Ask the students to identify any suggestions that name things that people must have to live.

Study the Vocabulary

NEW WORDS	DISCUSSION WORDS
needs	*healthy*
food	*protects*
clothing	
shelter	
wants	

■ Have the students look up the New Words in the Picture Glossary, pp. 212–216. Discuss the meaning of each word. Discuss how the pictures and the sentences help to define the words.

■ Have the students write sentences using the New Words and draw pictures to illustrate the words.

60

What Are Needs and Wants?

All people have **needs**.

A need is something people must have to live.

Food is a need.

People eat food to be healthy.

60

Optional Activities

PREVIEWING LESSON VOCABULARY

NAME _____

PREVIEWING LESSON VOCABULARY

UNIT **3**

Classifying

LESSON 1 VOCABULARY MASTER

* NEEDS are things we must have to live. Food, clothes, and shelter are NEEDS. Find words in the box at the bottom of the page that are NEEDS. Write them in the blanks where they belong.

NEEDS

Food	Clothes	Shelter
pear	shirt	house

* WANTS are things people would like to have but can live without. Toys, pets, and trips are WANTS. Find words in the box below that are WANTS. Write them in the blanks where they belong.

WANTS

Toys	Pets	Trips
bike	cat	beach

| beach | bike | pear | cat | shirt | house |

Think and Do: Draw a picture of your favorite food. Use the back of this sheet.

Use with textbook pages 60–63. 21

Review Master Booklet, p. 21

Clothing is a need.
Clothing protects people
from the weather.
All people need a **shelter**.
A shelter is a place to live.

Read and Discuss
Text pages 60–63

To help the students differentiate between needs and wants, have them read pp. 60–63 and answer these questions.

1. **What are three kinds of needs?**
(Food, clothing, shelter, *pp. 60–61*)

2. **How do our needs help us?**
(Food gives us health; clothing gives us protection; shelter gives us a place to live. *pp. 60–61*)

3. **Do all people have the same wants?**
(No, the pictures on pp. 62 and 63 show the people wanting books, a pet, a new car. *pp. 62–63*)

Thinking Critically **Why do people have different wants?** (Hypothesize)
(Answers may include that wants are based on the individual and that each person is different. *p. 62*)

VISUAL THINKING SKILL

Comparing the Photographs

Have the students children look at the pictures on pp. 60–61. **Which picture shows the three basic needs?**
(The picture on p. 60 shows food, clothing, and shelter.)

PREVIEWING LESSON VOCABULARY

NAME _____
PREVIEWING LESSON VOCABULARY **UNIT 3**

Identifying LESSON 1 VOCABULARY MASTER

✶ FOOD is what you eat to be healthy.
CLOTHING protects you from the weather. A SHELTER is a place to live. Look at the pictures below. Write FOOD, CLOTHING, or SHELTER in the blank next to each picture.

food

shelter

clothing

Think and Do: What kind of shelter do you live in? Draw a picture of it on the back of this sheet.

22 Use with textbook pages 60–65.

Review Master Booklet, p. 22

Cooperative Learning

Making a Mobile Have the students work in groups of four. Have each group brainstorm to list items that are needs and wants. One student should keep the list.

● Once the list is compiled, each student should be responsible for drawing the items in one group on a square of construction paper. Each student must label his or her square *Food, Clothing, Shelter,* or *Wants.* One student should be responsible for checking the labels.

● One student should gather a hanger and string, precut to the apppropriate lengths, from the supply table. Each student should tie his or her square on the hanger.

● One student should present the mobile to the class. Group members should evaluate how well they listened to each other and did their jobs.

Optional Activities

Meeting Individual Needs

Concept:
Changes in Wants

Although everyone has the same basic needs, wants may vary according to age.

◆EASY Have the students work in small groups. Each student should list several items that a baby, a child, or an adult might want.

The group should guess who would want those items.

◀▶AVERAGE Have each student fold a piece of 12″ × 18″ paper into thirds. Label the parts *Baby*, *Child*, and *Adult*.

Have each student cut out of magazines and catalogs a person for each category. Then have the student cut out three wants the person in each group might have.

◀▮▶CHALLENGING Have each student take a birthday survey.

Have the student ask five people below age five, five peers, and five adults to name one gift that they would like for their birthday.

The responses for each age group should be written on a separate page and illustrated.

The pages should be bound into a booklet.

VISUAL THINKING SKILL

Comparing the Photographs

■ Look at the pictures on pp. 62–63. **How are the wants different?**
(The children wanted different books, the boy or family wanted a new dog, and a family wanted a new car.)

People have **wants** too.

A want is something a person would like to have.

Wants are not the same for all people.

62

Optional Activities

Writing to Learn

Showing Needs and Wants Have each student fold his or her paper into thirds. In the center section, the student should draw himself or herself. In one empty section of the paper, the student should draw and list his or her wants. In the other empty section, the student should draw and list his or her needs.

Class Riddle Book

● Have each student write three clues to describe a want that is not a basic need. Then have the student draw and label the want on a separate piece of paper. Assemble the riddles into a book so that the answer is seen after turning a page.

Mary's family would like a new car.
What is a want that you have?

Lesson 1 ——— Review ———

Read and Think

1. How are wants and needs different? **(Analyze)**

2. What wants does your class have? **(Synthesize)**

Skills Check

Find the new words on pages 60 and 61.
Put the words in ABC order.

63

Answers to Read and Think
1. People must have their needs met to live. Wants are things that people would like to have.

2. Accept all answers that are wants.

Answer to Skills Check
Clothing, food, needs, shelter

Answer to Lesson Title Question

Ask the lesson title question, found at the beginning of the lesson:
What are needs and wants?
(Food, clothing, and shelter are needs. People must have these things to live. Wants are items that people would like to have but do not need to live.)

Additional Practice

You may wish to assign the ancillary materials listed below.
Understanding the Lesson p. 23
Workbook p. 13

Reteaching Main Objective

⭐ *Differentiate between needs and wants.*

- Have each student draw and label a picture of a want or a need on an index card. Collect, shuffle, and distribute the cards.

- Ask one student to stand and show his or her card. Ask all students who can identify the picture as a need or a want to stand. The first student with the correct answer shows his or her card next. Play continues until all the cards have been shown.

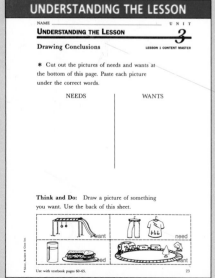

UNDERSTANDING THE LESSON

NAME _____

UNDERSTANDING THE LESSON   U N I T
                                        3

Drawing Conclusions   LESSON 1 CONTENT MASTER

✱ Cut out the pictures of needs and wants at the bottom of this page. Paste each picture under the correct words.

NEEDS   WANTS

Think and Do: Draw a picture of something you want. Use the back of this sheet.

Use with textbook pages 60–65.   23

Review Master
Booklet, p. 23

Optional Activities

63

CITIZENSHIP AND AMERICAN VALUES

How Can We Help Other People?

Objectives

1. **Identify** reasons why some people need our help and why it is important to help them.
2. **Identify** ways to help other people.

Guided Reading

To identify the fact that some people need our help, and some of the ways we can help them, ask students the following questions after they read pp. 64–65.

1. **How did Trevor help the man without a home?**
   (He gave him a pillow and a blanket so he could stay warm. *p. 64*)

2. **How did other people help Trevor?**
   (They gave him food and blankets to give to the people without homes. *p. 65*)

Trevor Ferrell heard about a problem.

The problem was that some people needed homes.

Trevor wanted to help the people.

One cold night he met a man without a home.

He gave the man a pillow and a blanket.

Trevor wanted the man to stay warm.

64

Optional Activities

Current Events Activity

● Discuss with the students what it would be like to be homeless. Discuss some of the things that homeless people need to live; food, clothing, a place to sleep, and so on.

● Have the students cut out pictures from magazines of things they would like to give a homeless person.

● Have the students explain how the items they selected would help to meet some of the basic needs of a homeless person.

More people needed Trevor's help.

Trevor wanted to help them too.

He asked other people to work with him.

They gave Trevor food and blankets.

Trevor gave them to people without homes.

Thinking for Yourself

1. Why did some people need Trevor's help?

2. Why, do you think, did other people help Trevor?

3. How can you help other people?

65

Answers to Thinking For Yourself

1. Some people needed Trevor's help because they had no homes.

2. Answers may include because they saw Trevor doing something nice for other people and they wanted to help; they felt sorry for the people with no homes and they wanted to help them.

3. Answers may include helping schoolmates with their homework, assisting a family member with a project or a problem, helping people in the community such as the aged or the disabled, and so on.

For Your Information

Trevor Ferrell was 11 years old when he began helping the homeless. His efforts have resulted in Trevor's Campaign for the Homeless, a non-profit organization located in Philadelphia, PA which provides food, shelter, clothing, and social services to the poor and homeless. He also founded a 33-room shelter called "Trevor's Place, A Home for the Homeless," and a thrift shop where homeless people can get food, clothing, furniture, and books.

Trevor has received many awards for his work. In 1985, the President's Volunteer Action Award was presented to Trevor at the White House by President Reagan.

Optional Activities

What Kinds of Shelters Are There?

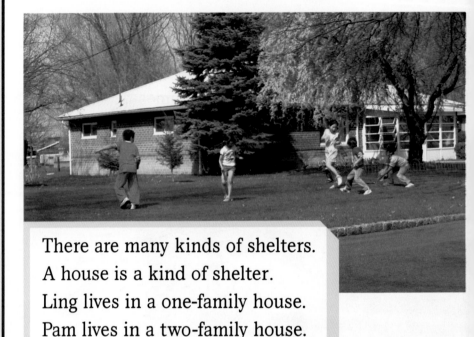

What Kinds of Shelters Are There?

Objectives

★**1. Name** at least three kinds of shelters.

2. Identify the kinds of shelters in your community.

3. Associate different climates with the type of shelters built.

1 STARTING THE LESSON

Motivation/ Prior Knowledge

■ Have the students each draw a picture of their home. Display the pictures in the classroom.

■ Have the students compare and contrast the types of homes in regard to size, color, and building materials.

Study the Vocabulary

NEW WORDS	DISCUSSION WORDS	ORAL VOCABULARY
apartment	two-family house	materials climate

■ Cut a large piece of paper into the shape of a house. Have the students name different kinds of shelters. List the shelters on the paper (house, duplex, apartment, tent, tepee, igloo, and so on).

■ Review each type of shelter with the students. Name one salient point about each shelter. Post the list for easy reference.

There are many kinds of shelters.
A house is a kind of shelter.
Ling lives in a one-family house.
Pam lives in a two-family house.

66

Optional Activities

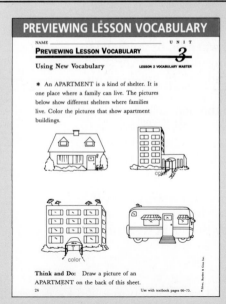

PREVIEWING LESSON VOCABULARY

NAME

PREVIEWING LESSON VOCABULARY

UNIT **3**

Using New Vocabulary

LESSON 2 VOCABULARY MASTER

✴ An APARTMENT is a kind of shelter. It is one place where a family can live. The pictures below show different shelters where families live. Color the pictures that show apartment buildings.

Think and Do: Draw a picture of an APARTMENT on the back of this sheet.

24

Use with textbook pages 66–73.

Review Master Booklet, p. 24

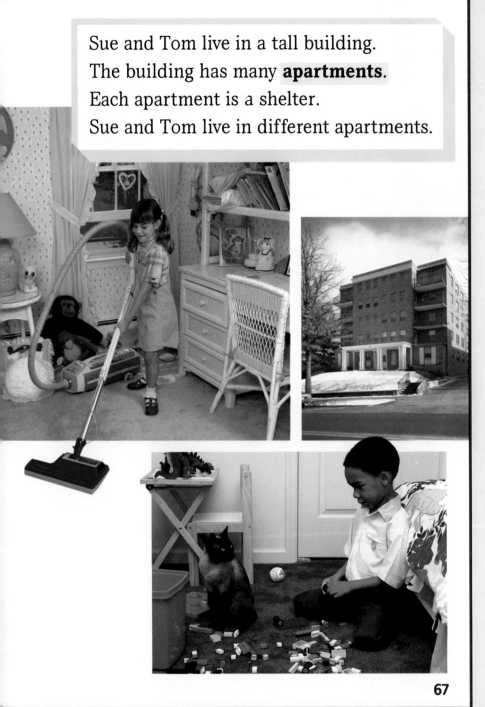

Sue and Tom live in a tall building.
The building has many **apartments**.
Each apartment is a shelter.
Sue and Tom live in different apartments.

67

2 DEVELOPING THE LESSON

Read and Discuss
Text pages 66–69

To help the students identify the differences in housing structures, have them read pages 66–69.

1. **What is another word for house?**
   (Shelter *p. 70*)

2. **What is an apartment?**
   (An apartment is one shelter in a tall building with many shelters. *p. 71*)

3. **Where can you find shelters?**
   (In warm and cold places *pp. 72–73*)

   Thinking Critically How are shelters in cold places and shelters in warm places alike? (Evaluate)
   (Answers may include that both have walls, roofs, and windows and protect people from the weather. *pp. 66–69*)

VISUAL THINKING SKILL

Comparing the Photographs

■ Look at the pictures on pp. 70–71. **How are the apartment building and Pam's house the same?**
(They both have more than one story and were built for more than one family. Both have a small play area.)

Using the Globe to Learn About Climates

Gather pictures of shelters in warm and cold climates. Using a globe, find the locations where the different kinds of shelters are found. For example, there are homes with thatched roofs in Myanmar, formerly Burma.

Have the students tell whether each shelter would be found in a warm or cold climate. Mark each location on the globe with a small piece of red clay for warm climates and blue clay for cold climates.

● Once all of the shelters have been marked, help the students recognize that the warm climates are near the Equator and that the cold climates are near the Poles.

● Draw a sphere with a 4′ diameter on white paper. Mark the Equator and the Poles. Have each student draw a picture of a shelter. Have the student attach the picture to the correct climate zone on the paper.

Optional Activities

Meeting Individual Needs

Concept:
Shelters and Climates

Shelters are constructed differently and with different materials according to the climate.

◆**EASY** Have the students find pictures in books or magazines of places in hot or cold, wet or dry climates.

Have the students draw themselves and an appropriate shelter in a climate that they would like to visit.

◀▶**AVERAGE** Have the students review pictures of different climates and select a climate to describe.

Have them write at least three sentences about the climate selected and the type of shelters found in that climate.

Have the students each draw a picture of the shelter and the surrounding environment. Attach the descriptions to the backs of the pictures.

Ask the other students to identify the climates from the descriptions.

◀▮▶**CHALLENGING** Prepare blank books in the shapes of tepees, igloos, apartment buildings, houses, and so on.

Have the children select a shelter and write about living in it. The story should mention the type of climate surrounding the shelter.

GEOGRAPHY THEME

Location

■ Have the students turn to the Atlas map on pp. 206–207 and locate Arizona and Alaska on it.

■ Have the students turn to pp. 208–209 and find the United States as a point of reference. Then ask the students to locate Norway and Myanmar.

There are other kinds of shelters.
Some of the shelters are in warm places.

68 Myanmar

Optional Activities

Writing to Learn

Maintaining a Shelter Ask the students to name jobs that must be done to keep homes in good condition. Examples may include fixing the roof, painting the house, and cleaning the house.

● List the jobs on the chalkboard. Have each student draw a picture of someone doing one of the jobs. Then have the student write one or two sentences about the picture.

e of the shelters are in cold places.
are the shelters different?

on 2

Review

Read and Think

1. Name three kinds of shelters. (Analyze)
2. Which shelter is like your shelter? (Evaluate)

Skills Check

Look at the pictures on page 68.

How can you tell the shelters are in warm places?

69

Answers to Read and Think

1. Three types of shelters are a one family house, a two family house, and an apartment.

2. Answers will vary but must compare a shelter with a student's home.

Answer to Skills Check

The buildings in warm climate have thinner walls. One shelter uses mainly straw for its walls. The adobe is painted white to keep the building cool.

Answer to Lesson Title Question

Ask the lesson title question, found at the start of the lesson:

What kinds of shelters are there?

(The shelters discussed in this lesson are a one-family house, a two-family house, an apartment building, an adobe house, a bamboo and thatch house, and a cabin. These shelters can also be described as appropriate for warm or cold climates.)

Additional Practice

You may wish to assign the ancillary materials listed below.

Understanding the Lesson p. 25
Workbook p. 14

Reteaching Main Objective

⭐ *Name at least three kinds of shelters.*

- Mount and number on heavy paper, pictures of different types of shelters. Then write the name of each shelter on an index card. Put the number of the picture it matches on the back of the card.

- Have all the class members work together to match the names and the shelters. After practicing, have the students name the shelters without using the word cards.

Review Master
Booklet, p. 25

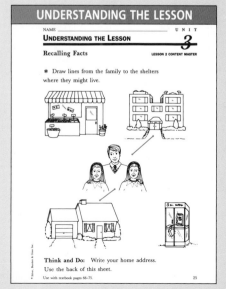

UNDERSTANDING THE LESSON

NAME

UNDERSTANDING THE LESSON UNIT 3

Recalling Facts LESSON 2 CONTENT MASTER

✳ Draw lines from the family to the shelters where they might live.

Think and Do: Write your home address. Use the back of this sheet.
Use with textbook pages 66-75.

25

Optional Activities

69

Use the information below to help students better understand the literature selection found on pp. 70–75.

Selection Summary

This is the story of two ducks in search of a place to make their home and raise their ducklings. They know they need to find a place that has water to swim in, and a good supply of food, where their ducklings will be safe. Their search takes them to a small island in the Charles River in Boston.

After their ducklings are born, Mrs. Mallard trains them to survive in the city. When they are ready, she takes them on their first expedition. Mrs. Mallard takes the ducklings to a small island in the Public Garden. They are protected from the traffic by kind-hearted policemen and are welcomed by all of the people they meet. The ducklings decide to live in the Public Garden.

FROM

MAKE WAY FOR DUCKLINGS
BY ROBERT McCLOSKEY

Optional Activities

...ople and animals need homes.

...e ducks in this story need a home.

...here do you think they will look?

...o they flew over Beacon Hill and round the
...ate House, but there was no place there.

1. **What do the ducks see as they fly over the city?**
   (Large buildings, streets with a lot of traffic, some trees, bushes, and grass.)

2. **What are the ducks looking for?**
   (They are looking for a home.)

Optional Activities

Why don't they live in Louisburg Square?
(There is no water to swim in.)

72

Optional Activities

Creating a Shelter

- Discuss with the students some of the things people consider when they are looking for a home, such as its location, the neighborhood it is in, its size, and so on.

- Tell the students to pretend they have built a home. Have them draw a picture of it and discuss with the class why people would want to live in the home they have built.

They looked in Louisburg Square, but
there was no water to swim in.

Optional Activities

1. **How do the cars get across the river?**
   (They drive over the bridge.)

2. **Where do the ducks decide to make their home?**
   (On the island in the river.)

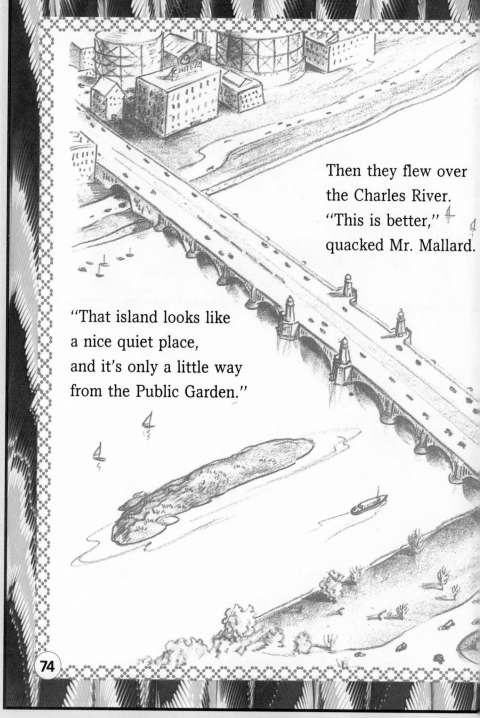

Then they flew over the Charles River. "This is better," quacked Mr. Mallard.

"That island looks like a nice quiet place, and it's only a little way from the Public Garden."

74

Optional Activities

Curriculum Connection

Literature   Have students match the appropriate animals with their homes.

- Discuss with the students various habitats in which animals live.

- Write a list of animals and their homes on the board. Examples may include nests (birds), caves (bats), water (fish), and so on.

Yes," said Mrs. Mallard, remembering the peanuts.
"That looks like just the right place
to hatch ducklings."

What Do You Think?

Why was the island the best place for a home?

How do people choose their homes?

75

Divide the class into two groups. Have one group use construction paper to make the habitats and the other group make the animals that would live in them.

When completed, have students match the animals with the habitats and display them on a bulletin board or mural.

What Do You Think?
Answers may include because there was water to swim in, it was not far from the Public Garden, and they would not be near the traffic.

Answers may include by the way the home looks, how much money it costs, how close it is to where they work or go to school, how big it is, and so on.

Where Do We Get Food?

Objectives

★ **1. Describe** three places where food may be purchased.

2. Distinguish between raw and processed food.

3. Record and **read** information on a bar graph.

1 STARTING THE LESSON

Motivation/ Prior Knowledge

■ Pack a grocery bag with boxed food, canned food, dairy products, and fresh vegetables.

■ Unload each item and ask the students where they think the food was purchased. Explain that in this lesson they will learn about several places to buy food.

Study the Vocabulary

NEW WORDS	DISCUSSION WORDS	ORAL VOCABULARY
bar graph	*supermarket* *buy* *sell* *bakery* *fresh*	*processed*

■ Label each object in the shopping bag with a 1, 2, or 3. Then give a few students some math counters and ask each one to buy an item as if in a store. Explain that food is bought and sold.

■ Ask the student buying each item whether the food grows that way or if it has been changed before people buy it.

■ Tell the students that a bar graph is one way to show how much or how many. A bar graph could show how many food items were bought by the members of the class.

76

Lesson 3

Where Do We Get Food?

The Roberts family buys food in different places. Sometimes the family goes to a supermarket. A supermarket has many kinds of foods.

76

The family goes to special stores too.
Special stores sell one kind of food.
A bakery is a special store.
A cheese shop is a special store.

77

Taking a Trip to a Supermarket

● Make a pretend grocery list consisting of a wide variety of foods.

● Take the class to the supermarket. Find each item on the list. Have the students note the different sizes of products and how the products are grouped within each aisle.

● Write a class story about the trip to the supermarket. Have the students illustrate the story.

Optional Activities

Read and Discuss
Text pages 76–79

Help the students name the places where food may be purchased by reading pp. 76–79 and asking the questions below.

1. **What type of store sells many kinds of foods?**
(Supermarket *p. 76*)

2. **What are two examples of special stores?**
(Bakery, cheese shop *p. 77*)

3. **What are two places where farmers may sell their crops?**
(Stores, farm stands *pp. 78–79*)

Thinking Critically Why, do you think, do farmers grow food for many people? (Hypothesize)
(Answers may include that farmers earn money by growing food and that many people do not have land to grow food.)

Thinking Critically Why, do you think, do some people buy fruits and vegetables at a farm stand instead of at a supermarket? (Hypothesize)
(Answers may include that a farm stand might be nearby and that the food is very fresh at a farm stand.)

VISUAL THINKING SKILL

Analyzing the Photograph

■ Tell the students that many kinds of food are sold at supermarkets. Have the students name the food in the Roberts family's shopping cart shown on p. 76. (Eggs, milk, bread, and fruit)

■ Have the students draw a picture of the foods that they would buy at a supermarket.

77

Analyzing the Photographs

■ Tell the students that a farmer needs to be able to walk and move around easily in his or her fields. Have the students look at the top picture on p. 78. Then ask the following question.

How is the lettuce planted so that the farmer can move around?

(The lettuce is planted in rows.)

■ The farmer needs to gather his or her crops once they are grown so that they can be sold. Have the students look at the bottom picture on p. 78. Then ask the students this question.

How are the crops being collected from the field?

(Workers have pulled the carrots from the ground and made piles of them. The workers then load the carrots onto a truck to be taken out of the field.)

Some farmers grow food for many people. The farms have large fields for their crops. Farmers sell their crops to stores.

78

Optional Activities

Graphic Organizer

To help the students recognize where different kinds of food are available, draw the graphic organizer on the chalkboard. Have the students name the answers for each category. Add their answers to the board. Possible answers are shown here.

SUPERMARKET
cereal
crackers
soup

CHEESE SHOP
Swiss cheese
Cheddar cheese

PLACES TO BUY FOOD

FARM STAND
apples
tomatoes

BAKERY
rolls
bread

Some farmers have farm stands too.
The farmers sell food from the farm.
The Roberts family likes fresh vegetables.
The family buys vegetables at a farm stand.

Meeting Individual Needs

Concept:
Understanding Bar Graphs

To help the students become more comfortable using and creating bar graphs, assign one of the activities described below.

◆**EASY** Have the students work in pairs for this activity. Prepare bar graphs with the boxes shaded and the categories noted. Have each pair add a title to its graph and tell which category has the most colored boxes and which category has the fewest.

◀▶**AVERAGE** Have the students work in pairs to complete this activity. Give each pair the outline for a graph and a bag containing circles, triangles, squares, and rectangles cut out of construction paper. Have the students draw a shape in each row and graph the contents of the bag. Then have the students write one or two sentences to summarize the information in the graph.

◀▮▶**CHALLENGING** Have the students work in pairs to complete a bar graph. Give each pair a blank graph with spaces for the category names, the boxes, and a line for the title. Have the students decide what they want their graph to show and make up data for their graph. Have the pairs summarize the information for the class.

Cooperative Learning

Making a Categorizing Activity Have the students work in groups of three to make an activity about places to buy food. Each group should select three places to include in the activity.

Have each group member cut out pictures from magazines and newspapers of food that can be purchased at one of the three places.

Group members should concur that the pictures selected for each place are correct. Have them mount each picture on paper.

● Each group member should decorate and label a container to hold the food pictures for one of the three places.

● Mix all the food pictures together and have the group members sort the pictures one by one into the correct container.

● Each group should evaluate how throughly it prepared its activity and how well the its members did when sorting the pictures. Have the groups play each other's activities.

Read and Discuss
Text pages 80–81

To help the students learn about bar graphs, have them read pp. 80–81. Then ask these questions.

1. **What does a bar graph tell you?**
   (It tells a story. It also tells how much or how many.)

2. **What does the bar graph on p. 80 tell?**
   (It tells how many trips were made to different types of food stores.)

3. **How is each trip to a place shown on this bar graph?**
   (A box is colored in.)

   Thinking Critically **Why, do you think, were more trips were made to special stores than to the supermarket?** (Hypothesize)
   (Answers may include that people can buy more kinds of food in one trip to a supermarket.)

VISUAL THINKING SKILL

Interpreting the Bar Graph

■ Help the students learn to read bar graphs by having them look at the bar graph on p. 80 and answer this question. **How many more times did the family go to special stores than to the supermarket?**
(Two)

This is a **bar graph**.
A bar graph tells a story.
It tells how much or how many.
This graph tells how many trips the Roberts family made for food.
One box is colored for each trip to a place.
How many trips were made to the farm stand?

Trips to Buy Food in a Week

Supermarket

Special Stores

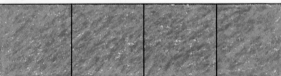

Farm Stand

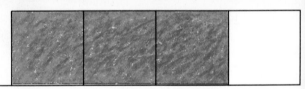

Making a Class Bar Graph

● List *bananas, apples, oranges,* and *grapes* on the chalkboard. Ask the students to choose their favorite.

● Draw a bar graph with 4″ rows on heavy paper. Give each student a 4″ × 4″ box to color. Label a row for each fruit. Have the students attach their boxes to the bar graph. Add a title to the graph such as "Our Class' Favorite Fruits."

● Have the students count the number of boxes for each type of fruit and compare the numbers.

Writing to Learn

Drawing a Place to Buy Food Have the students think about the places where their families buy food. Have the students each draw a picture of one place where their families shop. Have the students list at least two food items that can be bought there.

Bill likes bar graphs.
He is ready to make a graph.

Review

Read and Think

1. Where does the family buy food? (Recall)
2. Where do you buy food? (Synthesize)

Skills Check

Look at the graph on page 80.

How many trips were made to the supermarket?

81

---

3 CLOSING THE LESSON

Lesson 3 Review

Answers to Read and Think
1. The family buys food at the supermarket, special stores, and farm stands.
2. Specialty shops, the supermarket, and farm stands are possible answers.

Answer to Skills Check
Two trips were made to the supermarket.

Answer to Lesson Title Question

Ask the lesson title question, found at the beginning of the lesson:
Where do we get food?
(The supermarket; specialty stores, such as cheese shops and bakeries; and farm stands are all places to purchase food.)

Additional Practice

You may wish to assign the ancillary materials listed below.
Understanding the Lesson p. 27
Workbook p. 15

SKILL TRACE:	Understanding Bar Graphs	
INTRODUCE PE, p. 80	**PRACTICE** PE, p. 81 TE, p. 79 RMB, p. 26	**TEST** Unit 5 Test, TMB

Reteaching Main Objective

⭐ *Describe three places where food may be purchased.*

- Ask the students where raw carrots may be purchased. Answers should include the supermarket, a farm stand, and a fruit and vegetable store. Continue to name foods and ask where they can be purchased. More than one place may be named for some foods.

- Then name a place to buy food and have the students list the types of foods that can be purchased there.

Review Master
Booklet, p. 27

UNDERSTANDING THE LESSON

NAME
UNDERSTANDING THE LESSON   U N I T **3**

Making Comparisons   LESSON 3 CONTENT MASTER

✱ Here is a list of items. Which ones can you get in the supermarket? Which ones can you get at other places? Put a check in the correct boxes.

Items	Super-market	Bakery	Farm Stand	Cheese Shop
1. Apple	✓		✓	
2. Loaf of Bread	✓	✓		
3. Swiss Cheese	✓			✓
4. Dog Food	✓			

Think and Do: Draw a picture of the place where you can get *many* different types of food. Use the back of this sheet.
Use with textbook pages 76–81.   27

81

Optional Activities

How Do We Get Clothing?

Objectives

★**1. Name** three ways to get clothing.

2. Identify the component parts of clothing.

3. Sequence the process of sewing a garment.

1 STARTING THE LESSON

Motivation/ Prior Knowledge

■ Hold up two pieces of baby clothing. Have the students identify who the clothes are meant for.

■ Ask the students if the baby clothes would fit them now. Explain that as people grow they need bigger clothes. Ask the students to name other reasons that they might need new clothes.

■ Have the students identify where they go to get new clothes.

Study the Vocabulary

DISCUSSION WORDS	ORAL VOCABULARY
size	*thread*
sweater	*needles*
yarn	*scissors*
sews	*pattern*
cloth	*leather*

■ Have the students name the tools and materials that help people make clothing. Cloth, needles, and a pattern are a few examples.

■ Then list *cloth*, *yarn*, and *leather* on the chalkboard. Have the students name articles of clothing that are made from each.

Lesson 4

How Do We Get Clothing?

Jon and his father are at a clothing store.
The store sells clothes in many sizes.
Jon needs bigger clothes.
They will buy the size he needs.

Optional Activities

Current Events

● Have the students cut out pictures of clothes and items that are needed to make clothes from newspapers and circulars. Create three posters in the classroom with the titles "Clothing from Stores," "Sewing Tools and Materials," and "Clothes Made by Hand." Have the students attach each picture to the correct poster.

Mrs. Smith works with yarn.

She knits sweaters.

She sells some of her sweaters.

Other sweaters she gives to her family.

Mrs. Smith made a sweater for Kevin.

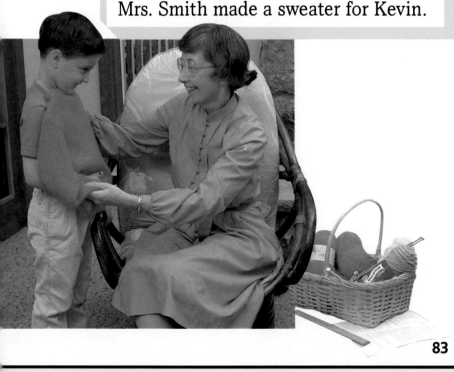

Read and Discuss
Text pages 82–85

Help the students learn about the different ways to get clothing by having them read pp. 82–85 and answer the questions below.

1. **What are two ways to get new clothes?**
   (Buy them or make them. *pp. 82–85*)

2. **Where do people go to buy clothing?**
   (Clothing store *p. 82*)

3. **How can you tell if clothes fit you?**
   (You try them on. *p. 85*)

   Thinking Critically If you were able to get your own clothes, where or how would you get them? (Hypothesize)
   (Answers might include buying them at a store or buying materials to make them.)

VISUAL THINKING SKILL

Analyzing the Photograph

■ Tell the students that new clothing items must be paid for. Have the students look at the top photograph on p. 83.
What machine helps Mrs. Smith find the sum for each sale?
(Cash register *p. 83*)

83

Using Source Materials

Reviewing Photographs Have the students bring in photographs from home of their grandparents when they were younger. Have the students ask their families how the clothes shown in the pictures were obtained.

Have the students show the photographs to their classmates and share the information about the clothes. Have the students comment on how the style of clothing has changed since the pictures were taken. Summarize how the clothes shown in the pictures were obtained.

SKILLBUILDER REVIEW

Understanding Order On pp. 56–57 the students learned how to sequence a chain of events, using the order words *first*, *next*, *then*, and *last*. Have the students use this skill and apply it to selecting and purchasing an item of clothing, as discussed on pp. 82–85.

● Have the students draw pictures that show four steps involved in purchasing clothing-choosing an item, trying it on, paying for it, and wearing it. Have the students label each picture with an order word or a sentence containing the appropriate order word.

Optional Activities

Meeting Individual Needs

Concept: Sequencing

Help the students learn to sequence steps properly by assigning one of the three activities below.

EASY Draw three sizes of paper doll cutouts and three matching sizes of dresses or shirts and pants. Have the students color and cut out the dolls and the clothing pieces. Have the students glue the clothes to the correct dolls. Then have the students mount the dolls, from smallest to largest, on a piece of construction paper.

AVERAGE Have the students plan and draw a simple design on a styrofoam meat tray. Then have the students stitch their designs using yarn and plastic needles. Finally, have the students write the steps they followed to complete their project.

CHALLENGING Give each student a paper doll. Have the student draw a clothes pattern for the doll, using white paper. Then have the student cut out the pattern and trace it on construction paper. Have the student cut out the clothes and glue them onto the doll.

VISUAL THINKING SKILL

Analyzing the Photographs

- To sew your own clothes you cut the cloth into pieces. Look at the top picture on p. 84.
  How does Mrs. Long know how big to cut each piece of cloth?
  (She is using a pattern. *p. 84*)

Mrs. Long sews clothes for her family.
She buys some cloth.
Then she cuts the cloth into pieces.
Mrs. Long sews the pieces together.

84

Optional Activities

Writing to Learn

Writing about Clothes With the students make a list of words about clothing. Then create a list of words that describe clothing, such as scratchy, soft.

- Have the students write a diary entry in which they describe the clothes that they are wearing for that day and how they got them. For example, *Today I am wearing a soft brown shirt and my scratchy blue jeans. My clothes are from a clothing store.*

Jen tries on her new skirt.
The new skirt fits her well.

Lesson 4

Review

Read and Think

1. Where does Jon get his clothes? (Recall)
2. Where do you get your clothes? (Synthesize)

Skills Check

Look at the pictures on pages 84 and 85.

List three things Mrs. Long needs to make a skirt.

85

Lesson 4 Review

Answers to Read and Think

1. Jon gets his clothes at a clothing store.
2. Answers will vary but may include at clothing store or have them made.

Answer to Skills Check

Answers may include a pattern, scissors, needles, a sewing machine, and a pin cushion.

Answer to Lesson Title Question

Ask the lesson title question, found at the beginning of the lesson:
How do we get clothing?
(There are several ways to get clothing. Buying clothes at a store is one option. Sewing or knitting clothes are additional options.)

Additional Practice

You may wish to assign the ancillary materials listed below.
Understanding the Lesson p. 28
Workbook p. 16

Reteaching Main Objective

⭐ *Name three ways to get clothing.*

● Have the class participate in a game of charades in which one student demonstrates a way to get clothing and the rest of the students guess the method he or she is demonstrating. For example, a student might pretend to cut out fabric, knit with yarn, or pay a store clerk. Prepare index cards with ideas to pantomime in case a student needs an idea.

Review Master
Booklet, p. 28

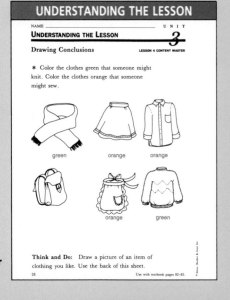

UNDERSTANDING THE LESSON

NAME _____
UNDERSTANDING THE LESSON

UNIT 3

Drawing Conclusions   LESSON 4 CONTENT MASTER

✳ Color the clothes green that someone might knit. Color the clothes orange that someone might sew.

green   orange   orange

orange   green

Think and Do: Draw a picture of an item of clothing you like. Use the back of this sheet.

28   Use with textbook pages 82–85.

Optional Activities

85

Using the New Words

The vocabulary terms in this review were introduced in the unit. Some students may have difficulty distinguishing between similar concepts. Discuss the meaning of each word in relation to the pictures before having the students match the words to the pictures.

Suggested Answers

1. C

2. E

3. F

4. D

5. A

6. B

7. G

Accept other responses if students can explain their choice.

UNIT 3 PUTTING IT ALL TOGETHER

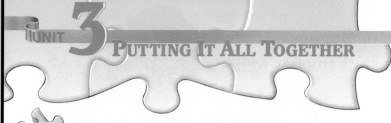

A. Using the New Words

Find the picture that best matches each word.

1. needs ____

2. apartment ____

3. clothing ____

4. shelter ____

5. bar graph ____

6. wants ____

7. food ____

A.

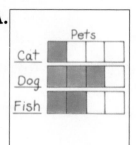

B.

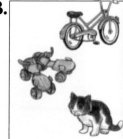

C.

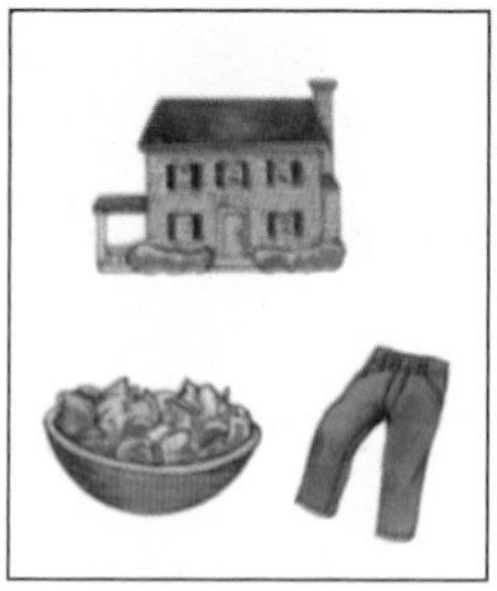

D.

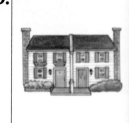

E.

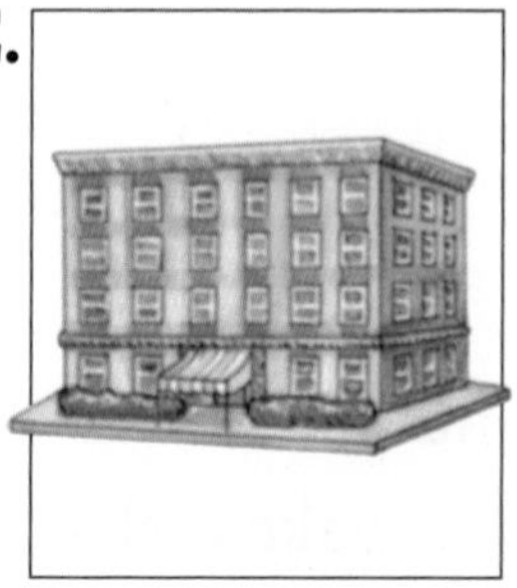

F.

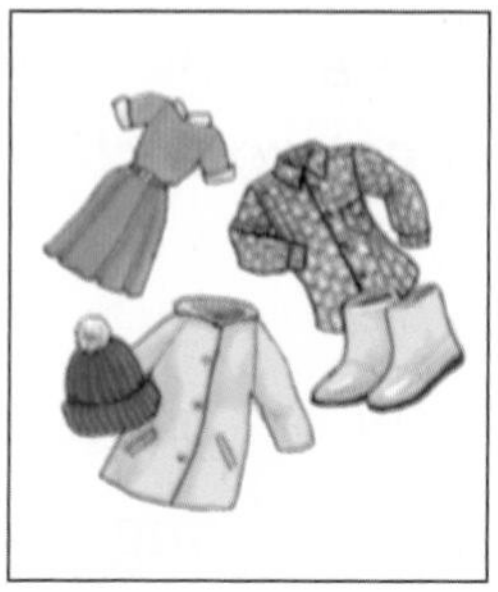

G.

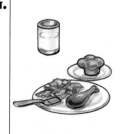

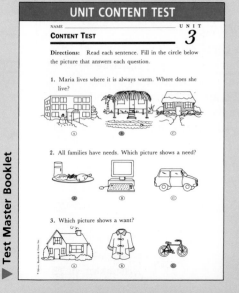

86

UNIT CONTENT TEST

NAME ____ UNIT 3

CONTENT TEST

Directions: Read each sentence. Fill in the circle below the picture that answers each question.

1. Maria lives where it is always warm. Where does she live?

2. All families have needs. Which picture shows a need?

3. Which picture shows a want?

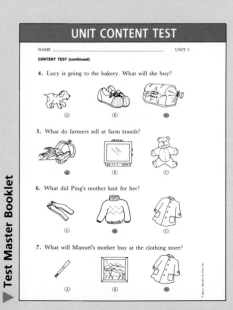

Test Master Booklet

UNIT CONTENT TEST

NAME ____ UNIT 3

CONTENT TEST (continued)

4. Lucy is going to the bakery. What will she buy?

5. What do farmers sell at farm stands?

6. What did Ping's mother knit for her?

7. What will Manuel's mother buy at the clothing store?

Test Master Booklet

B. Remembering What You Read

Answer these questions about the unit.

1. Name three kinds of needs.
2. How are shelters alike and different?
3. Why are people's wants different?

C. Summarizing the Unit

A.   **B.**   **C.**

Look at the pictures above.

Use the letters to put the pictures in order.

First _____   Next _____   Last _____

Where could the family buy the food it needs?

87

Remembering What You Read

Answer these questions about the unit.

1. Food, clothing, and shelter are three kinds of needs.
2. All shelters protect people and give them a place to live. Shelters are different sizes and shapes. Some shelters are in cold places, and some are in warm places.
3. People's wants are different because no two people are exactly alike. Each person is special. People like different things.

Summarizing the Unit

Have the students look at the pictures and put them in sequential order.

First C   Next A   Last B

The family could buy its food at the supermarket, a special store, or a farm stand.

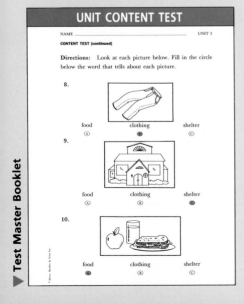

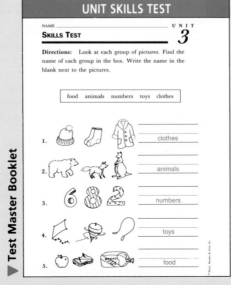

▶ **Test Master Booklet**

UNIT CONTENT TEST

NAME _____ UNIT 3

CONTENT TEST (continued)

Directions: Look at each picture below. Fill in the circle below the word that tells about each picture.

8.

food   clothing   shelter
Ⓐ   ●   Ⓒ

9.

food   clothing   shelter
Ⓐ   Ⓑ   ●

10.

food   clothing   shelter
●   Ⓑ   Ⓒ

▶ **Test Master Booklet**

UNIT SKILLS TEST

NAME _____ **U N I T**
SKILLS TEST **3**

Directions: Look at each group of pictures. Find the name of each group in the box. Write the name in the blank next to the pictures.

food   animals   numbers   toys   clothes

1. clothes
2. animals
3. numbers
4. toys
5. food

87

Objectives

1. **Identify** that words in a group have something in common.

2. **Name** words that belong in a given word group.

3. **Label** a word group based on the words the group contains.

Why Do I Need This Skill?

Help the students recognize that by putting words into groups we can understand them better. Write the following words on the chalkboard: *shoe, doll, sneaker, ball, boot, game.* Tell the students that these words can be made into two word groups; then ask the following questions.

1. **What words can we put in a group called "Things We Wear on Our Feet"?**
(Sneaker, boot, and shoe)
p. 88

2. **What would we call the group that has the words *ball, doll,* and *game* in it?**
(Answers should reflect that they are things children play with.)

Learning the Skill

Review with the students that a need is something we must have to live and a want is something we would like to have but don't need to live.

Have the students read the words in the box on p. 88; then ask the following questions.

1. **Why are the words *food, clothing,* and *shelter* listed together in the word group called *Needs*?**
(They are all things we need to live.)

2. **Why are the words *book, bike,* and *game* listed together in the word group called *Wants*?**
(They are all things we may want, but we do not need them to live.)

88

A | Why Do I Need This Skill?

Sometimes we can make word groups.
The words in the group are alike in some way.
The groups help us learn about the words.

B | Learning the Skill

You learned about needs and wants.
Here are word groups for needs and wants.

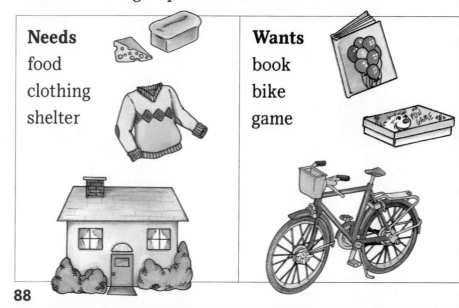

Needs
food
clothing
shelter

Wants
book
bike
game

88

Curriculum Connection

Art Have each student draw a picture for a word that belongs in a given word group and match the picture with the correct group.

- Give each student a piece of paper with a word on it. The word will belong in one of these four groups: *Food, Clothes, Animals, People.*

- Have each student draw a picture to go with the word on his or her paper.

- Post the name of each word group in a corner of the classroom. Have each student read his or her word, show the class the picture, decide which group the word belongs in, and go to that corner of the room.

Optional Activities

 C **Practicing the Skill**

Look at the word groups on this page.

People	Places
teacher	school
nurse	home

1. Copy the groups onto a piece of paper.

2. Put these words in the correct group.

friend   park   store   principal

3. Think of more people and places.
Put each one in the correct group.

 D **Applying the Skill**

Look at the words in the box below.

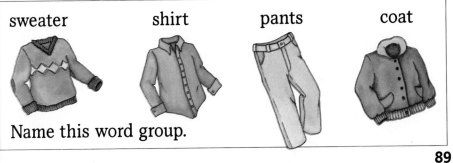

sweater   shirt   pants   coat

Name this word group.

89

Practicing the Skill

Have the students match the words with the correct word groups.

People	Places
teacher	school
nurse	home
friend	park
principal	store

If students have difficulty with this concept, you may wish to assign the reteaching activity.

Applying the Skill

Have the students read the words that accompany the pictures on p. 89. Have them identify that these are all things people wear and would be in a word group named *Clothes* or *Things We Wear*.

SKILL TRACE:	Classifying and Categorizing Words	
INTRODUCE	**PRACTICE**	**TEST**
PE, p. 88	PE, p. 89	Unit 3 Test,
	TE, p. 110	TMB
	RMB, p. 21	

Reteaching Activity

- List the words *red, yellow,* and *blue* on the board. Ask the students how these words are alike. Write the word *Colors* above the list and tell the students this is the name of the word group.

- Ask the students to name other words that belong in this group. Write their responses on the chalkboard.

Optional Activities

Unit 4 Resource Center

Work
(pp. 90–111)

Unit Theme: Work is completed in a variety of places. Some jobs produce goods. Other jobs provide services.

UNIT RESOURCES
Unit 4 Test

 SOCIAL STUDIES LIBRARY: *Mike Mulligan and His Steam Shovel*
Whose Hat Is That?

LESSON *1* What Are Goods and Services?
(pp. 92–95)
Theme: Some workers produce goods; others provide services.

LESSON RESOURCES
Workbook, p. 17
Review Master Booklet
  Previewing Lesson Vocabulary,
  p. 29
Understanding the Lesson, p. 30

SOCIAL STUDIES LIBRARY: *Mike Mulligan and His Steam Shovel*
Up Goes the Skyscraper!

LESSON *2* Where Do People Work?
(pp. 96–99)
Theme: People work in indoor and outdoor settings. Some places are designed for many workers. Others are planned for just a few workers.

LESSON RESOURCES
Workbook, p. 18
Review Master Booklet
  Previewing Lesson Vocabulary,
  p. 31
Understanding the Lesson, p. 32

SOCIAL STUDIES LIBRARY: *Up Goes the Skyscraper!*

LESSON *3* How Are Sneakers Made?
(pp. 100–107)
Theme: Sneakers are produced in a factory by many workers each performing a small task.

LESSON RESOURCES
Workbook, p. 19
Review Master Booklet
  Understanding the Lesson, p. 33

LESSON *4* How Do People Travel to Work?
(pp. 108–111)
Theme: In the past, people relied on horses and trains for travel. Today, cars, buses, trains, planes, and boats are possible modes of transportation.

LESSON RESOURCES
Workbook, p. 20
Review Master Booklet
  Previewing Lesson Vocabulary,
  p. 34
Understanding the Lesson, p. 35

PACING GUIDE

September	October	November	December	January	February	March	April	May
UNIT	UNIT	UNITS	UNIT	UNIT	UNIT	UNITS	UNIT	UNIT
1	2	2–3	3	4	5	5–6	6	7

Annotated Bibliography

Books for Teachers

Hill, Susan. *Books Alive! Using Literature in the Classroom.* Portsmouth, NH: Heinemann Educational Books, 1986. ISBN 0-435-08513-1. Four approaches to using literature with children are presented: responding to text, focusing on a particular author, focusing on the story, and experiencing the "great books."

McElmeel, Sharron L. *My Bag of Book Tricks.* Englewood, CO: Teachers Ideas Press, 1979. ISBN 0-872-87722-1. This book categorizes books by themes and gives suggestions for literature-related activities to do with children.

Books for Read Aloud

Arnold, Caroline. *How Do We Travel?* New York: Franklin Watts, 1983. ISBN 0-531-04507-2. Describes the different kinds of vehicles used within a community, including bikes, motorcycles, cars, trucks, buses, trains, boats, airplanes, and helicopters.

—— *Who Works Here?* New York: Franklin Watts, 1982. ISBN 0-531-04443-2. The text and photographs show how diverse jobs add to the vitality of the community.

Potter, Beatrix. *The Tailor of Gloucester.* New York: Frederick Warne, 1968. ISBN 0-723-20594-9. When the tailor becomes sick and cannot finish the coat for the mayor, mice finish it.

Sharmat, Marjorie Weinman. *Nate the Great.* New York: Coward McCann & Geoghegan, 1972. ISBN 0-698-20218-X. Nate the Great, a detective, solves the mystery of the missing picture.

Spier, Peter. *Firehouse.* New York: Doubleday. ISBN 0-385-15728-2. Picture book depicting a firefighter's job.

Worthington, Phoebe. *Teddy Bear Baker.* New York: Frederick Warne, 1979. ISBN 0-723-22339-4. This story follows an industrious baker through his busy day.

Filmstrips and Videos

Doctor DeSoto (and other stories). Weston, CT: CC Studios, 1985. 35-minute video. Dr. DeSoto, a dentist, consents to help a fox with a mean toothache, even though he never treats animals that are potentially harmful to mice.

The Tailor of Gloucester. Rabbit Ears Productions, Sony, 1988. 30-minute video. When a tailor becomes sick and cannot finish a coat for the mayor, mice finish it.

Computer Software

The Market Place, Apple II. St. Paul: Minnesota Educational Computing Corp.

Bulletin Board Idea

WORK   WORK   WORK

A teacher helps the students learn.

Farmers grow food and care for animals.

Factory workers work together to make goods.

The store clerk helps the people who need to buy something.

Student Activity

Have the students work in groups to make construction paper models of places where people work. Then have them draw the workers who work in those places. Have the students write descriptions for their workers. Use pieces of string to connect the workers to their workplaces.

Travel Then and Now

Why do people travel?

In Unit 4 the students will learn how people travel to their jobs. They will also learn that travel has changed since long ago when people used horses and trains. Improvements in travel enable people today to live farther from their jobs and commute to work. In the following activities the students will expand their knowledge of how travel has changed. They will also explore the different purposes and means of travel in our world.

SOCIAL STUDIES

Geography Show students a map of the United States. Have a volunteer find the state in which he or she lives and mark that state with a colored pin. Have another volunteer find the major city nearest the place where he or she lives and mark that city with a pin. (You may wish to use different colored pins for states and cities.)

■ Ask the students whether they have ever traveled to another state. Vacations and visiting relatives are two possible reasons for travel. Have volunteers locate on the map the states they have traveled to. Ask them to mark those states with pins.

■ Have the students track the path from their home state to the states they visited and tell how they traveled. Discuss whether they could have traveled another way. Ask, **What would be alike and what would be different about your trip if you had traveled by bus instead of by airplane?**

■ You may wish to repeat or adapt this activity, using a map of your state and discussing where and how students have traveled.

Economics Select a city in your state. Tell the students that they are going to travel by bus to visit a friend in this city. Show the students a road map of the state and have a volunteer track the path of the trip on the map. Discuss how people purchase bus tickets. Lead the discussion by asking questions such as these.

1. **What do you say to the person at the ticket counter?**
2. **Do you think that you will need a one-way or a round-trip ticket?**

■ Have two volunteers show in words and in pantomime a person purchasing a bus ticket for the trip.

Global Awareness Explain that travelers often prepare for a trip outside of their country by learning some of the customs of the country and a few words in the language of the country that they will visit.

■ Tell students to pretend that they are traveling to Japan. Tell them that in Japan, people greet each other by bowing. Have the students exchange Japanese greetings with each other. Suggest that the students prepare for their trip by learning to say "thank you" in Japanese. Teach students that the Japanese word for "thank you" is *arigato*.

■ You may wish to tell them how to say "thank you" in other languages as well. Tell them that "thank you" is *gracias* in Spanish, *merci* in French, and *danke* in German.

LITERATURE

■ Read to the students part or all of *The Little Prince* by Antoine Saint-Exupéry (New York: Harcourt Brace Jovanovich Inc., 1982, ISBN 0-156-46511-6). Discuss the story's relationship to travel and ask the students the following questions.

1. Why did the little prince set out from his planet?

2. What did he learn on his travels?

3. What do you think was the most important thing that he learned?

MATHEMATICS

■ Ask the students to pretend they are part of a family that is going camping. Each family member is taking two bags on the trip. How many bags will a family of 2 take? How many bags will families of 3, 5, and 8 members take?

ART

■ Tell the students that some people use travel brochures to find out where they would like to go on vacation. Show the students one or two travel brochures. Read the text to the students and discuss with them how the brochure could help a person decide whether or not to visit the place that it describes. (A local travel agent is a good source for travel brochures.) Then have the students create their own travel brochure, using the real ones as models.

LANGUAGE ARTS

■ Ask the students to think of various places where travelers can stay overnight. Write these places on the chalkboard. Motels, tents, and the homes of friends are possible answers. Then have the students silently recall one such place where they have stayed.

■ Ask each student to describe these places to the class. Give the students several minutes of silence to plan what they will say.

Make a School-Supplies Box

INSTRUCTIONS FOR THE TEACHER:

Focus In this unit the students will learn about occupations, places of employment, how and where products are made, and transportation to and from the workplace. Lesson 1, "What Are Goods and Services?" teaches the students to distinguish between workers who make a good and workers who provide a service. Lesson 3," How Are Sneakers Made?" shows the role of different workers in an assembly-line process. These concepts are abstract. Help the students grasp them by creating their own good. Remind the students that goods are often made in shops or factories.

If members of any students' families work in factories or produce things on their own, it would be interesting for them to come to class and describe their jobs. This would be a good introduction to the idea of a student-produced item.

Warm-up Activity Collect and mount on construction paper magazine pictures of people doing their jobs. For example, you might wish to show a cook, a truck driver, an artist, a carpenter.

On a sheet of chart paper, write the headings *Makes A Good* and *Provides a Service*. Discuss with the students how some workers make a product for sale, while other workers provide a service. Service workers do not produce products. Tell the students that a potter makes a good and that a doctor provides a service.

Show the pictures to the class one at a time. Ask the students to identify the worker and describe his or her job. Have the students explain whether or not they would like each job and why. Have them tape each picture under the appropriate heading on the chart paper.

Refer to the workers listed under *Makes a Good*. Draw or cut out pictures of the goods that these workers make. Refer to the workers listed under *Provides a Service*. Draw or cut out pictures of the tools that the service workers use to perform their jobs. Paste each picture on an index card. Show each card to the students. Have them name the corresponding occupation and attach the card to the chart paper next to the correct worker.

ACTIVITY FOR THE STUDENTS:

Procedure Ask each student to bring an empty shoe box, complete with its lid, to school. Collect a few extra boxes for those students who are not able to bring one in. Explain to the students that today they are going to play the role of artists. They are going to create goods—unique and colorful supply boxes.

Making the School-Supplies Box Using glue and construction paper, colored wrapping paper, or foil, show the students how to cover the outsides of their boxes. You may wish to create your own box to help illustrate this step for the students. Help students glue the paper to the sides of the box, allowing time for the glue to dry before continuing.

Have the students use glitter, yarn, construction paper, tissue paper, felt-tip markers, and crayons to decorate their boxes. Each student should create a unique design. Remind students to put their names somewhere on their finished products.

End the lesson by discussing with students how they produced their boxes in much the same way that a worker would produce a product for sale.

Follow-up Discussion Have each student show his or her finished product to the class and explain how it was decorated.

Extension Have the students think of other times at which they might produce a box like this. To whom would they give it, and for what reason? You may wish to collect a few extra boxes to allow the students to create special boxes for different occasions.

Workbook Pages

GOODS AND SERVICES

Classifying

✳ Write "goods" or "service" under each picture to tell whether the worker is making goods or doing a service.

goods

service

service

goods

Unit 4, pages 92–95

17

HOW MANY ARE THERE?

Graphing

✳ A pictograph uses pictures to show how many or how much. Answer the questions. Then in the correct rows on the pictograph, draw one 👤 for each boy and girl in your family.

1. How many girls are in your family? _____

2. How many boys are in your family? _____

Girls and Boys in My Family	
Girls	
Boys	

18

Unit 4, pages 96–99

BAKING BREAD

Sequencing

✳ Number the pictures in the correct order.

3

1

4

2

Unit 4, pages 100–107

19

GETTING TO WORK

Alphabetizing

✳ Start at A and follow the letters of the alphabet to connect the dots.

✳ Write two other ways of getting to work.

1. Suggested answers are provided.

_____ train _____

2. _____

_____ car _____

20

Unit 4, pages 108–111

U4-G

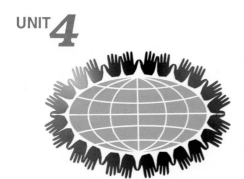

MULTICULTURAL PERSPECTIVES

Work Around the World

(pages 96–99)

List on the chalkboard a few types of workers who travel great distances in their work. These workers may include the following.

- Airline personnel
- Armed services personnel
- Scientists
- Musicians
- Actresses and actors

Ask the students if they can name any other occupations that take workers to other countries.

Ask the students what things might be different if you lived in another country. Their answers might include the following.

- the laws of the country
- the customs of the country
- holidays and events in the country
- currency used in the country
- language
- clothing
- foods

Ask the students whether they would like to do a type of work in which travel to another country is involved. Ask them where they might like to go.

90

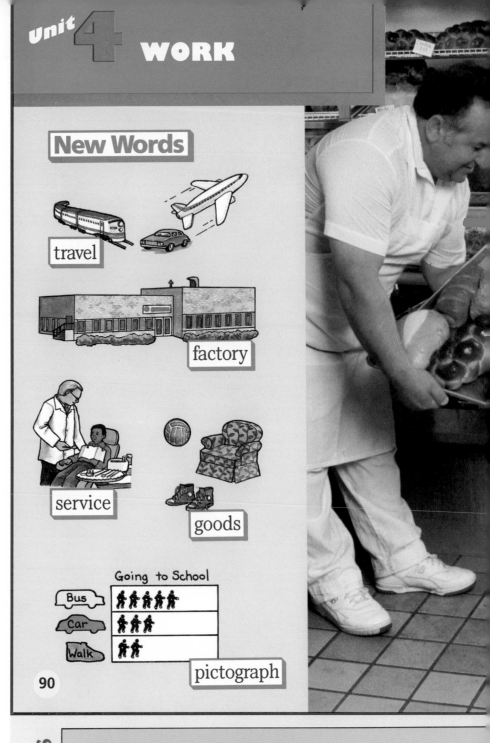

Unit **4** WORK

New Words

travel

factory

service

goods

Going to School

Bus	👤👤👤👤👤👤
Car	👤👤👤
Walk	👤👤

pictograph

90

Optional Activities

Making a Class Book

- Have the students look at the picture on pp. 90–91. Ask them what kind of job the man in the picture has. Have them identify the clothes he is wearing and what he is holding in his hands.

- Ask the students to name the jobs they have read about or have seen people do. List their responses on the chalkboard. Have at least as many jobs as there are students in the class.

Modes of Transportation

(pages 108–111)

There are many modes of transportation available to people today. Some forms of transportation were developed long ago and are still in use today. Other forms of transportation have developed more recently.

Gather pictures of the following forms of transportation.
- Rickshaw
- Gondola
- Bicycle
- Horse and carriage

Have the students discuss how the forms of transportation were helpful to people. Examples are that the bicycle was faster than walking, and the gondola took advantage of the plentiful water supply.

Have the students use a world map to find the area associated with the development of each form of transportation.
- Rickshaw—Japan
- Gondola—Italy
- Bicycle — France and England (These countries are known for the first bicycle and for a successful safety bicycle with both wheels of the same size.)
- Horse and carriage—Europe

Ask the students to consider forms of transportation that are used today around the world. Gondolas are still used in Italy, bicycles are used for enjoyment and for commuting to work, and people still enjoy a leisurely horse-and-carriage ride. The students may also mention the use of automobiles, buses and subways, trains and bullet trains, airplanes, and boats for transportation.

91

- Have each student choose one of the jobs and draw a picture of a worker doing that job. Have each student label his or her picture.

- Assemble all of the labeled pictures in alphabetical order to make a book of jobs that the students can refer to throughout the year.

Optional Activities

What Are Goods and Services?

Objectives

★1. **Distinguish** between jobs that produce goods and jobs that perform services.

2. **Name** jobs where goods are produced and jobs where services are performed.

3. **Explain** why both types of jobs are needed.

1 STARTING THE LESSON

Motivation/ Prior Knowledge

■ Prepare a list of occupations for the students to pantomime, such as a doctor, a teacher, a bus driver, and an artist. Assign the occupations to the students.

■ Have the students rehearse their pantomimes and then present them to the class. Have the other students name each occupation.

■ Tell the students that this lesson is about different kinds of jobs.

Study the Vocabulary

NEW WORDS	DISCUSSION WORDS	ORAL VOCABULARY
goods	*machines*	*producer*
service		

■ Copy the lists of occupations and tools shown below on the chalkboard.

Occupations	Tools
nurse	bus
bus driver	thermometer
artist	stove
chef	paints

■ Have the students match each worker to the correct tool.

■ Have the students place check marks next to the tools that are machines.

■ Have the students identify which workers make something. Explain that these workers are producers.

92

What Are Goods and Services?

Many people work each day.
The work they do is their job.
There are different kinds of jobs.
Some people make things.
The things they make are
called **goods**.

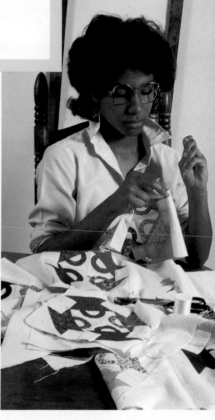

92

Optional Activities

PREVIEWING LESSON VOCABULARY

NAME _____   UNIT

PREVIEWING LESSON VOCABULARY   **4**

Classifying   LESSON 1 VOCABULARY MASTER

✱ Things that people make are called GOODS. Things that people do for others are called SERVICES. Write GOODS under the pictures that show workers making GOODS. Write SERVICE under the pictures that show workers doing a SERVICE.

goods	service
service	goods

Think and Do: Write the name of a job that you would like to have. Write whether you would make GOODS or do a SERVICE. Use the back of this sheet.

Use with textbook pages 92–95.   29

Review Master Booklet, p. 29

These workers are making goods.
Machines help them work faster.
Sometimes many people work
together to make goods.
Each job is important.

93

Read and Discuss
Text pages 92–95

To help the students learn to differentiate the types of jobs people perform, have them read pp. 92–95, and answer the questions below.

1. **How do machines help workers do their jobs?**
   (They help them work faster. *p. 93*)

2. **What kind of jobs ask the workers to do something for people for their job?**
   (Service jobs *p. 94*)

   Thinking Critically **How do you think the workers learn their jobs?** (Hypothesize)
   (Answers may include going to school and learning from others. *pp. 92–95*)

VISUAL THINKING SKILL

Comparing the Photographs

■ Have the students examine the photographs on p. 92. Tell them that both workers are making goods. Then ask them the following question.
What tools are the workers using to do their jobs?
(The man is using a blowtorch and a rod. The woman is using a needle and scissors.)

Cooperative Learning

Making a Directory   Have the students work in pairs to make a directory that shows goods and services. Have them begin by first discussing and then listing five goods and five service workers.

● Have the students draw pictures for each good. Then have them draw pictures that show the service workers performing their services. Each picture should be on a separate page and should contain a label. The drawing responsibilities should be evenly divided.

● Have the students color borders around the edge of each paper. One color should be used for the goods and one color should be used for the service workers.

● Have the students arrange the goods pages and then the service pages in alphabetical order. Have them design and draw a cover together.

● Have each pair of students present their directories to the class. Then ask the pair to evaluate how well they discussed and followed through on their plans.

Optional Activities

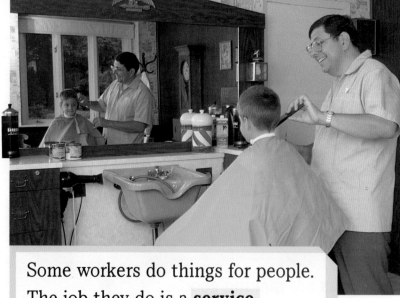

Meeting Individual Needs

Concept:
Using Machines

Many workers use machines to help them complete their jobs. Assign one of the activities below to help the students understand how often machines are in use.

◆ **EASY** Have the students draw pictures of three machines. Have them write the names of the machines and the worker that uses each machine below the picture.

◀▶ **AVERAGE** Have each student draw a design for a new machine and create a name for it. Have the student present the drawing to the class and explain how a worker would use it.

◀▮▶ **CHALLENGING** Have the students think of a new kind of job and design a machine to help a worker perform the job. Have the students describe the job and the machine below the picture.

VISUAL THINKING SKILL

Interpreting the Photograph

■ Tell the students to look at the photograph on p. 95. Ask them the following questions.
1. **Why, do you think, are the children smiling at the delivery person?**
(One of the packages he has could be for them.)
2. **What, do you think, could be in the packages?**
(Answers should be appropriate for size of the packages.)

Some workers do things for people.
The job they do is a **service**.
A barber cuts hair.
A doctor helps you stay healthy.

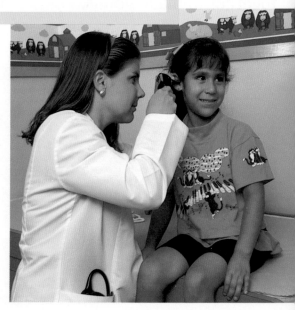

Optional Activities

Writing to Learn

Making a Good Have the students select a good that they would like to make. Have them explain whether they will be making the entire good or completing part of the production process. Have the students write why they would want to make that particular good.

Many people send packages to each other.
This worker brings people their packages.

Lesson 1

─── **Review** ───

Read and Think

1. What are goods? **(Recall)**
2. Name some other service jobs. **(Synthesize)**

Skills Check

Look at the pictures on pages 92 and 93.
How are the goods being made?

95

Lesson 1 Review

Answers to Read and Think
1. Goods are things that people make.
2. Answers may include teachers, secretaries, and gardeners.

Answer to Skills Check
Workers are using a blowtorch, a rod, scissors, a needle, a drill, and conveyor belts to help make goods.

Answer to Lesson Title Question

Ask the lesson title question, found at the beginning of the lesson:
What are goods and services?
(Goods are things that workers make. Services are jobs that need the worker to do something for another person.)

Additional Practice

You may wish to assign the ancillary material listed below.
Understanding the Lesson p. 30
Workbook p. 17

95

Reteaching Main Objective

★ *Distinguish between jobs that produce goods and jobs that perform services.*

● Give each student two index cards and have each label one card with a *G* and one card with an *S*.
● Call out the names of different occupations such as veterinarian, artist, secretary, potter, and sales clerk. Have the students raise the card with a *G* if the worker makes a good, and the card with an *S* if the worker performs a service.

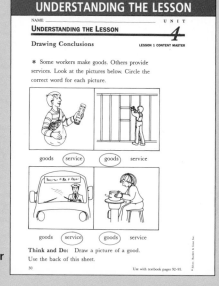

UNDERSTANDING THE LESSON

NAME _____
UNDERSTANDING THE LESSON   U N I T
                                         4
Drawing Conclusions   LESSON 1 CONTENT MASTER

✻ Some workers make goods. Others provide services. Look at the pictures below. Circle the correct word for each picture.

goods (service)   (goods) service

goods (service)   (goods) service

Think and Do: Draw a picture of a good.
Use the back of this sheet.

Review Master Booklet, p. 30

Optional Activities

95

Where Do People Work?

Objectives

★1. **Identify** at least five locations where people can work.

2. **Compare** and **contrast** different environments.

3. **Define** and **read** a pictograph.

---

1 STARTING THE LESSON

Motivation/ Prior Knowledge

■ Ask the students to name the places where people go to buy food. (Answers may include the supermarket, a farm stand, and a vegetable store.)

■ Then ask them where people go to get money. (Bank)

■ Tell the students that, in this lesson, they will be learning about some of the different places people work.

Study the Vocabulary

NEW WORDS	DISCUSSION WORDS	ORAL VOCABULARY
factory pictograph	stores bank dock broken	repair

■ Review the vocabulary words above and list them on the chalkboard. Have the students use the words to complete the sentences below.

A _____ makes many goods at one time. (factory)

Ships are unloaded at a _____ . (dock)

Many people sell goods in _____ . (stores)

My machine is _____ ; it does not work. (broken)

Some workers fix or _____ broken machines. (repair)

A _____ uses pictures to show information. (pictograph)

Lesson 2

Where Do People Work?

People work in different places.
A school is one place to work.
A **factory** is another place to work.
The workers in a factory make goods.

96

PREVIEWING LESSON VOCABULARY

NAME _____

PREVIEWING LESSON VOCABULARY   U N I T **4**

Understanding New Vocabulary   LESSON 2 VOCABULARY MASTER

✳ A FACTORY is a place where goods are made. A PICTOGRAPH uses pictures to show how much or how many. Look at the PICTOGRAPH. It shows how many factories are in Terrytown and what they make. Answer the questions below.

FACTORIES IN TERRYTOWN			
Shoe factory	👟	👟	👟
Clothes factory	👕	👕	👕 👕
Tool factory	🔧	🔧	

👟 = 1 factory

How many clothes factories does the town have?   4

How many tool factories does the town have?   2

Think and Do: Name another good that is made in a FACTORY. Write your answer on the back of this sheet.

Use with textbook pages 96–99.   31

Review Master Booklet, p. 31

Some people work in stores.
Others work in banks.
Some people load and unload
ships at a dock.
There are many places to work.

97

2 DEVELOPING THE LESSON

Read and Discuss
Text pages 96–99

To help the students learn to use a picto-graph and name different working environ-ments, have them read pp. 96–99 and an-swer these questions.

1. **What are some places where people can work?**
   (School, factory, farm, bank, and stores *pp. 96–98*)

2. **What do pictographs show?**
   (Pictographs show how much or how many with pictures. *p. 98*)

   Thinking Critically How, do you think, do people decide where they want to work? (Hypothesize)
   (Answers will vary. Encourage the stu-dents consider whether they like to work with people or to make things. *pp. 96–99*)

VISUAL THINKING SKILL

Comparing the Photographs

■ Have the students look at the photo-graphs on p. 97 and notice that some people work inside and others work out-side.

■ Have the students draw a picture of an-other worker who works outside.

Making Puzzles
● Have the students draw a picture of a place to work. Have them use markers or crayon heavily. Have the students mount the pictures on cardboard.

● Have the students cut their pictures into ten pieces. Have them put their puzzles in envelopes. Have the students solve each other's puzzles.

Curriculum Connection
Mathematics Have students make one pictograph showing their birthdays. Have each student draw a picture of a balloon for a symbol on the pictograph.

● Draw the outline of the graph on chart paper for the students. Have the students write the month labels and the title of the pictograph. Then have them attach their symbols.

● Discuss the pictograph by comparing the number of birthdays in certain months and in groups of months.

Optional Activities

 stands for one worker.

Mrs. Johnson's class talked about workers.
The children made a **pictograph** about
workers in their families.
A pictograph uses pictures to show how
much or how many.
There is one for each worker.
How many store workers are there?

98

Meeting Individual Needs

Concept:
Understanding Pictographs

To help the students understand pictographs, assign one of the activities below.

◆**EASY** Draw the grid for a pictograph to show the number of rainy days in March, April, and May. Write the title and the months on the grid. Have the students draw in seven raindrops for March, six raindrops for April, and four raindrops for May.

Then have the students use their graphs to answer these questions.

What month had the fewest rainy days? (May)

How many days did it rain in April and May together? (Ten)

◀▶**AVERAGE** Give the students a grid for a pictograph with the title *Balloons Sold* and *Thursday*, *Friday*, and *Saturday* listed on the graph. Have the students draw in balloons to match this information.

Four balloons were sold on Thursday.
Six balloons were sold on Friday.
Eight balloons were sold on Saturday.

Have the students answer these questions.

How many balloons were sold altogether? (Eighteen)

How many more balloons were sold on Saturday than on Thursday? (Four)

◀❙▶**CHALLENGING** Give the students blank grids. Ask them to complete the grid on a topic of their choice. Then have them summarize the information in the graph.

VISUAL THINKING SKILL

Interpreting a Pictograph

■ Have the students look at the pictograph on p. 98 to answer these questions.
  1. **What is the title of the pictograph?** (Places Where People in Our Families Work)
  2. **How many people work in a bank?** (Two)

98

Optional Activities

Writing to Learn

Selecting a Workplace Have the students decide whether they would like a job where they work inside or outside. Have the students explain their preferences.

Describing Workplaces Have the students list three of the workplaces described in this lesson and write one or two sentences about each one.

This worker does not work in one place.
He fixes broken machines in many places.
He carries his tools to fix the machines.

Lesson 2

Review

Read and Think

1. What is made in a factory? (Recall)
2. Tell where you would like to work and why.
(Evaluate)

Skills Check

Look at the pictograph on page 98.
How many more people work in factories than on farms?

99

Answers to Read and Think

1. Goods are made in a factory.

2. Answers will vary, but they must include an explanation.

Answer to Skills Check

Three more people work in factories than on farms.

Answer to Lesson Title Question

Ask the lesson title question, found at the beginning of the lesson:
Where do people work?
(Farms, schools, stores, factories, and banks are places where people work.)

Additional Practice

You may wish to assign the ancillary materials listed below.
Understanding the Lesson p. 32
Workbook p. 18

SKILL TRACE:	Understanding Pictographs	
INTRODUCE PE, p. 98	**PRACTICE** TE, p. 98 WB, p. 18 RMB, p. 31	**TEST** Unit 4 Test, TMB

Reteaching Main Objective

⭐ *Identify at least five locations where people can work.*

- Have one student select a place where people can work. Have the other students ask questions that can be answered by a yes or no to deduce the selected workplace. Encourage the students to ask questions that describe a feature of the workplace. For example, *Do many people work in this place?*

- Give each student a turn to select a workplace. Encourage the students to select a variety of places.

Review Master Booklet, p. 32

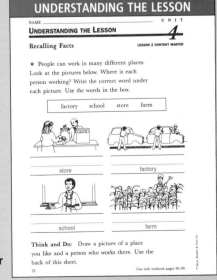

UNDERSTANDING THE LESSON

NAME _____
UNDERSTANDING THE LESSON   UNIT **4**

Recalling Facts   LESSON 2 CONTENT MASTER

✳ People can work in many different places. Look at the pictures below. Where is each person working? Write the correct word under each picture. Use the words in the box.

| factory | school | store | farm |

store

factory

school

farm

Think and Do: Draw a picture of a place you like and a person who works there. Use the back of this sheet.

Optional Activities

99

LESSON 3 PAGES 100–107

How Are Sneakers Made?

Objectives

★**1. Explain** the relationship between an assembly line worker in a factory and the finished product.

2. Explain why some goods are made in factories.

3. Describe why a sequence of steps is needed to produce goods.

1 STARTING THE LESSON

Motivation/ Prior Knowledge

■ Show the students a canvas sneaker. Ask them to name some of the parts of the sneaker, such as the sole, the sides, and the shoelaces.

■ Ask the students to name the materials used in making sneakers, such as rubber and cloth or canvas.

■ Tell the students that this lesson describes some of the steps followed when making sneakers.

Study the Vocabulary

DISCUSSION WORDS	ORAL VOCABULARY
rubber	order
recipe	assembly line

■ Ask the students how their families get ready for dinner. Have them identify and order the steps that must be completed before the family can eat.

■ Tell the students that many workers in factories must follow steps in the right order to make goods.

100

Lesson 3

How Are Sneakers Made?

Mrs. Johnson's class went to a factory.
The factory makes sneakers.
Many workers are needed to make sneakers.

① Rubber is used for the bottoms of sneakers.
A worker reads a recipe for yellow rubber.
The recipe tells him how to make the rubber.

100

For Your Information

● Four carts like the one shown in photograph 1 are needed for each batch of rubber. The rubber ingredients are combined in a mixer and then sent through a series of rollers to continue the mixing process.

● The rubber is dipped in a soap and water solution before it is folded into a pile. The soap prevents the folds of rubber from sticking together.

● The rubber strip in photograph 2 is cut into bars. Each bar is pressed in a mold to form an outsole.

Optional Activities

③ Each piece makes the bottom of a sneaker.

② The rubber is folded into a pile. Then the pile is cut into pieces.

Curriculum Connection

Art Draw a tracer for the side of a sneaker. Have the students trace the shape on a piece of construction paper. Then have them draw and color a new design for a sneaker.

● Have the students punch holes for laces along the angled edge of the sneaker. Then have them lace their sneaker with yarn and tie a bow.

● Have the students present their designs. Display the sneakers in the classroom.

Optional Activities

2 DEVELOPING THE LESSON

Read and Discuss
Text pages 100–101

To help the students learn about the assembly line process in a factory and, specifically, how the rubber soles of the sneakers are produced, have the students read pp. 100–101 and answer these questions.

1. **Where are sneakers made?**
   (Sneakers are made in a factory. *p. 100*)

2. **What tells the worker how to make the rubber?**
   (A recipe tells the worker how to make the rubber. *p. 100*)

3. **Why is the rubber cut into pieces?**
   (Each piece is used to make the bottom of a sneaker. *p. 101*)

   Thinking Critically Why, do you think, are many workers needed to make sneakers? (Hypothesize)
   (Answers may include that the factory makes many sneakers each day and more than one worker is needed for each job. *pp. 100–101*)

VISUAL THINKING SKILL

Analyzing the Photograph

■ Remind the students that a recipe tells you what to mix together. Ask the students to look at the photograph on p. 100. Then ask the following questions.

1. **How does the worker know how to mix the rubber correctly?**
   (He keeps the recipe in front of him so he can refer to it when he needs to.)

2. **What is another time when people use recipes?**
   (People use recipes when they cook food.)

Read and Discuss
Text pages 102–103

To help the students understand how the cloth in sneakers is prepared, have the students read pp. 102–103 and answer these questions.

1. **How is the cloth cut?**
   (A worker uses a machine to cut it. *p. 102*)

2. **What two ways do the workers in the factory use to attach the pieces of the sneaker together?**
   (They sew and glue the pieces together. *pp. 102–103*)

   Thinking Critically **What would happen if the worker did not glue the cloth to the cushions?** (Hypothesize)
   (Answers may include that the sneaker will fall apart. *p. 103*)

④ Another worker cuts the cloth for the sneakers.

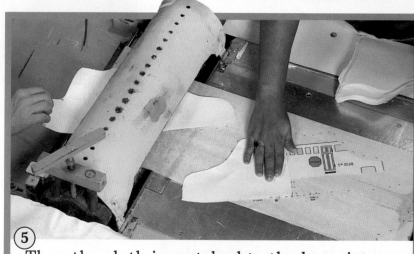

⑤ Then the cloth is matched to the bus picture.

Optional Activities

For Your Information

- The machine in photograph 4 is an electric knife. It can cut through 48 layers of cloth at one time. The machine in picture 5 uses heat to transfer the picture onto the cloth.

- Several workers are involved with sewing the canvas. The sides or quarters of the shoes are sewn, then the topstitching is done. Finally, the tongue is sewn in.

- The machine that glues the canvas and the cushions together is the most difficult to operate.

6
Someone sews the cloth.

7
There are cushions
in sneakers.
A worker glues the
cloth to the cushions.

103

VISUAL THINKING SKILL

Interpreting the Photograph

■ The gluing process is very important. Have the students look at the photograph on p. 103. Then ask this question. **How is the glue put on the cushions?** (A worker glues the cloth to the cushions.)

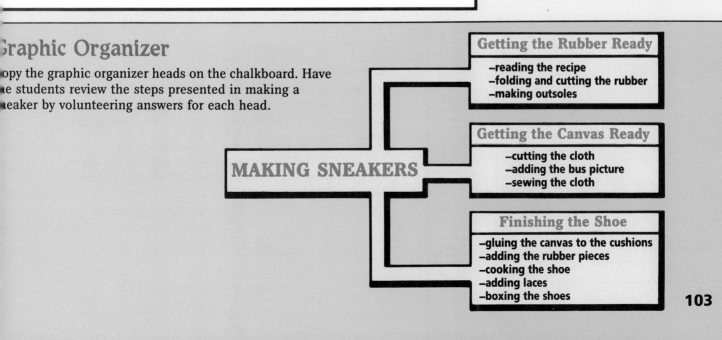

Graphic Organizer

Copy the graphic organizer heads on the chalkboard. Have the students review the steps presented in making a sneaker by volunteering answers for each head.

MAKING SNEAKERS

Getting the Rubber Ready
–reading the recipe
–folding and cutting the rubber
–making outsoles

Getting the Canvas Ready
–cutting the cloth
–adding the bus picture
–sewing the cloth

Finishing the Shoe
–gluing the canvas to the cushions
–adding the rubber pieces
–cooking the shoe
–adding laces
–boxing the shoes

Optional Activities

103

Read and Discuss
Text pages 104–105

To help the students recognize the many steps involved in the production process, have them read pp. 104–105 and answer these questions.

1. **What happens before the sneakers are cooked?**
   (The rubber pieces are added to the sneaker. *p. 104*)

2. **What happens after the sneakers are cooked?**
   (Shoelaces are added to each pair. *p. 105*)

   Thinking Critically **Why do the rubber pieces stick to the sneaker?** (Infer)
   (The sneakers are dipped in glue. *p. 104*)

VISUAL THINKING SKILL

Interpreting the Photographs

■ Explain to the students that for some of the steps in the production process, the sneaker is kept on a metal mold shaped like a foot and is called a *last*. Have the students look at the photographs on p. 104 and answer these questions.
Why, do you think, is the last shaped like a foot?
(The finished sneaker will be the right shape if it is made with a last.)

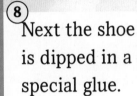

Next the shoe is dipped in a special glue.

Then rubber pieces are added to the sneakers.

104

Optional Activities

For Your Information

● Raw rubber is slightly sticky and will stretch without returning to its original shape. The cooking process shown in picture 10 alters the rubber so that it retains its shape. The sneakers are in the oven for more than an hour.

● The lasts or metal inserts, are removed from the shoes after the shoes are cooked. The shoes are placed in bins and stored until they are boxed.

10 The sneakers are cooked in an oven.

11 Shoelaces are added to each pair of sneakers.

105

Read and Discuss
Text pages 106–107

To help the students understand the packaging and distribution processes for the sneakers, have them read pp. 106–107 and answer these questions.

1. **What do the workers do with each pair of sneakers?**
(They put them in boxes. *p. 106*)

2. **How do the sneakers get to the stores?**
(Trucks deliver them. *p. 106*)

   Thinking Critically **How do you choose the sneakers you buy?**
   (Analyze)
   (Answers may include that they fit, that they have a nice design, and that they are reasonably priced. *p. 107*)

VISUAL THINKING SKILL

Analyzing the Photograph

■ Discuss with the students how people purchase shoes and sneakers at stores. Have the students look at the picture on p. 107. Then ask these questions.

1. **What are the children doing before they take their new sneakers home?**
(They are trying them on first to make sure that they fit their feet correctly.)

2. **Who is helping them try on their sneakers?**
(The salesperson who works in the shoe store)

⑫ Some workers put the sneakers in boxes.

⑬ Trucks take the sneakers to many stores.

106

Optional Activities

For Your Information

● The workers in photograph 12 are stamping the size onto the box, wrapping the sneakers in tissue paper, and packing the individual boxes into large boxes for shipment.

● The end of the packaging line is near the loading docks in the factory. It is a short distance to get the shoes onto the trucks.

(14)

The class has seen the sneakers in stores.
Pam's friends each bought a pair of sneakers.

Lesson 3

Review

Read and Think

1. How do workers help to make the sneakers? **(Analyze)**

2. Why is it important for all the workers to do their jobs? **(Evaluate)**

Skills Check

You are going to work in a sneaker factory.
Write about your new job and what you will do.

107

3 CLOSING THE LESSON

Lesson 3 Review

Answers to Read and Think

1. Workers make rubber, cut and sew the cloth, glue the pieces together, and package the sneakers.

2. Each job is necessary for the shoes to be made properly.

Answer to Skills Check

Stories should describe a job needed in order to produce sneakers.

Answer to Lesson Title Question

Ask the lesson title question, found at the beginning of the lesson:

How are sneakers made?

(Sneakers are made with the combined effort of many workers. Workers mix the rubber, attach the pieces, box the sneakers, and deliver them to stores.)

Additional Practice

You may wish to assign the ancillary materials listed below.

Understanding the Lesson p. 33

Workbook p. 19

Reteaching Main Objective

⭐ *Explain the relationship between an assembly line worker in a factory and the finished product.*

● Divide the class into groups of six. Within the group assign each member a crayon color and a shape to draw. Give each group a sheet of white paper. Have the group members draw their shapes on the paper.

● Have the groups do a second copy of their design. Instruct one member per group to skip his or her job.

● Have the groups compare the originals to the copies and identify the missing elements.

● Have the students explain how the assembly process works and why each job must be done.

Review Master Booklet, p. 33

UNDERSTANDING THE LESSON

NAME _____

UNDERSTANDING THE LESSON   UNIT **4**

Putting Events in Order   LESSON 3 CONTENT MASTER

✱ How are sneakers made? Number the pictures in the correct order. Write the number in the box in the corner of each picture.

```
┌──────────┬──────────┐
│          │          │
│    2     │    3     │
├──────────┼──────────┤
│          │          │
│    4     │    1     │
└──────────┴──────────┘
```

Think and Do: Draw a pair of sneakers. Use the back of this sheet.
Use with textbook pages 100–107.   33

107

Optional Activities

How Do People Travel to Work?

Objectives

★1. **Identify** five modes of transportation.

2. **Compare** the modes of transportation used long ago with those available today.

1 STARTING THE LESSON

Motivation/ Prior Knowledge

■ Ask the students to name the ways their families get to school and to work each day. List their responses on the chalkboard.

■ Tell the students that this lesson is about the ways people travel to work.

Study the Vocabulary

NEW WORD	DISCUSSION WORD
travel	*horses*
	airplane

■ Explain to the students that travel means "to go from one place to another." Have the students compare the speed of a horse to that of an airplane.

■ Have the students use the following words in sentences: *horse, train, car, boat,* and *airplane.*

108

How Do People Travel to Work?

Travel means to go from one place to another.
Long ago travel took a long time.
People had to live near their jobs.
People used horses and trains to travel.

108

Optional Activities

PREVIEWING LESSON VOCABULARY

NAME _____

PREVIEWING LESSON VOCABULARY   U N I T **4**

Identifying   LESSON 4 VOCABULARY MASTER

✳ TRAVEL means to go from one place to another. There are many ways to TRAVEL. Pictured below are some ways to TRAVEL. Write the word from the word box that goes with each picture.

car	bus	train	bicycle	airplane	boat

bus   boat   train

bicycle   airplane   car

Think and Do: Draw your favorite way to TRAVEL. Use the back of this sheet.

34   Use with textbook pages 108–111.

Review Master Booklet, p. 34

Today many people must travel to work.
They do not live near their jobs.
Cars and buses help people travel to work.
Mr. Hill rides a bus to his job.
Mrs. Hill drives a car to her job.

109

Writing to Learn

Sequencing a Trip Have the students describe the series of steps that they would have to follow to take a trip on a bus, a train, or an airplane.

- Have the students use the sequencing terms *first*, *next*, *then*, and *last* in their descriptions.

- Have the students illustrate each step.

Read and Discuss

Text pages 108–111

The ways people travel have changed. Ask the students to read pp. 108–111 and to answer these questions.

1. **What does *travel* mean?**
   (*Travel* means "to go from one place to another." *p. 108*)

2. **How do people travel to work today?**
   (People use cars, buses, boats, trains and airplanes to travel to work. *pp. 109–111*)

3. **How did people travel to work long ago?**
   (They used horses and trains. *p. 109*)

   Thinking Critically How are a wagon and a car similar? (Analyze)
   (Answers may include that they were both designed to hold families and their belongings rather than large numbers of people. *pp. 108–109*)

VISUAL THINKING SKILL

Comparing the Photographs

■ There are many buses and cars on our roads today. Have the students look at the photographs on p. 109 and answer these questions.
Which can carry more people to their jobs—the car or the bus? Why?
(The bus can carry more people. It is much larger than the car.)

Concept:
Recognizing Conditions for Travel

Different modes of travel require different elements for operation. Assign one of the activities below to help the students understand these differences.

◆**EASY** Have the students work in groups of five to design a transportation riddle book. Have the students work together to think of clues for a train, a car, a bus, an airplane, and a boat. For example, *I ride on tracks* may be a clue for a train.

Each student should write one of the clues and illustrate it on a sheet of paper. Then have each group assemble the pages into a book. Have the students print the answers on the back of the pages.

◀▶**AVERAGE** Have the students work in pairs to list three elements needed to operate each of the following: a train, a car, a boat, an airplane, and a bus. For example, tracks, cars, and a ticket collector can be associated with a train.

◀▮▶**CHALLENGING** Have the students list ways that a car and a wagon are alike in their requirements for operation. Then have them list ways that they are different.

VISUAL THINKING SKILL

Interpreting the Photographs

■ Discuss with the students that trains and boats operate on schedules. Have the students look at the photographs on p. 110. Then ask them these questions.

1. **Are the three people waiting for a train or for a boat to pick them up?**
   (A train)

2. **How do you know they are waiting for a train?**
   (They are standing next to train tracks.)

There are other ways to travel too. Some workers take a boat to work. Other workers take a train.

Optional Activities

SKILLBUILDER REVIEW

Grouping Words On pp. 56–57, the students learned to make word groups. Have the students review this skill by sorting selected words into the following categories: car, train, boat, and airplane.

● Write these words on the chalkboard for the students to categorize: *water*, *track*, *runway*, *road*, *train station*, *airport*, *garage*, and *dock*.

People travel on airplanes too.
An airplane is another way to go places.
Airplanes are much faster than cars.

Review

Read and Think

1. Name some ways people travel. **(Recall)**

2. Which way do you like to travel and why?
(Evaluate)

Skills Check

Look at the pictures on page 108.

How are the train and the wagon different?

111

---

3 CLOSING THE LESSON

Lesson 4 Review

Answers to Read and Think

1. People travel in cars, in buses, on trains, on airplanes, and on boats.

2. Answers will vary, but the students must include reasons for their answers.

Answer to Skills Check

Answers may include that wagons move on roads and trains move on tracks, and the vehicles move by different means.

Answer to Lesson Title Question

Ask the lesson title question, found at the beginning of the lesson:
How do people travel to work?
(People use cars, buses, trains, boats, and occasionally airplanes to travel to work.)

Additional Practice

You may wish to assign the ancillary materials listed below.
Understanding the Lesson p. 35
Workbook p. 20

Reteaching Main Objective

⭐ *Identify modes of transportation.*

- Give each student five 5″ × 8″ index cards. On one half have the student draw a mode of transportation. On the other half have the student label the form of transportation.

- Have the students cut their cards in half, mix up the cards, and then match the drawings to the labels.

Review Master Booklet, p. 35

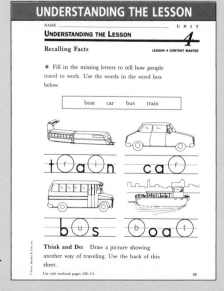

UNDERSTANDING THE LESSON

NAME

UNDERSTANDING THE LESSON

UNIT 4

Recalling Facts

LESSON 4 CONTENT MASTER

* Fill in the missing letters to tell how people travel to work. Use the words in the word box below.

| boat | car | bus | train |

t r a i n   c a r

b u s   b o a t

Think and Do: Draw a picture showing another way of traveling. Use the back of this sheet.

Use with textbook pages 108–111.   35

Optional Activities

111

Using the New Words

The vocabulary terms in this review were introduced in the unit. Some students may have difficulty distinguishing between similar concepts. Discuss the meaning of each word in relation to the pictures before having the students match the words to the pictures.

Suggested Answers

1. C
2. E
3. B
4. A
5. D

Accept other responses if students can explain their choice.

A. Using the New Words

Find the picture that best matches each word.

1. factory _____
2. travel _____
3. pictograph _____
4. goods _____
5. service _____

A.

B.

C.

D.

E.

112

UNIT CONTENT TEST

NAME _____

CONTENT TEST UNIT **4**

Directions: Read each sentence. Fill in the circle below the picture that best completes each sentence.

1. Sneakers are made in a _____ .

2. Clothes are sold at a _____ .

3. One service worker is a _____ .

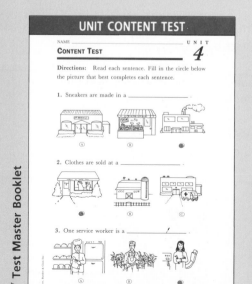

▶ **Test Master Booklet**

UNIT CONTENT TEST

NAME _____ UNIT 4

CONTENT TEST (continued)

4. Goods are made by a _____ .

5. Long ago people traveled by _____ .

6. Many people in a city travel by _____ .

7. A fast way to travel is by _____ .

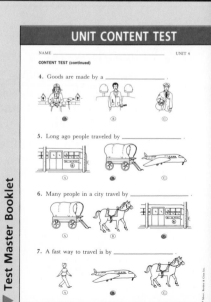

▶ **Test Master Booklet**

B. Remembering What You Read

Answer these questions about the unit.

1. Name some places where people work.
2. How do people travel today?
3. How is working in a factory different from working in a bank?

C. Summarizing the Unit

Write a story about a job you would like.

1. Where would you work?
2. Why would you like that job?

113

Remembering What You Read

Answer these questions about the unit.

1. People work in schools, in factories, in stores, in banks, on docks, and on farms. Accept all reasonable answers.

2. Today, people travel in cars, in buses, on trains, on boats, and on airplanes.

3. One difference between working in a factory and working in a bank is that a worker in a factory makes *goods,* while a worker in a bank provides a *service.* Accept all reasonable answers.

Summarizing the Unit

Have the students look at the picture on p. 113. Tell them to think of something they enjoy doing, such as drawing, playing a sport, or being around animals.

Tell the students to each think of a job in which they could do what they enjoy. Have them write stories about the place they would work and explain why they would like their job.

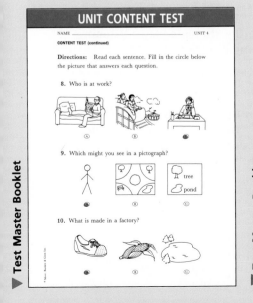

Following Directions

Objectives

1. **Identify** why directions are important.
2. **Follow** directions correctly to complete a task.

Why Do I Need This Skill?

To help the students recognize why directions are important, ask the following questions.

1. **Can you think of some things that you have at home that have directions on them?**
   (Answers may include such things as food labels, games, computers, clothing, appliances, and so on.)

2. **Why, do you think, do these things come with directions?**
   (Answers should reflect the understanding that the directions tell us how to use the items correctly.)

Learning the Skill

To help the students understand why it is important to follow directions, ask the following questions.

1. **Before the workers can glue the pieces together, what must they do?**
   (They must make the rubber and cut the cloth for the sides.)

2. **Why is it important for the workers to follow the directions when they make the sneakers?**
   (So that the sneakers are made correctly)

SKILL TRACE:	Following Written Directions	
INTRODUCE PE, p. 114	PRACTICE PE, p. 115 TE, p. 120 WB, p. 21	TEST Unit 4 Test, TMB

114

 A ## Why Do I Need This Skill?

Directions tell you what to do.
Following directions helps you do things the right way.

 B ## Learning the Skill

Directions helped the workers make sneakers.

 The workers had to do their jobs in order.
Here are some of the directions.

1. Use the recipe to make the rubber.
2. Cut the cloth for the sides.
3. Glue the pieces together.
4. Cook the sneakers.

114

Optional Activities

Curriculum Connection

Listening Skills   Have the students play a listening game that involves following directions.

● Explain to the students that sometimes they will need to listen to directions instead of reading them.

● Have each student listen to and follow a short string of oral directions, such as "Walk to the bookcase, find a blue book, put it on my desk, wave to the class, and sit down at your desk again."

Practicing the Skill

Follow the directions below.

1. Get out a piece of paper.
2. Write your name on the top.
3. Draw a sneaker with your pencil.
4. Color the sneaker blue or red.

 ## Applying the Skill

Write the directions for making a sandwich.

Ask a friend to read your directions.

Practicing the Skill

Have the students follow the directions at the top of p. 115.

Each student should write his or her name at the top of a piece of paper, draw a picture of a sneaker and color it blue or red.

If students have difficulty with this concept, you may wish to assign the reteaching activity.

Applying the Skill

Have the students look at the picture on p. 115. Tell them to write the directions for making their favorite sandwiches.

Their directions should include taking two slices of bread and putting some kind of filling on the slices. Have them trade papers with neighboring students and read each other's directions.

Reteaching Activity

● Supply the students with paper and crayons or markers. Write the directions below on the chalkboard and have students read and follow them.

1. Draw a circle.
2. Color the circle yellow.
3. Draw a square.
4. Color the square red.
5. Write your name in blue.

Optional Activities

SOCIAL STUDIES LIBRARY: *The Little Red Lighthouse and the Great Gray Bridge*

Neighborhoods and Communities
(pp. 116–143)

Unit Theme: Neighborhoods are small groups of homes. Communities are composed of neighborhoods and provide special services for the residents.

UNIT RESOURCES
Unit 5 Test

 SOCIAL STUDIES LIBRARY: *Old Henry*

LESSON *1*   What Is a Neighborhood?
(pp. 118–121)

Theme: A neighborhood is composed of a group of homes and the people living in them. Neighbors can work and play together.

LESSON RESOURCES
Workbook, p. 21
Review Master Booklet
  Previewing Lesson Vocabulary,
  p. 36
  Understanding the Lesson, p. 37

LESSON *2*   How Is a Map Like a Picture?
(pp. 122–125)

Theme: A map shows the same features as a picture, but the features are represented with symbols.

LESSON RESOURCES
Workbook, pp. 22–23
Review Master Booklet
  Understanding the Lesson, p. 38

LESSON *3*   What Is a Community?
(pp. 126–129)

Theme: A community is composed of neighborhoods and provides special services to help the residents.

LESSON RESOURCES
Workbook, pp. 24–25
Review Master Booklet
  Previewing Lesson Vocabulary,
  p. 39
  Understanding the Lesson, p. 40

SOCIAL STUDIES LIBRARY: *Whose Hat Is That?*

LESSON *4*   Who Are Community Workers?
(pp. 134–137)

Theme: Community workers, such as police officers and road crews, provide services to community members and work to make the community a safe place to live.

LESSON RESOURCES
Workbook, p. 26
Review Master Booklet
  Understanding the Lesson, p. 41

LESSON *5*   What Kinds of Communities Are There?
(pp. 138–143)

Theme: Farms and cities represent two types of communities.

LESSON RESOURCES
Workbook, p. 27
Review Master Booklet
  Previewing Lesson Vocabulary,
  p. 42
  Understanding the Lesson, p. 43

PACING GUIDE

September UNIT	October UNIT	November UNITS	December UNIT	January UNIT	February UNIT	March UNITS	April UNIT	May UNIT
1	2	2–3	3	4	5	5–6	6	7

Annotated Bibliography

Books for Teachers

Polette, Nancy. *Picture Books for Gifted Programs.* Metuchen, NJ: Scarecrow Press, 1981. ISBN 0-810-81461-7. This book presents information about the special needs of gifted children. It lists a number of picture books with bibliographic information and provides various activities to facilitate communication skills, productive thinking, and critical thinking.

Trelease, Jim. *The Read Aloud Handbook,* 2nd ed. New York: Penguin Books, 1985. ISBN 0-140-46727-0. The author presents reasons why reading aloud to children is essential at all ages. In addition, he has compiled a list of good read-aloud books, complete with descriptions of each.

Books for Read Aloud

Arnold, Caroline. *What Is a Community?* New York: Franklin Watts, 1982. ISBN 0-531-04444-0. Takes a look at the various aspects, characteristics, and needs of communities which are made up of families living in neighborhoods.

Brown, Marcia. *Stone Soup.* New York: Charles Scribner's Sons, 1947. ISBN 0-684-92296-7. A group of soldiers teach a community how to work together to make a meal for everyone.

Galdone, Paul. *The Little Red Hen.* New York: Seabury Press, 1973. ISBN 0-816-43099-3. The little red hen finds none of her lazy friends willing to help her plant, harvest, or grind wheat into flour, but all want to eat the cake she makes from it.

Pearson, Tracey Campbell. *Old MacDonald Had a Farm.* New York: Dial Books for Young Readers, 1984. ISBN 0-803-70068-7. The inhabitants of the farm are described verse by verse, with beautiful illustrations added.

Stevens, Janet. *The Town Mouse and the Country Mouse.* New York: Holiday House, 1987. ISBN 0-823-40633-4. A town mouse and a country mouse exchange visits and discover that each prefers his own home.

Filmstrips and Video

Rosie's Walk. Weston, CT: Weston Woods. 5-minute video. Although unaware that a fox is after her, Rosie the hen takes a walk around the farmyard.

Computer Software

Sticky Town Bear. Apple II. Norfolk, CT: Weekly Reader Family.

Bulletin Board Idea

The ABC's of a Community

A — Apartment
An apartment is a place to live.

F — Fire Station
The fire engines are kept at the fire station.

H — House
A house is a kind of shelter.

L — Library
A library shares its books with the community members.

P — Park
A park is a place to play.

Police Station
The police officers work at the police station. The officers help keep the area safe.

S — School
Children go to a school to learn.

Store
A store sells things for people to buy.

Student Activity
Have the students work in small groups to draw and color an apartment building, a fire station, a house, a library, a park, a police station, a school, and a store. Then have the groups make labels for the places and write sentences that explain why the place is needed in the community.

Communities Around the World

How are communities around the world alike and how are they different?

In Unit 5 the students will learn about typical city and farm communities in our country. In the following activities the students will build on their knowledge by exploring life in communities around the world.

SOCIAL STUDIES

History Discuss how people celebrate the Fourth of July in their community by asking the following questions.

1. Did you do anything special, such as go to a picnic or barbecue, to celebrate the holiday?
2. Did you see any fireworks?
3. Why, do you think, do people like to watch fireworks on the Fourth of July?

■ Point out that celebrations in communities change over time. Mention to the students that the Fourth of July is the anniversary of our country's independence. It is considered our nation's birthday.

■ Have the students ask older members of the community how the Fourth of July was celebrated when they were young. Then ask the students to draw pictures showing the differences in the way they celebrate the Fourth of July and the way people celebrated the holiday long ago.

Economics Obtain currency (in low denominations) from several countries, including the United States. (You may wish to call several banks in your area to find out which ones exchange currencies, then compare rates of exchange.) Show the students the money from different countries and discuss how it is alike and how it is different.

Global Awareness Ask students what people in their community say when they greet someone. Tell the students that people in communities around the world speak different languages. Ask the students if anyone knows how to say "hello" in more than one language. Write the students' answers on the chalkboard.

■ Teach the students some greetings in other languages. "Hello" or "good day" is *buòn giorno* in Italian, *guten Tag* in German, *buenos días* in Spanish, and *shalom* in Hebrew. Have the students walk around the room and greet each other in the languages that they learned.

LANGUAGE ARTS

Writing a Class Letter Have the class write a letter to an imaginary first grade class in a school in another country. Have the students make a list of the questions they would want to ask the children. The list of questions might include the following.

1. What is your school like?
2. What does your town or village look like?
3. What do you do for fun?
4. How many people are in your family?
5. What is your home like?

■ Then ask the students to answer those same questions as if the student from the other country asked them. Have the students respond orally to the questions.

Class Discussion Ask the students if their family eats any special foods that represent communities in other countries.

■ Have the students describe these dishes. Write their descriptions on the chalkboard. Supplement the list with any additional foreign dishes that you can describe. Suggest that students bring in recipes to exchange with one another.

■ Some students may wish to prepare one of the foods from the list at home and share it with the class.

MATHEMATICS

■ Poll the class to find out what communities around the country and around the world the students have visited. List these communities down the left side of a large piece of butcher paper. Have students make a pictograph by drawing a stick figure next to the names of the places they have visited. After the graph is completed, ask the following questions:

1. **How many places have been visited by members of the class?**

2. **What is the name of the place that the most students visited?**

3. **How many students have been to_____?** (Insert the name of one of the places.)

4. **Have more people been to _____or_____?** (Insert the names of two places on the list.)

ART

■ Have the students make figures that are dressed in the native costumes of several farm and city communities around the world. Students could use construction paper, glue, scissors, and felt-tip markers to make the figures. A travel agency is a good source for pictures that the students can use as references. Communities with distinctive dress, such as Lancaster County, Pennsylvania (farm), and Beijing, China (city), are recommended for this activity.

■ Display the figures on a bulletin board entitled *Can You Tell Where I Live?*

Build a Community Model

INSTRUCTIONS FOR THE TEACHER:

Focus In this unit the students will learn about neighborhoods and communities. The students will develop an awareness of maps, directions, and the important places in their neighborhoods and communities. The students will also learn that a group of neighborhoods form a community.

Prepare students for building their own community model by first reviewing the concepts learned in Lesson 1, "What Is a Neighborhood?" and Lesson 3, "What Is a Community?" The map skills presented in these lessons will help the students plan and describe the special places in the community that they will create. Establishing the special places in the community as well as using directions to explain where they are located in the community are key elements of this activity.

Warm-up Activity In advance, use a large piece of butcher paper and masking tape to make a city map showing a three-street by three-street grid. Label each street. Write the name of each main direction on an index card. The students will need these cards for reference during the activity. Then cut out from construction paper nine different shapes. The shapes should be large enough for the students to

hold easily, and each shape must fit within the dimensions of one city block on your grid.

Tell students that to follow or give directions, it is important to know the names of the four main directions and where the directions are located on a map. Place the butcher paper map on the floor. Have the students gather around the map. Have them help you place the four direction cards on the correct sides of the map. Then hold up one of the shapes and ask the students to place it on the map according to your oral direction. For example, "Place the circle north of Elm Street." Give directions until all the shapes are placed. Repeat this procedure until the students can easily place the shapes correctly. Then reverse the procedure. Place a shape on the map and have the students describe where the shape is located. Before proceeding, be sure that all of the students can use direction words readily.

ACTIVITY FOR THE STUDENTS:

Procedure Before starting this activity, collect or have the students bring in empty half gallon paper cartons and paper boxes of different sizes.

Tell the students that they will be making a model of a community. Ask them to name places that are found in commmunities. The students might name schools, houses, apartment buildings, factories, stores, parks, a library, a fire station, a police station, and a hospital. List all the ideas on the chalkboard. Have the students select which places they would like to include in their community. Assign each student a building to construct.

Give the students cartons and boxes, construction paper, crayons, markers, scissors, tissue paper, and glue to create and decorate their buildings.

Building the Community Model Once all the buildings are completed, draw a simple pattern of streets on a large piece of butcher paper. With the class, decide where to place each of the buildings. Once all the buildings are placed, name the community and the streets.

Assign groups of students to color the streets and the grass. Other students should make trees, bushes, traffic lights, stop signs, and street signs for the community. One group of students should make a sign to name the community.

Once the model is complete, make a map that shows the streets of your community. Have the students label the streets first. Then, with the class, decide what type of symbol will be used for each place in the community. Complete the maps together.

Follow-up Activity Ask the students to describe with direction words where different places in their new community are located. You may also play a guessing game with the students. Have a student select a place in the community and give a clue about the place to the rest of the class. The clue should contain a direction word. Have the class members guess the secret place.

Extension You may wish to make cars and buses for your community. Have the students place these vehicles on the road and follow the traffic safety rules. You may wish to build a train station, an airport, or dock area in or near your community. Discuss with the students any special land or water needs that must be accommodated. If you wish, have the students pretend to buy tickets at the train station or at the airport.

Workbook Pages

OUR NEIGHBORHOOD

Following Directions

✳ A neighborhood is a group of homes. Chris, Lee, and Maria live in the same neighborhood. Follow the directions below.

(blue)   (red)   (yellow) (green)

1. Chris lives next door to Lee. He also lives next door to Maria. Color his house red.

2. Lee's house has the most windows. Color his house blue.

3. A tree is next to Maria's house. Color her house yellow. Color the tree green.

© Silver, Burdett & Ginn Inc.

Unit 5, pages 118–121

21

A PICTURE AND A MAP

Understanding Pictures and Maps

✳ A picture and a map can both show the same place. Look at the picture of a neighborhood below. Draw a map of that neighborhood on the next page. Use the map key.

22

Unit 5, pages 122–125

© Silver, Burdett & Ginn Inc.

A PICTURE AND MAP *CONTINUED*

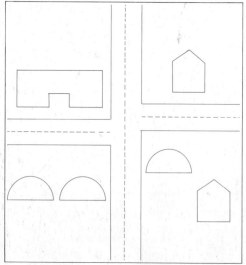

Map Key

⌂ house   ⊓ school   ◠ store   --- road

© Silver, Burdett & Ginn Inc.

Unit 5, pages 122–125

23

PLACES IN THE COMMUNITY

Following Directions

✳ Every community has many different places. You go to different places for different things. Look at the map. Follow the directions on the next page.

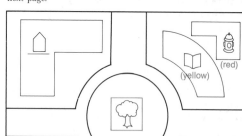

(red)

(yellow)

(blue)

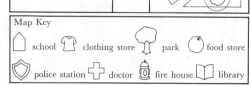

Map Key

⌂ school   👕 clothing store   🌳 park   🍎 food store

🛡 police station   ✚ doctor   fire house   📖 library

24

Unit 5, pages 126–133

© Silver, Burdett & Ginn Inc.

U5-G

Workbook Pages

NAME ______________________ UNIT 5

PLACES IN THE COMMUNITY *CONTINUED*

1. Circle the place you go to buy food.
2. Put an X on the place you go when you are sick.
3. Put a line under the place you go to learn.
4. Put a red △ around the place you go to buy a new coat.
5. Find the place where fire trucks are kept. Color it red.
6. Find the place you would call if you needed a police officer. Color it blue.
7. Put a ☐ around the place where you go to play.
8. Find the place where you can borrow books. Color that place yellow.

NAME ______________________ UNIT 5

SOME COMMUNITY WORKERS

Observing

* Some community workers drive special cars or trucks. Find the special cars or trucks hidden in the puzzle. Color them. Their names are written in the word box.

mail truck	fire truck	police car
garbage truck		city bus

NAME ______________________ UNIT 5

TWO KINDS OF COMMUNITIES

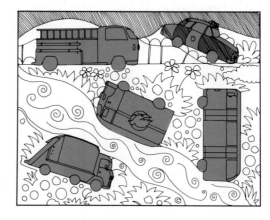

Classifying

* Connect the dots in the two pictures. Start with the number 1 and complete the pictures. Write **farm** next to the picture that shows something you see on a farm. Write **city** next to the picture that shows something you see in a city.

farm

city

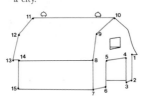

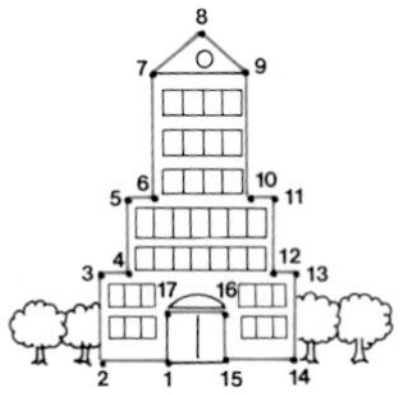

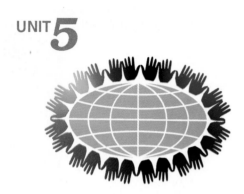

MULTICULTURAL PERSPECTIVES

Sounds You Hear *(pages 118–121)*
The enjoyment of music varies from person to person. Within a neighborhood, people may enjoy different types of music. A person's background may influence the type of music that he or she listens to.

Share with your students the music of different cultures. Obtain from the library or music center several records, compact discs, or audiocassettes of music from various cultures. The following are some suggestions for music forms, with the cultures in which they originated.

- calypso—Trinidadian
- reggae—Jamaican
- zydeco (ZYE duh koh)—Cajun, southern Louisianian
- polka—Polish
- salsa—Puerto Rican and African-Cuban

As you play each of these forms, show students pictures of people from these cultures in festive apparel. This will enable students to appreciate more of the cultural flavor of the music.

With the students, locate the area related to each culture on a map. Then discuss the area with the students.

Unit 5
NEIGHBORHOODS AND COMMUNITIES

New Words

community

directions

neighbor

neighborhood

city

THE POSTMA

Kinds of Clothing

Clothing	Summer	Winter
Shorts	X	
Mittens		X

table

116

Optional Activities

Class Discussion

- Have the students look at the picture on pp. 116–117. Have them identify the children as Little League players and the man at the left as a police officer. Ask them if they think the children know the police officer. How can they tell?

- Ask the students to name some activities they participate in with people in their neighborhood. These may include sports, Scout meetings, activities in various clubs, religious events, and so on.

Living in Cities *(pages 138–143)*
Many large cities have park areas for their residents to enjoy. Ask the students to consider whether they would enjoy playing in a park if they lived in a city. Ask them to explain their reasoning.

Mention to the students some famous parks of the world, such as the following.

Mount Royal Park, Montreal, Canada
This park has paths for carriage rides and sleigh rides, a playhouse for performances, and a lake for ice-skating.

Royal Parks, London
Five parks exist in central London. The lands for the parks were once part of royal estates. These parks contain different features which include walking paths, formal gardens, and a lake.

Tivoli Gardens, Copenhagen, Denmark
This park has rides and also performance areas for ballets and concerts.

Ueno (WAY noh) Park, Tokyo, Japan
This park is well-known for cherry-blossom and lotus-blossom displays. It has a concert hall, museums, a zoo, a temple and shrine, and the tombs of Japanese rulers.

Ask the students to consider features that they would like to have in a park. Have them work alone or in small groups to design parks with these features. Have them describe their parks to the rest of the class.

Optional Activities

What Is a Neighborhood?

Objectives

★1. **Name** the direction words and **explain** the relationships between north, south, east, and west.

2. **Use** direction words to find places on a street map.

3. **Define** *neighborhood* and *neighbor*.

1 STARTING THE LESSON

Motivation/ Prior Knowledge

■ Have the students describe the area near their homes and the people who live near them.

■ Explain to the students that these areas are called neighborhoods and that they will be learning about neighborhoods as part of this lesson.

Study the Vocabulary

NEW WORDS	DISCUSSION WORDS
neighbor	*opposite*
neighborhood	*north*
directions	*south*
	east
	west

■ Make arrows with the directions north, south, east, and west. Postion them in appropriate places in the room.

■ Have the students stand. Give them oral directions to move a few steps in each direction. Continue to give directions until all of the students can follow them correctly.

118

Lesson 1

What Is a Neighborhood?

A **neighborhood** is a group of homes. The homes are near each other. People who live near each other are **neighbors**.

118

Optional Activities

PREVIEWING LESSON VOCABULARY

NAME _____   UNIT

PREVIEWING LESSON VOCABULARY   **5**

Completing Sentences   LESSON 1 VOCABULARY MASTER

 ★ A NEIGHBORHOOD is a group of homes. NEIGHBORS are people who live near each other. DIRECTIONS tell you which way to go to find places. Use NEIGHBORHOOD, NEIGHBORS, or DIRECTIONS to complete each sentence below.

1. My ____neighborhood____ has many homes.

2. I use ____directions____ to find places.

3. Megan and Avi live near me. They are my

   ____neighbors____

4. My school is close to my house. It is in my

   ____neighborhood____ .

Think and Do: Draw a picture of one of your neighbors. Use the back of this sheet.

36   Use with textbook pages 118–121.

Review Master Booklet, p. 36

Neighbors can help each other.
Mrs. James will help her neighbor
rake leaves.
Neighbors can work together too.
These neighbors are building a play area.
The children will soon have a new
place to play.

119

Read and Discuss
Text pages 118–121

To help the students understand and use the vocabulary terms presented in this lesson, have the students read pp. 118–121. Then have them answer the following questions.

1. **What is a group of homes?**
(Neighborhood *p. 118*)

2. **What do neighbors do together?**
(Work and help each other *p. 119*)

3. **Which directions are opposites?**
(North-south; east-west *p. 120*)

   Thinking Critically How is your neighborhood like Jane's neighborhood? (Evaluate)
   (Answers may include that there are houses or apartments, or several blocks. *p. 120*)

VISUAL THINKING SKILL

Analyzing the Photographs

■ Have the students look at the bottom photograph on p. 119. Then ask this question.
How are the neighbors working together?
(Holding beams and sharing tools)

Creating Neighborhoods

Have the students use construction paper to cut out shapes that will represent their home and their neighbors' homes.

Have the students draw or color a street or streets on a sheet of 12″ × 18″ paper. Then ask them to glue their home and their neighbors' homes in place.

Have the students label the street or streets in their pictures. Have them add the title "My Neighborhood" to the pictures.

Comparing Neighborhoods

● Have the students work in pairs for this activity. Ask the students to describe to each other their neighborhoods and what they do in their neighborhoods.

● Have the students create a list of ways that their neighborhoods are alike and a list of ways that their neighborhoods are different.

● Then have the students compare the events that occur between neighbors in the two neighborhoods.

Optional Activities

Meeting Individual Needs

Concept:
Using Directions

An understanding of directions is necessary to use maps. Help the students with this concept by assigning one of the activities below.

◆ **EASY** Give the students a sheet of graph paper with 1″ squares. Have the students make an X in a box in the center of the paper. Then have them mark *north*, *south*, *east*, and *west* on the sides of their papers. Then give the students oral directions, using direction terms, for example, "Draw a heart to the south of the *X*." Correct the papers with the students.

◀▶ **AVERAGE** Label the walls of the classroom *north*, *south*, *east*, and *west*. Have the students write sentences that use the direction words and compare two objects in the room. Have the students use each direction word at least once.

◀▮▶ **CHALLENGING** Give the students a blank sheet of paper and a 2″ strip of cardboard to act as a unit measure. Have the students mark the directions on the sides of the paper and an X in the center of the paper.

Prepare for the students a sheet containing directions such as "Go two units north." Have the students draw the lines according to the written directions. Include the terms *north, south, east,* and *west* in the written directions.

GEOGRAPHY THEMES

Location

■ Have the students use the map on p. 120 to answer this question.
How can you get to Pine Street from Jane's house?
(Go north on Hillside Ave. Go west on Elm street. Pine Street is to the south of Elm Street.)

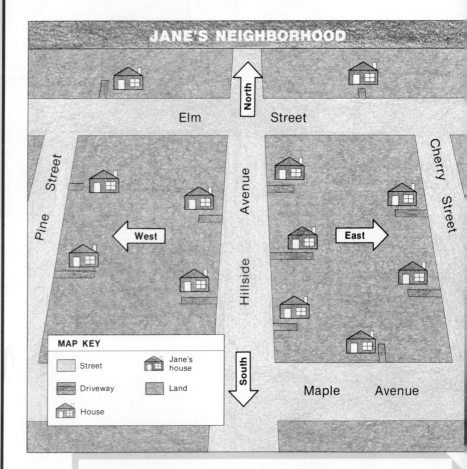

Look at the map on this page.
It shows Jane's neighborhood.
There are **directions** on this map.
Directions help people find places.
North, south, east, and west are directions.
North and south are opposite directions.
East and west are opposite directions.

Optional Activities

Writing to Learn

Identifying Neighbors Have the students write the names of two of their neighbors. Then have the students draw a picture of something that they do with those neighbors.

Thinking about Opposites Have the students work in pairs to list two pairs of opposites such as big-little.

● Give the students drawing paper to illustrate their opposite pairs. Each pair should be labeled and illustrated on a sheet of paper. Bind the papers into a class book of opposites.

Use the map on page 120.
Kim is on Maple Avenue.
In which direction will she walk
to go to Jane's house?

Lesson 1

Review

Read and Think

1. Name the four directions. **(Recall)**

2. What do you do with your neighbors? **(Analyze)**

Skills Check

Look at the map on page 120.
Which street is east of Jane's house?

121

Lesson *1* Review

Answers to Read and Think

1. North, south, east, and west

2. Answers will vary but may include going to the park or out to play.

Answer to Skills Check

Cherry Street is east of Jane's house.

Answer to Lesson Title Question

Ask the lesson title question, found at the beginning of the lesson:
What is a neighborhood?
(A neighborhood is a group of homes that are near each other. The people that live in the homes are neighbors. Neighbors sometimes work together or help each other.)

Additional Practice

You may wish to assign the ancillary materials listed below.
Understanding the Lesson p. 37
Workbook p. 21

SKILL TRACE:	Understanding Directions: N, S, E, W	
INTRODUCE PE, p. 120	**PRACTICE** PE, p. 127 TE, p. 120 RMB, p. 37	**TEST** Unit 5 Test, TMB

Reteaching Main Objective

⭐ *Name the direction words and explain the relationships between north, south, east, and west.*

● Have the students name the four directions. List them on the chalkboard. Give each student four index cards. Have the students write one direction word on each card.

● Call out one direction. Have the students find that card. Then ask them to find the opposite direction and raise that card. Repeat this procedure several times.

Review Master Booklet, p. 37

UNDERSTANDING THE LESSON

NAME _____

UNDERSTANDING THE LESSON

UNIT **5**

Understanding Directions   LESSON 1 CONTENT MASTER

⭐ Kim, Sara, Joe, and Ramon live in the same neighborhood. Fill in the correct direction to complete each sentence below.

```
  Sara △   △      Key
             ○      ○ house
Joe ○      ○ Kim
  ○ △ △            North
                West ○ East
  △ Ramon  △        South
```

1. Sara lives __north__ of Ramon.

2. Joe lives __west__ of Kim.

3. Ramon lives __south__ of Sara.

4. Kim lives __east__ of Joe.

Think and Do: Draw something in your neighborhood. Use the back of this sheet.
Use with textbook pages 118–121.   37

Optional Activities

121

How Is a Map Like a Picture?

Objectives

★**1. Compare** and **contrast** a photograph with a map.

2. Identify Chile and **describe** the events in a Chilean coastal neighborhood.

1 STARTING THE LESSON

Motivation/ Prior Knowledge

■ Ask the students if they have ever ridden in a airplane. Then ask those that have ridden on a plane to describe what they saw when they looked out the window to the ground below.

■ Tell the students that in this lesson they will be looking at a picture taken from a helicopter, another kind of aircraft.

Study the Vocabulary

DISCUSSION WORDS	ORAL VOCABULARY
helicopter Chile	aerial

■ Give the students empty, small milk cartons. Have them use construction paper to decorate the carton like a house. Ask the students to describe their houses.

■ Then ask the students to stand and look down at their houses. Have the students describe how their houses look now.

■ Tell the students that the standing view is like the view from a helicopter. The view from a helicopter shows the tops of things.

■ Have the students turn to their Atlas map on p. 208 to find Chile. Tell them that they will be learning about a neighborhood in Chile today.

122

How Is a Map Like a Picture?

A helicopter flies high in the air. This picture was taken from a helicopter. The picture shows Ann's neighborhood.

122

Optional Activities

Cooperative Learning

Mapping a Neighborhood Have the students work in pairs to complete this activity. Have the pairs start by using blocks to create a neighborhood.

● Once the students have finished their block neighborhoods have them list the features that need to be included on their maps. The pairs should decide how each feature will be represented on the map and in the map key.

● Have the students draw and color a map to correspond to their neighborhoods. Display the maps next to the block arrangements. Have the pairs evaluate how closely their maps represent their block neighborhoods.

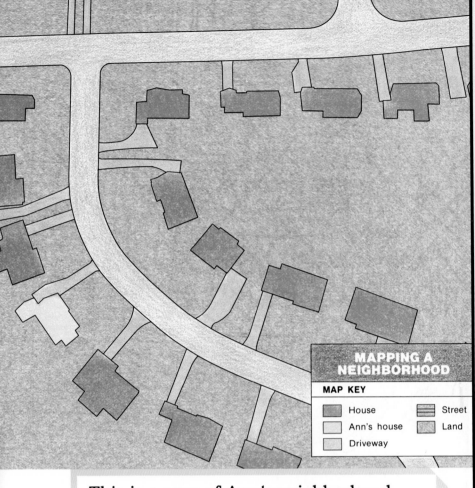

This is a map of Ann's neighborhood.
Use the map key to find Ann's house
on the map.
Ann's house is yellow on the map.
Can you find Ann's house in the picture?
How are the map and the picture alike?

MAPPING A NEIGHBORHOOD

MAP KEY

■	House	▤	Street
□	Ann's house	▦	Land
□	Driveway		

123

Writing to Learn

Writing to Rosa   Have the students write a letter to
Rosa that describes their neighborhood. Have the students
draw a picture of something that they have done with their
neighbors.

Optional Activities

2 DEVELOPING THE LESSON

Read and Discuss
Text pages 122–125

This lesson discusses maps in relation to
photographs and neighborhoods. Help the
students form the necessary comparisons
by reading pp. 122–125 and answering the
questions below.

1. **How can you find Ann's house on the
   map on p. 123 ?**
   (Use the map key. *p. 123*)

2. **What is Rosa's neighborhood like?**
   (Her neighborhood is near the water.
   Many people fish for their jobs. The
   neighborhood has a party in June for everyone who fishes. *p. 124*)

   Thinking Critically Why is it easier
   to find Ann's house on the map than
   in the picture?   (Analyze)
   (Her house is yellow on the map.
   p. 123)

   Thinking Critically How are Ann's
   and Rosa's neighborhoods different?
   (Analyze)
   (Rosa's neighborhood is near the water.
   Rosa's neighborhood has a party for the
   people who fish, while Ann's does not.
   Rosa's neighborhood is bigger than
   Ann's neighborhood. *pp. 122–124*)

GEOGRAPHY THEMES

Location

■ The map key is an important tool. Have
the students look at the map key on
p. 123. Then ask this question.
What does the map key show?
(House, Ann's house, driveway, street,
and land)

Meeting Individual Needs

Concept:
Using Aerial Perspective

Help the students grasp the concept of an aerial perspective by assigning one of the activities below.

◆ **EASY** Have the students mold a figure out of clay. Have them add details to the figure. Then have them write a description of the figure.

Have the students place their figures on the floor and look down on them. Have them write two ways that the figures look different.

◀▶ **AVERAGE** Prepare a map key for a map, showing a street, houses, and driveways. Then have the student draw a map that uses the symbols.

◀▮▶ **CHALLENGING** Have the students draw what they think a football field, a baseball diamond, and a swimming pool would look like from a helicopter.

VISUAL THINKING SKILL

Interpreting the Photograph

■ Have the students look at the bottom photograph on p. 124. Then ask this question.
What do you think the men do for a job?
(Answers may include that they fish. One man is holding a fish. They are wearing protective covering. They are standing on a pier.)

PEN PALS

Ann has a new pen pal named Rosa.
Rosa wrote to Ann about her neighborhood.

124

Dear Ann,

My family and I live in Chile.
Our neighborhood is near the water
My father catches fish for his job.
Many of our neighbors fish too.
Our neighborhood has a party in Ju
It is a party for people who fish.
We are thankful for the sea.

Your frie
Rosa

Optional Activities

For Your Information

● Chile is 2,650 miles long from north to south, but it is only 265 miles wide from east to west. The Andes Mountains are the boundary between Bolivia and Argentina and Chile.

● Chile has one of the world's largest fishing industries.

● The Festival of the Sea is celebrated by fishers each year on June 29. It is in honor of St. Peter.

Ann is busy working and playing
in her neighborhood.
She does many things with her neighbors.

Lesson 2

Review

Read and Think

1. How was the picture of Ann's
   neighborhood taken? (Recall)

2. Why does a map need a map key? (Evaluate)

Skills Check

Look at pages 122 and 123.

How is the picture different from the map?

125

Answers to Read and Think

1. The picture was taken from a helicopter.

2. People looking at the map need to know how to read the map.

Answer to Skills Check

Ann's house is a different color on the map. The trees are not shown on the map.

Answer to Lesson Title Question

Ask the lesson title question, found at the beginning of the lesson:

How is a map like a picture?
(A map is like a picture because it shows the important parts of the photograph. You can label parts of a map, so a map is like a labeled photograph.)

Additional Practice

You may wish to assign the ancillary materials listed below.
Understanding the Lesson p. 38
Workbook pp. 22–23

Reteaching Main Objective

⭐ *Compare and contrast a photograph with a map.*

● Have the students work in pairs and use pp. 122–123 for this activity.

● Have the students make two lists. One list should tell how the map and the photograph are alike. The second list should state how they are different. Have the pairs read their completed lists to the class.

**Review Master
Booklet, p. 38**

UNDERSTANDING THE LESSON

NAME _____

UNDERSTANDING THE LESSON

U N I T
5

A Picture and a Map   LESSON 2 CONTENT MASTER

✳ The picture and the map below show the same bedroom. Follow the directions under the map and picture.

Map Key

bed   dresser
chair
desk   bookcase

1. Put an x on the bed in the picture and on the map.

2. Circle the desk in the picture and on the map.

3. This ○ stands for a bookcase. Use this ○ to add a bookcase to the map. Then draw it in the key.

Think and Do: Draw a map of your bedroom. Make a map key. Use the back of this sheet.
38   Use with textbook pages 122–123.

Optional Activities

125

What Is a Community?

Objectives

★**1. Define** *community* and **name** five special places in a community.

2. Read and **use** a map containing abstract symbols.

---

1 STARTING THE LESSON

Motivation/ Prior Knowledge

■ Ask the students to name some of the places that they pass each day when coming to school. List the places on the chalkboard.

■ Have them identify how their families might use each place. For example, families buy things in stores.

Study the Vocabulary

NEW WORD	DISCUSSION WORDS	ORAL VOCABULARY
community	*post office library*	*service*

■ Copy the lists below on the chalkboard. Have the students match each word to its definition.

community   a place with many books
post office   a place to mail letters
library   a group of neighborhoods

■ Ask the students to name other places and describe each place with a phrase.

126

What Is a Community?

Juan lives in a neighborhood. His neighborhood is part of a **community**. A community is a group of neighborhoods. The map on page 127 shows Juan's community.

126

Optional Activities

PREVIEWING LESSON VOCABULARY

NAME _____   U N I T

PREVIEWING LESSON VOCABULARY   **5**

Answering Questions   LESSON 3 VOCABULARY MASTER

✱ A COMMUNITY is a group of neighborhoods. Communities have special places. Circle the pictures of special places that answer the questions below.

1. Where would you go to buy things?

2. Where would you go for help?

3. Where would you go to play?

Think and Do: Where would you go to have fun in your community? Draw a picture of this place. Use the back of this sheet.

Use with textbook pages 126–133.   39

Review Master Booklet, p. 39

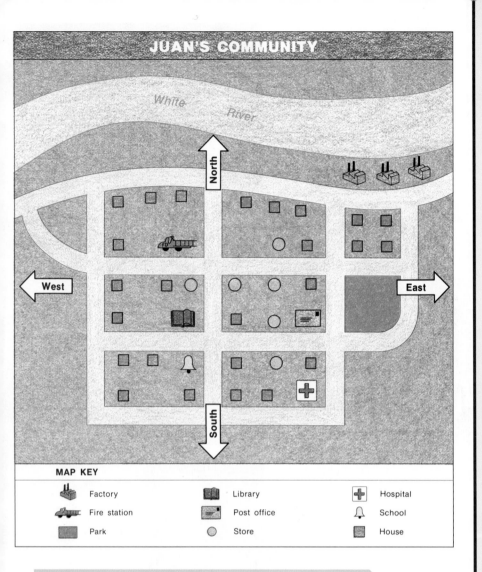

JUAN'S COMMUNITY

White River

North

West

East

South

MAP KEY

Factory	Library	Hospital
Fire station	Post office	School
Park	Store	House

The post office is one special place in the community.

What other special places do you see?

Curriculum Connection

Making a Mobile   Have the students work in pairs to create a mobile about their community. Ask each pair to draw pictures on construction paper of five places found in the community. Have the students cut out each picture and label it on the back. Encourage them to select a variety of places-specific stores; homes; and community buildings, such as a library.

● Have the students use yarn or string to attach the pictures to a hanger. Have them make a sign with the name of the community on it to attach to the hanger.

Optional Activities

② DEVELOPING THE LESSON

Read and Discuss
Text pages 126–129

To help the students develop their understanding of communities, have them read pp. 126–129 and answer these questions.

1. **What do we call a group of neighborhoods?**
   (Community *p. 126*)

2. **What are some of the special places in a community?**
   (Post office, schools, library, stores, park *pp. 127–129*)

   Thinking Critically Why, do you think, are some buildings shared by the whole community? (Hypothesize)
   (Answers may include that it would be too expensive to have buildings such as libraries or hospitals in each neighborhood or that not enough people would use them if they were built for each neighborhood. *pp. 126–129*)

GEOGRAPHY THEMES

 Location

■ Explain to the students that sometimes the map key does not show the items exactly as they appear in real life. Have the students look at the map on p. 127 and answer these questions.

1. **What places are shown in this map?**
   (Factory, fire station, park, library, post office, store, hospital, school, and house)

2. **How many stores are there in Juan's community?**
   (Six)

3. **Is the library north or south of the school?**
   (North)

Meeting Individual Needs

Concept:
Interpreting Maps

Help the students learn to work with abstract symbols on maps by assigning one of the activities below.

◆**EASY** Have the students choose five places in their community and draw map-key symbols for each one. Have them label each symbol.

◀▶**AVERAGE** Give each student a 12″ × 18″ sheet of paper. Ask the students to cut from colored construction paper different shapes to represent stores, houses, apartment buildings, and a school. Have the students create maps with their shapes. Ask the students to make map keys so that others can read their maps.

◀▮▶**CHALLENGING** Have the students draw maps of imaginary communities. The maps should contain at least five symbols. Have the students create map keys for their maps. Then ask the students to write three questions about their maps.

Have the students exchange maps and answer each other's questions.

VISUAL THINKING SKILL

Analyzing the Photograph

■ There are many kinds of stores in a community. Have the students look at the photograph on p. 128 of the people walking along the street. Then ask this question.
Look at the bags the people are carrying. What do you think the people bought?
(Answers might include wrapping paper, groceries, stationery, and sports equipment.)

The school is a place for children to learn.
The library is a place for everyone to learn.
The stores sell people the things they need.

128

Optional Activities

Writing to Learn

My Community Have the students list five places in their community. Then ask them to draw a picture of their favorite place in the community. Have the students write about why they like these places.

128

Some communities have places to play.
Juan likes to play in the park.

Lesson 3

Review

Read and Think

1. Name three special places in a community. (Recall)
2. Tell about your community. (Synthesize)

Skills Check

Look at the map on page 127.

Which direction is the post office from the park?

Lesson 3 Review

Answers to Read and Think
1. Answers may include: school, library, store, park.
2. Accept all reasonable answers about the students' community.

Answer to Skills Check
(The post office is west of the park.)

Answer to Lesson Title Question

Ask the lesson title question, found at the beginning of the lesson:
What is a community?
(A community is a group of neighborhoods. A community contains special places, such as schools, libraries, and stores as well as homes. People in a community share the special places.)

Additional Practice

You may wish to assign the ancillary material listed below.
Understanding the Lesson p. 40
Workbook pp. 24–25

Reteaching Main Objective

Define community and name five special places in a community.

- Have each student draw a picture of a place in a community. Have the students show their pictures. Ask the other members of the class to identify each place shown and tell why it is needed in the community.

- Summarize the discussion with statements about communities in general and the places found in a community.

Review Master
Booklet, p. 40

UNDERSTANDING THE LESSON

NAME _____
UNDERSTANDING THE LESSON

U N I T
5

Understanding a Map

LESSON 3 CONTENT MASTER

* A community is a group of neighborhoods.
Look at the map of a community. Then look at the map key. Answer the questions.

Map Key

△ Library 🏠 School Park ○ Store ⌂ House

1. How many stores are in this community? 10

2. How many parks are in this community? 2

3. What building is next to the school? Library

Think and Do: Draw a map of your street.
Use the back of this sheet.

40 Use with textbook pages 126–133.

Optional Activities

Thinking About Literature

Use the information below to help students better understand the literature selection found on pp. 130–133.

Selection Summary

This is the story of three hungry soldiers in a strange country looking for food and a place to sleep. The peasants in the town hide their food and tell the soldiers they have none to spare.

The soldiers devise a plan and tell the peasants that they will make a delicious soup from stones and proceed to fill a large pot with water and three stones and begin to cook it over a fire.

The peasants are so curious and amazed that they readily comply when the soldiers ask them for some "extra" ingredients to make the soup better. Soon the soup contains salt, pepper, vegetables, and meat all brought by the peasants.

With everyone cooperating and contributing some of the food they had hidden, the peasants soon have a delicious feast that they joyfully share with the soldiers.

LITERATURE
Read-Aloud

FROM
Stone Soup
BY MARCIA BROWN

Three hungry soldiers went to a poor village.
The people would not share their food.
The soldiers decided to make stone soup.
They started with a pot and some water.

"And now, if you please, three round, smooth stones."
Those were easy enough to find.
The peasants' eyes grew round as they watched the soldiers drop the stones into the pot.

(130)

Optional Activities

Curriculum Connection

Literature Have the students hang a large piece of roll paper on a wall to make a mural of the recipe for stone soup.

● Have students recall ingredients that went into the stone soup. List them on the chalkboard. The list should include water, stones, salt, pepper, cabbage, carrots, beef, and potatoes. Also ask students if they would like to add any other ingredients.

Any soup needs salt and pepper," said the

soldiers, as they began to stir.

children ran to fetch salt

and pepper.

Stones like these generally

make good soup.

ut oh, if there were carrots

would be much better."

Why I think I have a carrot

r two," said Francoise,

nd off she ran.

he came back with her

pron full of carrots from

he bin beneath the red quilt.

A good stone soup should have cabbage,"

aid the soldiers as they sliced the carrots

nto the pot.

But no use asking for what you don't have."

131

Guided Reading

1. **What did the children fetch to put in the soup?**
   (The salt and pepper)

2. **What did Francoise use to carry the carrots to the soldiers?**
   (She carried them in her apron.)

Optional Activities

- Have the students make a large pot and the listed ingredients out of construction paper. Have them also make labels for each item by copying the words from the board onto 3" x 5" index cards.

- Attach the pot to the mural and arrange the pictures of labeled ingredients around it.

Guided Reading

1. **How many cabbages did Marie bring to put in the soup?**
   (She brought three.)

2. **Where did the peasants hang their potatoes and sides of beef?**
   (In their cellars)

132

"I think I could find a cabbage somewhere,"
said Marie, and she hurried home.
Back she came
with three cabbages
from the cupboard
under the bed.

"If we only had a bit of beef and a few potatoes,
this soup would be good enough
for a rich man's table."
The peasants thought that over.

132

Optional Activities

They remembered their potatoes and the sides of beef hanging in the cellars.

They ran to fetch them.

A rich man's soup—and all from a few stones.

It seemed like magic!

What Do You Think?

What happened when the people worked together?

(133)

Classroom Cookbook

- Tell the students that people use recipes to make good things to eat.
- Have the students bring in a recipe from home of one of their favorite things to eat. Have them draw a picture to accompany the recipe and present it to the class.
- Put the recipe pages together to create a *Classroom Cookbook.*

Optional Activities

Who Are Community Workers?

Objectives

★1. **Name** three kinds of community workers and **describe** the jobs they perform.

2. **Describe** the equipment the workers use to do their jobs.

1 STARTING THE LESSON

Motivation/ Prior Knowledge

■ Ask the students to name workers who wear special uniforms, such as firefighters, police officers, astronauts, and bakers.

■ Tell the students that in this lesson they will learn about workers in the community and the equipment that the workers use to do their jobs.

Study the Vocabulary

DISCUSSION WORDS	ORAL VOCABULARY
firefighter	*equipment*
police officer	*uniform*
protect	*sanitation truck*
	road crew

■ Tell the students that protect means "to keep safe." Have the students describe how firefighters and police officers keep people safe.

■ Have the students draw pictures of firefighters or police officers doing their jobs.

Lesson 4

Who Are Community Workers?

"Mom, workers are fixing the road!" said Joe.

"They are community workers," said Mom. "Community workers help the community. It will be much easier for us to drive now."

Optional Activities

Creating a TV Viewer Show

● Have the students work in small groups to complete this activity. Assign each group a different community worker. Have each group draw one or two pictures of its community worker performing his or her job.

● Then have the students in each group work together to describe its worker and the job he or she performs. Have the groups write their descriptions.

● Assemble all of the pictures to make a roll for the TV viewer. (See the how-to article on p. U1-E–F for more complete directions.) Show the pictures in the viewer. Have the students tell about their workers when they see their pictures.

"Who else is a community worker?" asked Joe.

"Firefighters and police officers are community workers," said Mom. "They protect the community."

135

Read and Discuss
Text pages 134–137

Community workers ensure the smooth operation of processes that people in a community depend on. To help the students recognize the role these workers play in their community, have them read pp. 134–137 and answer these questions.

1. **Which kinds of community workers work with the roads in the community?**
   (The workers who fix the roads and the workers who sweep the streets *pp. 134, 137*)

2. **Which community workers protect us?**
   (Firefighters and police officers *p. 135*)

3. **What other workers help people in a community?**
   (Mail carriers and community center workers *p. 136*)

   Thinking Critically Why do we need so many community workers? (Hypothesize)
   (Today, our communities are structured so that we depend on others. One person cannot perform all the tasks necessary to maintain a community. Community workers work together to make communities nice places to live. *pp. 134–137*)

Making a Fishing Game

Make a fish pattern for the students to trace. Make the pattern large enough for the students to draw a small picture on one side.

Have each student select a community worker. Have each student trace the fish on construction paper and cut it out. Then have each student draw on one side of his or her fish a picture of the selected worker *or* a picture of the equipment that the worker uses. Have the student label the worker or the equipment on the other side of the fish.

- Once all of the fish are complete, have the students slide a paper clip onto each fish and arrange the fish on the floor with the pictures faceup.

- Have the students take turns using a string with a magnet attached to attract fish. Have the "fisher" identify the worker associated with the picture and check the answer on the back.

- The students keep any fish that they correctly identify. The winner is the student with the most fish when all of the fish have been caught.

Optional Activities

Concept:
Workers and Equipment

Help the students recognize community workers and the equipment they use by assigning one of the three activities below.

◆ **EASY** Have the students write riddles about two community workers. Have them include in their riddles descriptions of some equipment that the workers use.

Have the students draw pictures to illustrate their answers. Ask them to paste the pictures on the back of the riddles.

◀▶ **AVERAGE** Have each student use a paper lunch bag to make a hand puppet of a community worker. Have students decorate their puppets with construction paper, tissue paper, felt, yarn, and pipe cleaners.

Have the students present their puppets to the class and tell what equipment each kind of worker uses to do his or her job.

◀▮▶ **CHALLENGING** Have the students work in pairs, each pair creating a 3-D scene showing a community worker doing his or her job. The students should either cut and paste or draw a background for the picture. On a separate piece of paper, have them draw the worker doing his or her job. Have one student cut out the worker. Glue the figure to a small piece of plastic foam and then attach it to the correct place in the picture.

VISUAL THINKING SKILL

Interpreting the Photographs

■ There are several kinds of vehicles used by community workers. Have the students look at the photograph on p. 137 and identify the vehicle as a street cleaner.

■ Have each student draw a picture of another vehicle driven by a community worker.

"Our mail carrier is a community worker," said Mom.
"She brings our mail each day.
Mrs. Hall is another community worker.
She works in the community center."

136

Optional Activities

Writing to Learn

Writing about Community Workers Have each student select a community worker's job that he or she would like to hold. Ask the students to explain why they would want the jobs they chose and to name the equipment they would need to do the jobs.

● Have the students share their selections. Make a class bar graph to show which jobs were most popular. Have the students compare the numbers of classmates interested in the jobs.

"Workers cleaned the streets," said Joe.
"They must be community workers too.
The streets look much nicer now.
Many workers help our community."

Lesson 4

Review

Read and Think

1. Name some community workers. (Recall)
2. How do community workers help you? (Synthesize)

Skills Check

Write about a time you saw a community worker helping someone.

137

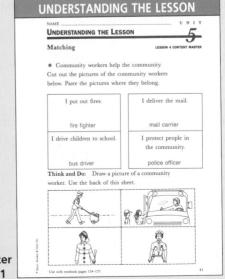
3 CLOSING THE LESSON

Lesson 4 Review

Answers to Read and Think
1. Police officers, firefighters, road crews, mail carriers, community center workers, and sanitation workers are all community workers.

2. Answers may include that community workers help protect the community and maintain common property.

Answer to Skills Check
(Stories should correctly name the community worker and describe the situation.)

Answer to Lesson Title Question

Ask the lesson title question, found at the beginning of the lesson:
Who are community workers?
(Community workers are workers who help the community. Firefighters, road crews, police officers, mail carriers, community center workers, and sanitation workers are examples of community workers.)

Additional Practice

You may wish to assign the ancillary materials listed below.
Understanding the Lesson p. 41
Workbook p. 26

Reteaching Main Objective

☆ *Name three kinds of community workers and describe the jobs they perform.*

● Prepare cards with different occupations written on them. Most of the cards should name occupations of community workers.

● Have some students pantomime the workers doing their jobs and have others name the jobs. Ask the students to explain how they determined their answers.

● Then have the students identify whether or not the worker is a community worker.

Review Master Booklet, p. 41

UNDERSTANDING THE LESSON

NAME _____ U N I T

UNDERSTANDING THE LESSON 5

Matching LESSON 4 CONTENT MASTER

✱ Community workers help the community. Cut out the pictures of the community workers below. Paste the pictures where they belong.

I put out fires.	I deliver the mail.
fire fighter	mail carrier
I drive children to school.	I protect people in the community.
bus driver	police officer

Think and Do: Draw a picture of a community worker. Use the back of this sheet.

Use with textbook pages 134–137. 41

137

What Kinds of Communities Are There?

Objectives

★1. **Define** *city* and **compare** and **contrast** city communities and farm communities.

2. **Read** and **use** information presented in a table.

3. **Record** information in a table.

1 STARTING THE LESSON

Motivation/ Prior Knowledge

■ Sing the song "Old MacDonald Had a Farm" with the students. Have them add the animals to sing about.

■ Tell the students that a farm community is one kind of community they will be learning about in this lesson.

Study the Vocabulary

NEW WORDS	DISCUSSION WORDS	ORAL VOCABULARY
city table	rooster tractor sounds	noise vendor

Have the students work in groups of four to list sounds that they hear at school, at home, and in their community.

Have the groups share their lists and make a master list on the chalkboard. Tell the students that a table would be another way to show this information and that they will be learning more about tables in this lesson.

Ask the students if they can name any other types of communities. Tell them that a city is a large and busy community.

138

Lesson 5

What Kinds of Communities Are There?

Jim lives in a farm community.
A farm needs a big piece of land.
Jim's neighbors live on nearby farms.
Most of the people in the community work on farms.
The workers live near their jobs.

Optional Activities

PREVIEWING LESSON VOCABULARY

NAME _____

PREVIEWING LESSON VOCABULARY

UNIT **5**

Understanding a Table   LESSON 5 VOCABULARY MASTER

★ A CITY is a large community. Many people live and work in a city. A TABLE is one way to list information. Look at the TABLE below. Put an X under CITY if the object is found in a CITY. Put an X under FARM if the object is found on a FARM. Some objects may be found in both places.

	CITY	FARM
Car	X	X
Tractor		X
Subway	X	
Barn		X
Skyscraper	X	
Apartment Building	X	

Think and Do: Draw a picture of something you would find in the CITY. Use the back of this sheet.

42   Use with textbook pages 138–143.

Review Master Booklet, p. 42

Robin lives in a **city**.

A city is a large community.

People live near each other in a city.

Robin's family lives in an apartment.

Robin sees many cars and buses from her home.

They help people travel around the city.

139

SKILLBUILDER REVIEW

Following Directions On pp. 114–115 the students learned how to follow directions to complete a task. Have the students review the information on tables on pp. 142–143.

● Have the students work in pairs to write three steps or directions people should follow to read a table.

Optional Activities

2 DEVELOPING THE LESSON

Read and Discuss
Text pages 138–139

To help the students compare farm communities and city communities, have them read pp. 138–139 and answer these questions.

1. **What does each farm need?**
(A big piece of land *p.138*)

2. **Where do most people in farm communities work?**
(They work on the farms. *p. 138*)

3. **What is a city?**
(A city is a large community. *p. 139*)

4. **How can people travel in cities?**
(They can travel in cars and buses. *p. 139*)

Thinking Critically Farm communities usually have fewer people in them than do city communities. Why, do you think, is this so? (Hypothesize)
(People live closer together in city communities. People are spread out in farm communities. *pp. 138–139*)

VISUAL THINKING SKILL

Comparing the Photographs

■ Farm communities and city communities are different. Have the students look at the photographs on pp. 138–139. Then have them answer this question.
How are the two communities different?
(The city community has tall buildings and many cars. The farm community has smaller buildings with more land in between them.)

Read and Discuss
Text pages 140–141

To help the students recognize the sounds that are present in different communities, have them read the poem on pp. 140–141 and answer these questions.

1. **What sound can you hear on a farm?**
   (A rooster crowing *p. 140*)

2. **What sounds can you hear in a city?**
   (You can hear the clatter of garbage cans , taxi horns tooting, bus engines roaring, and the delivery of newpapers in a city. *p. 141*)

   Thinking Critically **What other sounds might you hear in each kind of community?** (Hypothesize)
   (Answers may include the barking of dogs on the farm, and the sounds of machine engines and whistles in the city. *pp. 138–140*)

VISUAL THINKING SKILL

Analyzing the Drawing

■ There are different kinds of animals in the different communities. Have the students look at the drawing and answer this question.
   What animals are present in each kind of community?
   (A rooster, chickens, sheep, and pigs are present in the farm community. Only birds are shown in the city community.)

This poem is about a farm and the city. How are the two places different?

Wake Up!

In the country
Everyone knows
It's morning when
The rooster crows.

140

But the city's
A different matter!
You're sure to hear
Garbage cans clatter,
Taxis toot,
Buses roar,
A paper slap
Against your door.

In country or city,
Morning sounds say,
"Wake up! Here comes
Another day."

Eva Grant

141

Concept:
Understanding Tables

Help the students understand how to read and use tables by assigning one of the three activities described below.

◆ **EASY** Make a table that lists workers in three occupations and that has columns that are labeled *Goods* and *Service*. Have the students mark whether each worker makes goods or provides a service.

◀▶ **AVERAGE** Create a table with the title "Things I Do" and columns labeled *Home* and *School*. Make three rows in the table. Ask the students to list three things that they do, such as make their beds or swing on the swings. Have the students mark the table to show whether they do the activity at home or at school.

Have the students draw a picture of themselves doing one of the activities and then write a sentence about where they do the activity.

◀▮▶ **CHALLENGING** Have the students work in pairs to create a table about winter and summer. Give each pair a blank table and six pictures. Three of the pictures should be about winter. Three of the pictures should be about summer. Have the students list the pictures in the table and mark whether they show winter or summer.

Graphic Organizer

Help the students compare the sights and sounds of city communities and farm communities by completing as a class the graphic organizer shown here. Sample answers are provided with each category.

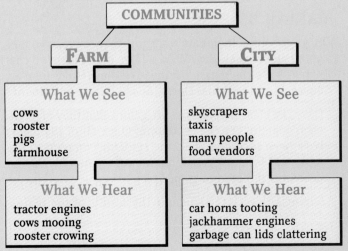

COMMUNITIES

FARM

What We See
cows
rooster
pigs
farmhouse

What We Hear
tractor engines
cows mooing
rooster crowing

CITY

What We See
skyscrapers
taxis
many people
food vendors

What We Hear
car horns tooting
jackhammer engines
garbage can lids clattering

Optional Activities

Read and Discuss
Text pages 142–143

To help the students learn more about tables, have them read pp. 142–143 and answer these questions.

1. **Why do we use tables?**
   (Tables are one way to tell about something.)

2. **Where will you hear the sounds made by what you see on p. 143?**
   (Vendor-city; jackhammer-city; pigs-farm)

   Thinking Critically Why, do you think, might people want to use tables? (Hypothesize)
   (Answers may include that tables group information together or that tables let people make comparisons quickly.)

VISUAL THINKING SKILL

Interpreting the Table

■ Have the students answer these general questions about the table on p. 142.

1. **What is the title of the table?**
   (Sounds You Hear in a Community)

2. **What things that make sounds are listed in this table?**
   (Bus, tractor, taxi, rooster, and cows)

SKILL TRACE:	Understanding Tables	
INTRODUCE PE, p. 142	PRACTICE PE, p. 143 TE, p. 141 RMB, p. 42	TEST Unit 5 Test, TMB

Sounds You Hear in a Community

Sounds	Farm	City
Bus		X
Tractor	X	
Taxi		X
Rooster	X	
Cows	X	

The poem tells about different sounds.
This **table** shows some of the sounds.
A table is one way to tell about something.
You will hear taxis and buses in a city.
You will hear roosters on a farm.
What else will you hear on a farm?

142

Optional Activities

Making a Table

- Have the class members work together to create a table about games they play. Make a large blank table on chart paper. Title the graph "Games We Play. Make four columns in the table: *Game, Sports, Card,* and *Board.*

- Have the class members name games that they play. List each game in the *Game* column. Once all of the games have been recorded, have the students come up to the table and for each game, mark an *X* in the column that describes the kind of game it is.

- Summarize with the students the results of the table.

Writing to Learn

Living in a Different Community Have the students select a type of community that they do not li in. Ask them to pretend that they are waking up to star the day in this new community.

- Have the students write a journal entry that describe what they see and hear. Then have the students hypothesize about the jobs or chores they would have do that day if they really lived in that community.

Look at the pictures above.
In which kind of community will
you find each picture?

esson 5

Review

Read and Think

1. How are cities and farms different?
2. Tell about your community.

Skills Check

Look at the table on page 142.
Where will you hear tractors?

Answers to Read and Think
1. Cities are larger and more crowded than farms. Farm communities are more spread out and contain fewer people.
2. Answers should reflect the students' community.

Answer to Skills Check
You will hear tractors on a farm.

Answer to Lesson Title Question

Ask the lesson title question, found at the beginning of the lesson:
What kinds of communities are there?
(Farm communities and city communities are two kinds of communities. Farm communities have large pieces of land between the homes. City communities have people living and working very close to each other.)

Additional Practice

You may wish to assign the ancillary materials listed below.
Understanding the Lesson p. 43
Workbook p. 27

Reteaching Main Objective

★ *Define* city *and compare and contrast city communities and farm communities.*

- Have the students work in pairs for this activity. Have one student draw a picture of a farm. Have the other student draw a picture of a city.
- Have the pairs list three ways that the communities are alike and three ways that they are different.

Review Master Booklet, p. 43

UNDERSTANDING THE LESSON

NAME _____

UNDERSTANDING THE LESSON

U N I T **5**

Understanding the Main Idea   LESSON 5 CONTENT MASTER

✳ Where do these children live? Write **farm** or **city** next to each sentence.

1. Joan lives on a busy street. _____ city

2. Todd helps feed the cows. _____ farm

3. Fran has a horse in a field near her house. _____ farm

4. Amar lives in an apartment building. _____ city

5. Al likes to play in the cornfield behind his house. _____ farm

Think and Do: Draw a farm animal. Then draw an animal people who live in the city can have. Use the back of this sheet.

Use with textbook pages 138-143.   43

Optional Activities

143

Using the New Words

The vocabulary terms in this review were introduced in the unit. Some students may have difficulty distinguishing between similar concepts. Discuss the meaning of each word in relation to the pictures before having the students match the words to the pictures.

Suggested Answers

1. C
2. F
3. D
4. B
5. A
6. E

Accept other responses if students can explain their choice.

A. Using the New Words

Find the picture that best matches each word.

1. city _____
2. table _____
3. community _____
4. neighbors _____
5. neighborhood _____
6. directions _____

A.

B.

C.

D.

E.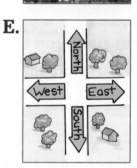

F.

144

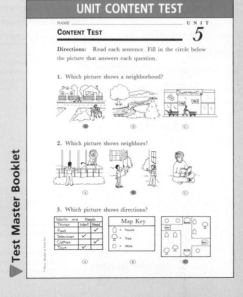

B. Remembering What You Read

Answer these questions about the unit.

1. Name at least three community workers.
2. How are neighborhoods alike?
   How are they different?

C. Summarizing the Unit

Look at the map below.

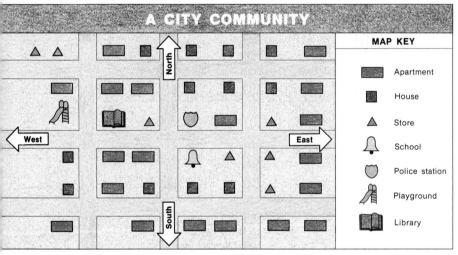

A CITY COMMUNITY

MAP KEY

Apartment
House
Store
School
Police station
Playground
Library

3. Is the police station north or south
   of the school?
4. How is this community different
   from your community?

145

Remembering What You Read

Answer these questions about the unit.

1. Firefighters, police officers, mail carriers, road crews, community-center workers, and street cleaners are all community workers. Accept all correct answers.

2. Answers may include that neighborhoods are alike in that they all have homes and neighbors who work and play together.

   Neighborhoods vary in size, location, types of shelter, and the activities in the neighborhood.

   Encourage the students to consider where community features are located in their community.

Summarizing the Unit

Have the students look at the map on p. 145. Have them identify the arrows pointing north, south, east, and west. Tell them to use the directions along with the map key to answer the questions.

1. The police station is north of the school.

2. Accept all reasonable answers.

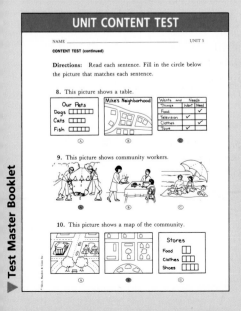

UNIT CONTENT TEST

UNIT SKILLS TEST

145

Objectives

1. **Identify** that main ideas tell what a story is about.
2. **Identify** the main idea in a story.
3. **Write** sentences related to a given main idea.

Why Do I Need This Skill?

To help the students recognize that a main idea tells what a story is about, write the following sentences on the chalkboard.

People travel to work in different ways.
Some people drive their cars to work.
Other people ride on the bus.
Boats take some people across the water to their jobs.

Have the students read the sentences, then ask the following questions.

1. **What is this story about?**
   (This story is about how people travel to work in different ways.)

2. **Which sentence tells us what this story is about?**
   (The first sentence)

Learning the Skill

Have the students read the sentences and look at the picture on p. 146; then ask the following questions.

1. **What is the main idea of this picture?**
   (The community workers are helping people.)

2. **How are the community workers helping people?**
   (The mail carrier is delivering mail. The police officer is giving the woman directions. The ambulance driver is helping someone who is sick or hurt.)

146

SKILLBUILDER

Finding Main Ideas

A Why Do I Need This Skill?

Main ideas tell what a picture or story is about.
They help us understand what we see or read.

B Learning the Skill

The picture below shows community workers.
The main idea is that these workers help us.
Most stories have a main idea too.
The main idea can be one sentence.
The other sentences tell about the idea.

146

Curriculum Connection

Language Arts Have each student write a main idea and a short story about a picture.

- Let each student choose a picture from a page in a magazine and cut it out.

- Have each student look at the picture he or she has chosen and write a sentence telling what the main idea is. Tell them to finish the story by writing three more sentences about the picture.

- Have each student show the class his or her picture, tell what the main idea is, and read the story.

Optional Activities

C Practicing the Skill

Read the story and find the main idea.

Communities have special places.
Schools are where children learn.
Stores sell things to people.
Parks are for playing or resting.
Factories and offices are for working.

D Applying the Skill

1. Draw a picture to show this main idea:
   "A neighborhood is a group of homes."
2. Write three sentences about the main idea.

147

Practicing the Skill

Have the students read the story and identify the main idea.

The main idea is that communities have special places.

If students have difficulty with this concept, you may wish to assign the reteaching activity.

Applying the Skill

Have the students read the sentence "A neighborhood is a group of homes.", and draw pictures to illustrate this main idea.

Have each student write three sentences about his or her picture that will tell more about the main idea.

SKILL TRACE:	Understanding Main Ideas and Details	
INTRODUCE PE, p. 146	PRACTICE TE, p. 147 TE, p. 157 RMB, p. 18	TEST Unit 5 Test, TMB

Reteaching Activity

- Write the following sentence on the chalkboard and have the students copy it onto a piece of paper.
  We learn many things at school.

- Tell the students that this will be the main idea of a story. Have the students finish the story by writing three sentences about things they learn at school.

- Have each student draw a box around the main idea and read his or her story to the class.

Optional Activities

Unit 6 Resource Center

Our Country
(pp. 148–175)

Unit Theme: Our country, its government, and its symbols are sources of pride for its citizens.

UNIT RESOURCES
Unit 6 Test

LESSON 1 Where Is Our Country?
(pp. 150–153)

Theme: Our country is part of the North American continent, with Canada to the north and Mexico to the south.

LESSON RESOURCES
Workbook, p. 28–29
Review Master Booklet
  Previewing Lesson Vocabulary,
    p. 44
  Understanding the Lesson, p. 45

LESSON 2 Who Are Our Country's Leaders?
(pp. 154–159)

Theme: The President, Congress, and state leaders make decision and laws concerning our country.

LESSON RESOURCES
Workbook, p. 30
Review Master Booklet
  Previewing Lesson Vocabulary,
    p. 46
  Understanding the Lesson, p. 47

SOCIAL STUDIES LIBRARY: *Georgia Music*

LESSON 3 What Makes Each State Special?
(pp. 160–163)

Theme: Each state has a capital city, where laws for the state are made. There are also special symbols for each state.

LESSON RESOURCES
Workbook, p. 31
Review Master Booklet
  Understanding the Lesson, p. 48

LESSON 4 What Are Our Country's Symbols?
(pp. 164–169)

Theme: There are several symbols of our country. Some symbols are found in many places. Other symbols are places and things that people visit.

LESSON RESOURCES
Workbook, p. 32–33
Review Master Booklet
  Previewing Lesson Vocabulary,
    p. 49
  Understanding the Lesson, p. 50

LESSON 5 What Are Natural Resources?
(pp. 170–173)

Theme: Air, water, and land are natural resources. We use those resources, but we must also protect them.

LESSON RESOURCES
Workbook, p. 34
Review Master Booklet
  Previewing Lesson Vocabulary,
    p. 51
  Understanding the Lesson, p. 52

PACING GUIDE

September	October	November	December	January	February	March	April	May
UNIT	UNIT	UNITS	UNIT	UNIT	UNIT	UNITS	UNIT	UNIT
1	2	2–3	3	4	5	5–6	6	7

Annotated Bibliography

Books for Teachers

Lima, Carolyn W. *A to Zoo: Subject Access to Children's Picture Books* 3rd ed. New York: R.R. Bowker, 1989. ISBN 0-835-22599-2. This book categorizes children's picture books by subject, author, illustrator, and title. It also gives brief bibliographic information about each book.

Lipson, Eden Ross. *The New York Times Parent's Guide to the Best Books for Children.* New York: Times Books, 1988. ISBN 0-812-91688-3. Books are categorized as follows: wordless, picture books, storybooks, early reading, middle reading, and young adult. Each title is accompanied by a description.

Books for Read Aloud

Carpenter, Allan. *Indiana.* Chicago: Childrens Press, 1979. ISBN 0-516-04114-2. Information is presented about the Indiana of both yesterday and today. This book is part of the Enchantment of America series, which has similar books about the other states.

Fisher, Leonard Everett. *The Statue of Liberty.* New York: Holiday House, 1985. ISBN 0-823-40586-9. Gives the history of the Statue of Liberty, a gift from the people of France to the people of the United States.

Knowlton, Jack. *Geography from A to Z.* New York: Crowell, 1988. ISBN 0-690-04616-2. This book describes the earth's physical geography, from the highest mountain to the deepest ocean, with colorful pictures and easy-to-understand text.

Siebert, Diane. *Heartland.* New York: Crowell, 1989. ISBN 0-690-04730-4. Describes the Midwestern section of the country in a flowing, rhythmic verse. Illustrations are beautiful.

Filmstrips and Videos

Learn To: States & Capitals. Troy, MI: Teacher's Discovery. 30-minute video (35EV). This video combines history and geography to teach students about the 50 states.

Let's Make a Map. Chicago: Britannica Films and Video. Video (4766). Designed to help young children learn how the physical world is represented on a map.

Computer Software

Lollipop Dragon's World of Maps and Globes. Apple II. Chicago: Society of Visual Education.

Bulletin Board Idea

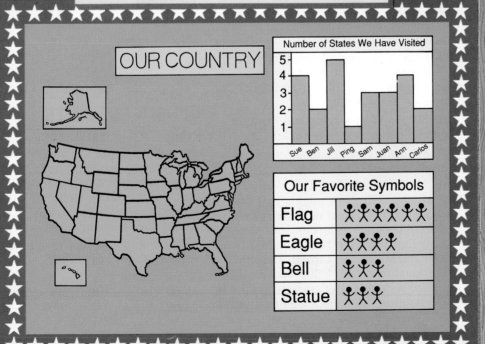

Student Activity

Have each student cut out several white paper stars for the bulletin board border. Have each student color a small figure to use in a class pictograph about favorite symbols.

Have the students find out how many states they have visited. Make a bar graph with this information.

A Tour of Washington, D.C.

What happened in the capital?

In Unit 6 the students will learn that Washington, D.C., is the capital of our country, the home of our President, and the place where Congress makes laws. Through the following activities the students will learn more about Washington, D.C.

SOCIAL STUDIES

Geography Obtain a map of Washington, D.C. (You may wish to call or write the Washington, D.C., Chamber of Commerce for a map and other materials, including guidebooks and brochures.) Put the map on a bulletin board.

■ Tell the students to look at the map of Washington, D.C. Ask them how it is similar and how it is different from the map of the United States in their textbook (p. 156).

■ Have volunteers find landmarks such as the Capitol Building, the Supreme Court Building, and the Pentagon on the map.

Political Science Help the students understand how government works by learning what goes on in the different buildings in Washington, D.C. Write the following list of buildings on the chalkboard and discuss with the students what takes place in each one.

■ White House (where the President lives and works)

■ Capitol (where the Senate and House of Representatives meet to make laws)

■ Supreme Court Building (where the Supreme Court meets to decide what is allowed by our governing document—the Constitution.

■ Bureau of Engraving and Printing (where paper money is made)

■ Pentagon (the headquarters of our armed forces)

History Tell the students that two of our country's most respected Presidents, Thomas Jefferson and Abraham Lincoln, have been honored by monuments in the capital. Describe the qualities and achievements of these Presidents. (Jefferson wrote the Declaration of Independence, and Lincoln freed the slaves.) Show the students pictures of these monuments.

■ You may wish to read to the class selections from the children's biography *Thomas Jefferson*, by Charles Patterson (New York: Franklin Watts, 1987, ISBN 0-531-10307-2) or *Abraham Lincoln*, by Larry Metzger, (New York: Franklin Watts, 1987, ISBN 0-531-10306-4.

LANGUAGE ARTS

Writing a Class Letter Have the class write a letter to one of the United States senators from your state. (Senate Office Building, Washington, D.C. 20510) Help the students decide what to say in the letter by asking the following questions.

1. What would you like to tell the senator about our class?

2. What would you like to know about the work that the senator does?

■ Write the inside addresses and salutation of the letter on the chalkboard. Have volunteers restate in sentences what the students have decided to say in the letter. Write these sentences on the chalkboard under the salutation. Solicit the students' help in revising and reordering the sentences as necessary. Add a closing to the letter. Ask one volunteer to copy the letter on a piece of paper and one volunteer to write the address and the return address on the envelope. Have each student sign the letter, then mail it.

■ You may wish to share your correspondence with the school by posting your letter and its response on a centrally located bulletin board.

Role-playing Have the students improvise a make-believe class visit to the White House through a skit. When assigning the roles, use the approach of Arena Stage, A D.C. theater company that casts actors of different races, physical ability levels, and ages in unexpected roles to enliven the action on stage. Students might portray the President's husband or wife, a cook, a housekeeper, guards, the teacher, and the students.

■ Help the class think about what it might say and do in the skit by asking questions such as these.

1. **What kinds of things would the President say to our class?**

2. **What might students want to say and do at the President's home?**

■ After the performance, discuss how it felt to have (for example) a girl portraying the President. Ask how the skit might have been the same and how it might have been different if people were cast in more predictable roles. (You may wish to repeat the skit with a traditional cast before comparing.)

MATHEMATICS

■ Tell the students that the Pentagon, the largest office building in the world, is a five-sided structure with 17.5 miles (28.2 km) of hallways. Explain that three branches of the armed forces, the Army, Navy, and Air Force, have headquarters in the Pentagon. Show students a picture of the Pentagon and explain the connection between its appearance and its name.

■ Using *pentagon* as a point of reference, explain the meaning of *hexagon*, *octagon*, and *decagon*. (All have the same number of sides as their Greek root words indicate.) Draw examples of these shapes on the chalkboard. Have the students copy and label the drawings on a paper entitled *SHAPES*. You may also want to make patterns for these shapes and have the students trace the patterns to form designs. Once the tracings are complete, the students can color them.

Make a 3-D Map

INSTRUCTIONS FOR THE TEACHER:

Focus In this unit "Our Country," the students will learn more about maps. They will learn how to distinguish between landmasses and bodies of water on maps. It is important for the students to recognize that we live on the earth and that many maps are flat models of the earth. Prepare the students to make their own 3-D map by reviewing the concepts learned in Lesson 1, "Where Is Our Country?" and the Skillbuilder on pp. 178–179. Explain to the students that they will make their own map from modeling clay.

Warm-Up Activity Have the students examine a globe. Explain that the globe is a round model of the earth. While examining the globe, remind students of the following facts:
• A globe is a round object that represents the earth.
• A globe is like a map in many ways.
• Many maps are flat. A globe is not flat.
  Review the terms *island*, *lake*, *hill*, and *mountain* with the students. Give the students four index cards each. Have them write one term on each card and draw a picture of the term. Have them cut each card in two pieces to make a puzzle. Then have the students exchange puzzles and complete them.

Explain the term *three-dimensional* to the class. Tell the students that they will be making three-dimensional (3-D) maps of islands.

ACTIVITY FOR THE STUDENTS:

Procedure Prior to starting this activity, you will need to gather modeling clay in four colors, 6″ × 8″ pieces of cardboard, and small plastic containers for water.

Making the 3-D Map Tell the students that they will work in pairs to make 3-D maps, or models, of an island. Give each pair a piece of drawing paper and a piece of cardboard. Have the partners trace the piece of cardboard on their paper. Tell them that they will be making an island that contains a lake, hills, and mountains. Have the partners draw their island on the drawing paper. The island should take up most of the available space. Then have them plan where they will place a lake, hills, and mountains on their island.
  Have the partners begin by tracing their island from the drawing paper on the cardboard. Then

have them use the clay to show the lake. Have them fill in the rest of land area on their island. Once a land base is completed, have the partners use different colors of clay to show hills and mountains. Finally, have the partners fill in the water around their island.

Follow-up Activity   Have each pair name its island and present it to the rest of the class. Each pair should identify the landforms on its map. Then have the partners write four directions to explain how they made their map.

Extension   Have the students write stories about events on their islands. Before assigning this task, you may wish to discuss some possible story ideas with the class. Once the stories are complete, have the students read them to the class. Then display the stories next to the maps.

Workbook Pages

AROUND THE WORLD

Identifying Continents

✳ Look at the map below. Write **North America** and **South America** on the correct continents. Color North America green. Color South America yellow.

(green)

North America

South America

(yellow)

28

© Silver, Burdett & Ginn Inc.

AROUND THE WORLD CONTINUED

✳ You learned about two continents on the last page. You will find the names of the other continents in the puzzle below. Write the correct letter above each number. Use the key.

Key

A	C	E	F	H	I	L	M	N	O	P	R	S	T	U
1	2	3	4	5	6	7	8	9	10	11	12	13	14	15

A N T A R C T I C A
1 9 14 1 12 2 14 6 2 1

A U S T R A L I A
1 15 13 14 12 1 7 6 1

A F R I C A
1 4 12 6 2 1

E U R O P E
3 15 12 10 11 3

A S I A
1 13 6 1

© Silver, Burdett & Ginn Inc.

ABOUT OUR COUNTRY'S LEADERS

Solving a Puzzle, Recalling Facts

✳ A mixed-up word is in each sentence. Unscramble the word so that each sentence is correct. Use the words in the word box to help you. The first letter of each answer is filled in for you.

Congress   law   capital   President   state

1. Leaders come to work in Washington, D.C., from every TAEST.

   State

2. The DSIPRNEET lives in the White House.

   President

3. A rule for our country is a WLA.

   law

4. Washington, D.C., is the ATLIPCA of our country.

   Capital

5. Many of our country's leaders are in SGOCSREN.

   Congress

30

© Silver, Burdett & Ginn Inc.

STATE FLAGS

Matching

✳ Each state has its own flag. Read the sentences. Then look at the flags below. Match each sentence to the correct flag. Write the name of the state under the correct flag.

Texas ---------- Alabama

Illinois ---------- Vermont

1. The flag of Alabama has a big X on it.
2. The flag of Illinois has an American eagle on it.
3. The flag of Texas has a star on it.
4. The flag of Vermont has a tree on it.

© Silver, Burdett & Ginn Inc.

Workbook Pages

AMERICAN SYMBOLS

✳ Our country has many symbols. Find the symbols hidden in the picture below. Use the word box to help. Circle the pictures of the symbols.

American flag	Statue of Liberty
American eagle	Liberty Bell

Unit 6, pages 164–169   © Silver, Burdett & Ginn Inc.

AMERICAN SYMBOLS *CONTINUED*

✳ Choose the words from the word box that finish the sentences about symbols. Write the words in the puzzle. Start each word at the number that matches the sentence number.

special	anthem	symbol	flag	freedom

ACROSS

1. The Liberty Bell is a symbol of _____ .
2. A _____ reminds us of something else.
3. "The Star Spangled Banner" is our national _____ .

DOWN

1. The American _____ is a symbol that waves in the wind.
2. Symbols say that our country is _____ to us.

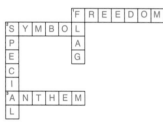

© Silver, Burdett & Ginn Inc.   Unit 6, pages 164–169

NATURAL RESOURCES

✳ What do we call land, water, and trees? To find out, color the spaces marked **A** green. Color the spaces marked **B** yellow. Color the spaces marked **C** red.

What does the hidden message say?

_____

_____ natural resources _____

Unit 6, pages 170–175   © Silver, Burdett & Ginn Inc.

U6-H

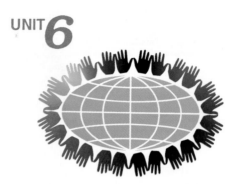

MULTICULTURAL PERSPECTIVES

Immigration and the Statue of Liberty (pages 150–153, 164–169)

Point to the country of France on a map of the world. Explain that in 1876 the United States was 100 years old. To celebrate this special birthday, the people of France gave the Statue of Liberty to the people of the United States. Two French architects, Frederic Auguste Bartholdi and Gustave Eiffel, and one American, Richard Morris Hunt, designed various parts of the statue. The French people paid for the statue and Americans paid for the base. Have the students examine the photograph on page 169 to see the two parts.

Only the right hand of the statue, holding a torch, was presented to the people of the United States on July 4, 1876. The completed statue was presented to the United States minister to France on July 4, 1884, in Paris.

The statue had to be taken apart and transported across the Atlantic Ocean to New York, where it was reassembled and its base was built. The statue was dedicated on October 28, 1886.

The statue stands on Liberty Island in New York Harbor. For many years, this statue has welcomed newcomers to this country. Many immigrants traveled to the United States by boat. The statue was one of the first sights they viewed as they sailed into New York Harbor.

Point to New York on the map. Have students note the locations of Europe and Africa in relation to New York.

Point to California on the map. Explain to your students that newcomers from countries near the Pacific Ocean came into the United States at Angel Island in San Francisco Bay.

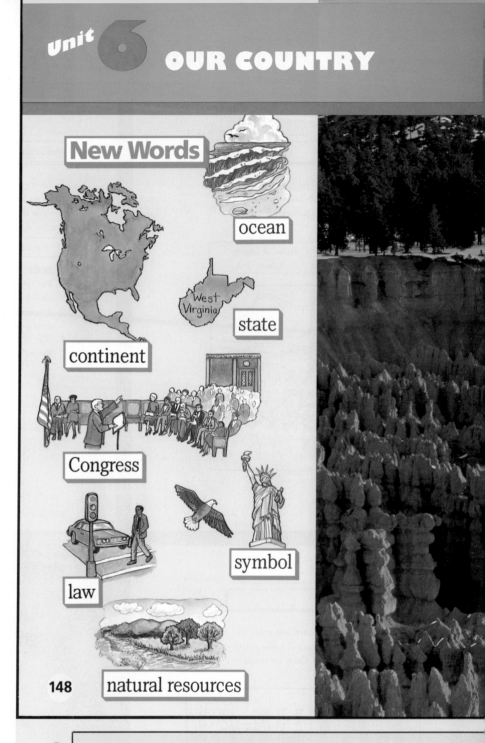

Unit 6 OUR COUNTRY

New Words

ocean

state

West Virginia

continent

Congress

law

symbol

148

natural resources

Optional Activities

Class Discussion

- Have the students look at the photograph on pp. 148–149 showing Bryce Canyon in Utah. Tell them that many people visit this place to see the interesting rocks and to look at the view.

- Have the students think of a special place nearby where they would like to take someone who was visiting them for the first time. Have them discuss why they would choose this place.

Optional Activities

Ask students to name and/or show on a map the places from which they or earlier generations of their families emigrated. Label these countries. Have the students identify the continent that each country is a part of.

Symbols *(pages 164–169)*
Gather the following items in preparation for a class discussion.
- Coins and paper currency of the U.S.
- Coins and paper currency of other countries
- A photograph of the United Nations headquarters with all the flags flying

Show the money to the students. Explain that the symbols of a country are often shown on its currency. Sometimes pictures of country leaders are shown on money.

Have the students describe the currencies that are displayed. Then have the students compare and contrast them. Make a chart on the chalkboard to record the features mentioned in the discussion.

The flag is introduced as a symbol of our country in this unit. Show the picture of the United Nations and tell students that every country in the world has its own flag. You may wish to show students pictures of several country's flags and help them locate the countries on a world map.

Leaders *(pages 154–159)*
Students need to understand that there are many different kinds of leaders. A leader is a person who is in charge of something.

Help the students consider the characteristics of a good leader. For example, the students may state that the person should be trustworthy. Help the students realize that leaders can be male or female and can come from different backgrounds.

Ask the students to name several kinds of community leaders, such as the following.
- Principal, leader of a school
- Mayor, leader of a town
- Head of a service organization
- Head of a house of worship

You may wish to collect some newspaper and magazine photographs of local and national leaders. Use the photographs to make a bulletin-board display about leaders.

149

Where Is Our Country?

Objectives

★ **1. Describe** where our country is located and **find** it on a map.

2. Define *continents* and *oceans* and **distinguish** between them on maps.

3. Identify the following places: *North America, Mexico,* and *Canada.*

1 STARTING THE LESSON

Motivation/ Prior Knowledge

■ Display a world map and a globe. Ask the students to compare them.

■ Discuss the fact that they both show land and water areas, although the map is flat and the globe is round.

Study the Vocabulary

NEW WORDS	DISCUSSION WORDS	ORAL VOCABULARY
continent ocean	North America map Mexico	globe Canada

■ Have each student draw a very large circle on a piece of construction paper. Have the students make several smaller shapes within their circles.

■ Have the students color the shapes different colors. Then have them color the rest of the area inside the big circle blue.

■ Explain to the students that the shapes stand for continents, or land, and that the blue stands for oceans, or water.

SKILL TRACE:	Understanding Continents and Oceans	
INTRODUCE	PRACTICE	TEST
PE, p. 150	PE, p. 153 TE, p. 152 WB, pp. 28–29	Unit 6 Test, TMB

150

Lesson 1

Where Is Our Country?

Mrs. Banks makes maps.

The maps show **continents** and **oceans**.

A continent is a large piece of land.

An ocean is a big body of water.

Our country is part of North America.

150

Optional Activities

PREVIEWING LESSON VOCABULARY

NAME _____

PREVIEWING LESSON VOCABULARY   U N I T **6**

Following Directions   LESSON 1 VOCABULARY MASTER

★ A CONTINENT is a large piece of land. An OCEAN is a big body of water. This globe shows some CONTINENTS and OCEANS. Color the CONTINENTS green. Color the OCEANS blue.

(green)

(blue)   (blue)

(green)

Think and Do: Draw a picture of a way to cross an OCEAN. Use the back of this sheet.

44   Use with textbook pages 150–153.

Review Master Booklet, p. 44

Find the United States of America on the map.
Mexico is south of the United States.
Which country is north of the United States?

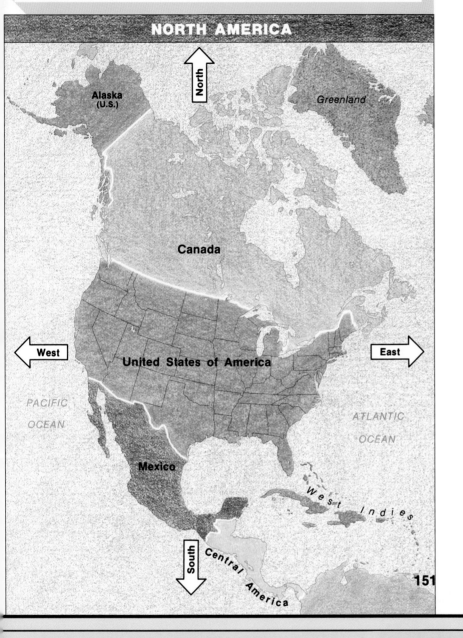

NORTH AMERICA

North

Alaska (U.S.)

Greenland

Canada

West

East

United States of America

PACIFIC OCEAN

ATLANTIC OCEAN

Mexico

West Indies

South Central America

151

Read and Discuss
Text pages 150–153

To help students understand the concepts of continents and oceans, have them read pp. 150–153 and answer these questions.

1. **What is an ocean?**
   (A large body of water *p. 150*)

2. **What continent is our country part of?**
   (North America *p. 150*)

3. **What country is south of the United States?**
   (Mexico *p. 151*)

   Thinking Critically Why do we need maps? (Hypothesize)
   (Accept all reasonable answers. Answers may include that we need maps to find places. *pp. 151–152*)

GEOGRAPHY THEMES

 Location

■ Ask the students to look at the map on page 151 and answer this question.
What country lies between two parts of the United States?
(Canada lies between the parts.)

Cooperative Learning

Making a Poster Have the students work in pairs for this activity. Assign each pair one of the following words: *continents, oceans,* or *world.* Each pair is to write a poem.

● Have the pair list words that start with the letters in the assigned word.

● Have one student write the assigned word vertically on a piece of paper. Have them write the appropriate words next to each letter. Then have them mount their work on posterboard and illustrate it.

● Have the students display their poems and evaluate how well they listened to each other's ideas.

(Sample poem)
W—whales, wind, wheat
O— oceans, onions, oil
R— roads, rivers, rice
L— land, lions, lettuce
D— ducks, dinosaurs, dirt

Optional Activities

Meeting Individual Needs

Concept:
Continents and Oceans

To help the students become more familiar with the concepts of continents and oceans, assign one of the activities below.

◆ **EASY** Have each student make a table that has the headings *Continents* and *Oceans*. Have the students complete the table with the information from the map on pp. 152–153.

◀▶ **AVERAGE** Have each student draw a picture of an underwater scene or of a land scene. Have the students write the names of the oceans under their underwater scenes and the names of the continents under their land scenes. Have each student write a sentence to define *ocean* or *continent*.

◀❙▶ **CHALLENGING** Have each student write an itinerary for a trip around the world. Tell the students that they would like to visit them. Have the students explain whether they will fly, sail, or take land transportation between the continents.

GEOGRAPHY THEMES

 Location

■ Look at the map on pp. 152–153.
What continents are near Asia?
(Africa, Europe, and Australia are near Asia.)

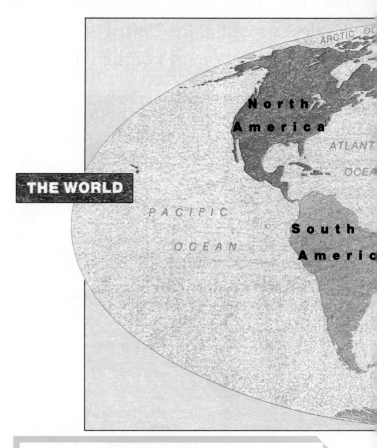

THE WORLD

Here is a world map.
Find the four oceans on the map.
Each continent is a different color on this map.
How many continents are there?

Optional Activities

Writing to Learn

Alphabetizing Have the students write the names of the seven continents in alphabetical order. Then have them write the names of the oceans in alphabetical order.

Current Events

Ask each student to bring in one newspaper article about something that happened on a continent other than North America. Have them share the article with the class.

● Make a list on the chalkboard of the continents written about in the articles.

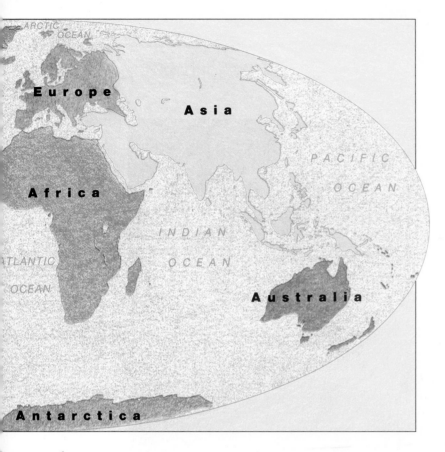

Europe

Asia

Africa

PACIFIC OCEAN

INDIAN OCEAN

ATLANTIC OCEAN

Australia

Antarctica

ARCTIC OCEAN

Lesson 1
Review

Read and Think

1. What is a continent? (Recall)

2. How many oceans are there? (Recall)

Skills Check

Look at the map on page 151.

What ocean is west of the United States?

153

Answers to Read and Think
1. A continent is a large piece of land.

2. There are four oceans.

Answer to Skills Check
The Pacific Ocean is west of the United States.

Answer to Lesson Title Question

Ask the lesson title question, found at the beginning of the lesson:
Where is our country?
(Our country, the United States, is located on the continent of North America. Mexico is south of our country. Canada is north of our country.)

Additional Practice

You may wish to assign the ancillary materials listed below.
Understanding the Lesson p. 45
Workbook pp. 28–29

Reteaching Main Objective

Describe where our country is located and find it on a map.

• Ask a group of five students to stand. Give four of the students a card with a direction word on it. Position the students holding the cards around the fifth student. Have the other students describe who is standing north, south, east, and west of the center student.

• Have the students look at the map on p. 151. Have them point to our country first. Then have them identify the land and water around our country.

Review Master Booklet, p. 45

UNDERSTANDING THE LESSON

NAME
UNDERSTANDING THE LESSON

UNIT
6

Recalling Facts
LESSON 1 CONTENT MASTER

✳ Use the words in the word box to answer the questions.

| ocean | Mexico | North America |
| continent | Canada | |

1. What is a large piece of land called? _____ continent

2. Our country is part of what continent? _____ North America

3. What is a big body of water called? _____ ocean

4. What country is south of the United States? _____ Mexico

5. What country is north of the United States? _____ Canada

Think and Do: Write the names of the four oceans. Use the back of this sheet.
Use with textbook pages 150–153.
45

Optional Activities

153

Who Are Our Country's Leaders?

Objectives

★1. **Identify** the President, Congress, and state level officials as some of the leaders of our country.

2. **Understand** that our country is composed of 50 states or parts and that Washington, D.C., is our country's capital city.

3. **Explain** that some of our leaders work to make laws or rules for our country.

1 STARTING THE LESSON

Motivation/ Prior Knowledge

■ Ask the students to name three or four songs. List them on the chalkboard.

■ Call out the title of each song. Have the students raise their hands to show which song they would like to sing. Record tally marks next to each title.

■ Explain to the students that they voted for the song they wanted to sing just as people vote for leaders.

Study the Vocabulary

NEW WORDS	DISCUSSION WORDS	ORAL VOCABULARY
state Congress laws	leaders vote White House Washington, D.C. capital	government

■ Present to the students an idea for a new classroom rule. Have the students discuss the rule and vote on it.

■ Explain to the students that Congress is a group of people who make the laws or rules for our country. Explain that each state or part in our country is allowed to vote on the laws just as each class member voted on the rule.

Lesson 2

Who Are Our Country's Leaders?

Our country has many leaders.
Sometimes many people want to be leaders.
The people in our country vote.
Voting is a way to choose leaders.
The people who get the most votes
become the leaders.

154

Optional Activities

PREVIEWING LESSON VOCABULARY

NAME _____

PREVIEWING LESSON VOCABULARY

UNIT **6**

Using New Words   LESSON 2 VOCABULARY MASTER

✱ Complete the sentences below. Use the letter key to help you.

A	C	E	G	L	N	O	R	S	T	W
1	2	3	4	5	6	7	8	9	10	11

The United States is made of 50 parts. Each

part is called a s t a t e . People
         9 10 1 10 3

from each state work in our nation's capital,

Washington, D.C. They are a group of leaders.

This group is called

 C o n g r e s s . Congress
 2 7 6 4 8 3 9 9

makes l a w s for our country.
     5 1 11 9

Think and Do: Where do you live? Write the name of your community and your state. Use the back of this sheet.

46   Use with textbook pages 154–159

Review Master Booklet, p. 46

Our President is an important leader.

We vote for our President every four years.

The President lives and works in the White House.

The White House is in Washington, D.C.

Washington, D.C., is the capital of our country.

Many leaders work in Washington, D.C.

155

Using Source Materials

Our Leaders Have students bring in pictures of elected leaders from newspapers and magazines.

● Discuss the names and jobs of the people in the pictures.

● Make a bulletin board of the pictures.

Hosting a Guest Speaker

● Invite a community leader to speak to the class. Have the students ask the leader to discuss how he or she was elected to office and what responsibilities followed the election.

● Write a class letter of thanks after the visit.

Optional Activities

2 DEVELOPING THE LESSON

Read and Discuss
Text pages 154–155

To help the students learn about some of our leaders, ask them to read pp. 154–155 and answer these questions.

1. **How do the people in our country choose leaders?**
   (They vote for them. *p. 154*)

2. **Where does the President live and work?**
   (In the White House in Washington, D.C. *p. 155*)

3. **What is the capital of our country?**
   (Washington, D.C. *p. 155*)

   Thinking Critically Why do we have to vote for our leaders?　(Hypothesize)
   (Answers may include that the leaders will not represent everyone if people do not vote. *p. 154*)

VISUAL THINKING SKILL

Interpreting a Photograph

■ The photograph on p. 154 shows a voting booth. Ask the students to look at the photograph and answer this question.
   Why, do you think, does the voting booth have a curtain?
   (Answers may include that the curtain gives the voter privacy.)

Meeting Individual Needs

Concept:
The President

It is essential that the students understand the importance of the President's role in our country. Assign one of the three activities below to help the students learn about the President.

◆ **EASY** Ask the students to cut out a picture of the President from a newspaper or a magazine. Have the students mount their picture on white or red construction paper and write the name of the President below the picture.

◀▶ **AVERAGE** Ask the students to work in small groups for this activity. Ask each group to discuss the qualities of a good leader. Have each group share its ideas with the rest of the class.

◀▮▶ **CHALLENGING** Have each student cut out a picture of the President from a newspaper or a magazine. Have each student mount the picture on a larger sheet of paper. Then, below the picture, ask each student to write a few sentences about the President.

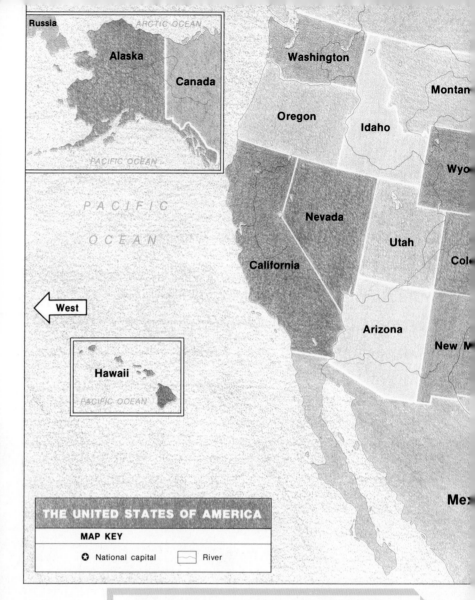

THE UNITED STATES OF AMERICA

MAP KEY

✪ National capital   ⬭ River

This is a map of the United States. Can you find Washington, D.C.?

156

Optional Activities

Graphic Organizer

To help the students learn state names and use direction words, have them use the map on pp. 156–157 to name states that are in each region of our country. Copy the graphic organizer below and list their responses.

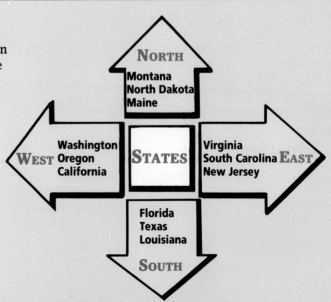

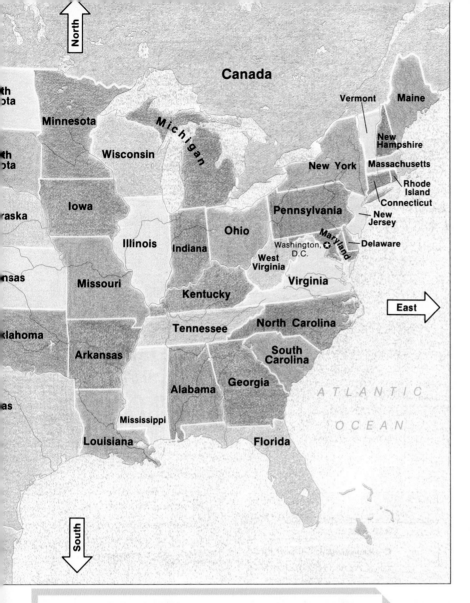

The United States has fifty main parts.
Each part is called a **state**.
Each state sends leaders to the capital.

157

To help students understand that our country is made up of 50 states and that each state has leaders have them read pp. 156–159 and answer these questions,

1. **How many states are in the United States?**
   (50 *p. 157*)

2. **What is the name of one group of leaders in Washington, D.C.?**
   (Congress *p. 158*)

3. **What is a law?**
   (A law is a rule for our country. *p. 158*)

Thinking Critically Why do state leaders travel around and talk to many people in their states? (Analyze)
(They need to know what the people in their states are thinking and what kinds of laws they may want and need. *p. 159*)

GEOGRAPHY THEMES

Location

- Have the students find the state of Nevada on the map on pp. 156–157. Ask them to name the states that border Nevada. (California, Oregon, Idaho, Utah, and Arizona)

- Have the students find the state that they live in and name the states that border it.

SKILLBUILDER REVIEW

Finding the Main Ideas On pp. 146–147 the students learned how to find the main ideas in pictures and stories. Have them use this skill by writing a main idea sentence about leaders followed by two supporting detail sentences.

● Have the students read their sentences to the class.

Optional Activities

Analyzing the Photographs

■ To help students understand the function of leaders, ask them to look at the photographs on pp. 158–159 and answer these questions.
What are the people in the picture on p. 158 doing?
(Meeting and talking with one another)

■ Leaders travel around their states to speak to the people living in their states. The picture on p. 159 shows Representative Patricia Schroeder of Colorado. Ask the students this question.
Where, do you think, could leaders go to meet people in their states?
(Answers may include parks, fairs, and special meetings.)

One group of leaders in Washington, D.C., is called **Congress**.

Congress makes **laws** for the whole country.

A law is a rule for our country.

158

Optional Activities

Writing to Learn
Assessing Leadership Qualities Ask the students to describe a good leader. Have the students draw a picture of the person doing something that illustrates that he or she is a good leader.

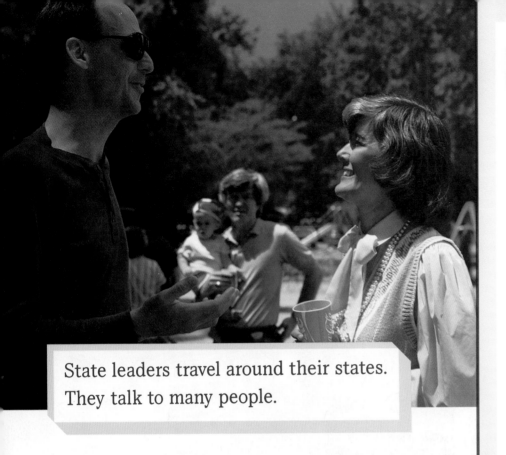

State leaders travel around their states.
They talk to many people.

Lesson 2
Review

Read and Think

1. Who makes laws for our country? (Recall)
2. Why should people vote for their leaders? (Evaluate)

Skills Check

Look at the map on pages 156 and 157.
What state is north of Oregon?

159

What Makes Each State Special?

Objectives

★ 1. **Recognize** that each state has leaders who make decisions on the state level.

2. **Explain** that each state has a capital city where the laws for the state are made.

3. **Recognize** that each state has state symbols, such as flag, tree, flower.

1 STARTING THE LESSON

Motivation/ Prior Knowledge

■ Have the students work together in small groups to assemble puzzles.

■ Then ask the students to describe the puzzle pieces. The answers may include that the pieces are different shapes and colors, and that all of the pieces are needed to make the puzzle.

■ Explain to the students that states are similar to puzzle pieces in that each one is different. The states are different sizes and shapes. Different leaders run each state.

Study the Vocabulary

DISCUSSION WORDS

capital city
Indiana
Indianapolis

■ Tell the students that decisions for the state are made in the capital city of the state.

■ Have the students look at the Atlas map on pp. 206–207 and use the map key to find the state capital of their state.

Lesson 3

What Makes Each State Special?

Washington, D.C., is our country's capital city.
Each state has a capital city too.
The leaders for each state meet in the capital city
They make laws for the state.
This picture shows the building where the
leaders in Indiana meet.

160

Optional Activities

Writing a Haiku Poem

● Write a class Haiku poem about the state. The first line should contain five syllables. The second line should contain seven syllables, and the last line should contain 5 syllables.

● Here is an example.

> New Jersey
> A land of gardens,
> Sandy beaches, lush green trees
> My wonderful state!

● Have the students draw pictures to accompany the poem.

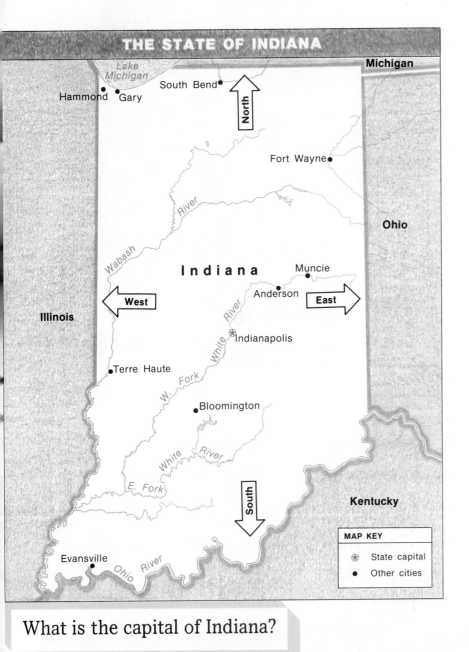

THE STATE OF INDIANA

Michigan

Lake
Michigan

Hammond • Gary • South Bend

↑ North

Fort Wayne •

Wabash River

I n d i a n a

Muncie •
Anderson •

⟵ West   East ⟶

Illinois

⊛ Indianapolis

White River

• Terre Haute

W. Fork

• Bloomington

White River

E. Fork

↓ South

Ohio

Kentucky

Evansville •   *Ohio River*

MAP KEY
⊛	State capital
•	Other cities

What is the capital of Indiana?

161

Read and Discuss
Text pages 160–163

To help students understand the concepts of capital cities and state symbols, have them read pp. 160–163 and answer the following questions.

1. **What is a state capital?**
   (A city in a state where the leaders meet to make laws. *p.160*)

2. **What is special about Indianapolis?**
   (It is the capital city of Indiana. *p. 161*)

3. **Name three things that each state has that are special to that state.**
   (Tree, flag, flower *pp. 162–163*)

   Thinking Critically Why, do you think, does each state need a state capital city?
   (Accept all reasonable answers. Answers may include that some issues are special to one state. *p. 162*)

GEOGRAPHY THEMES

Place

■ Ask the students to look at the map on page 161. Then ask this question.
Which city on this map is the farthest south?
(Evansville)

Cooperative Learning

Invent a Flag Have the students work in groups of three. Have each group work together to design a class flag. Emphasize that the flag should be symbolic; it should have something to do with what their class or school is like.

● Have students brainstorm ideas as a group and agree on one theme.

● Have one student draw an outline of the design on a piece of paper.

● Another member of the group should color in the design.

● The third group member should present the flag to the class and serve on a committee to create a bulletin board of the flag designs.

● Group members should evaluate how well they worked together to accomplish their task.

Optional Activities

Meeting Individual Needs

Concept:
State Features

Each state offers special features for its residents to enjoy. Have the students complete one of the activities below to recognize the special features in their state.

◆ **EASY** Have the students work in small groups to prepare a booklet about their state. Have the group prepare a list of special places that they have visited in their state. Have the students illustrate and label each place.

> You may wish to have the students do this activity so that the finished product can be shown on the TV Viewer as described on pp. U1-E–F.

> Have students choose a state other than their own. Ask them to draw an outline map of that state and find out what its capital city is.

> Have the students locate the capital city on the map and write its name with a gold star next to it.

◀▶ **AVERAGE** Have students choose a state other than their own. Ask them to draw an outline map of that state, mark the location of the capital city with a gold star and label it. Then ask them to write the names of all its border states around the outside of the map where they are located.

◀▶ **CHALLENGING** Have the students illustrate and describe three special places in their state. Have the students make a travel flyer with their work that encourages people to come and visit the state.

VISUAL THINKING SKILL

Analyzing the Photographs

■ Look at the picture on p. 163. What sport is the team playing? (Basketball)

Each state has a special tree and flower. There is a flag for each state too. These things are special to Indiana. Do you know what things are special to your state?

162

Optional Activities

Writing to Learn

Out-of-State Letter Ask each student write a letter to a person they know who lives in another state.

● Have them ask that person what it is like to live in that state and what they like most about it.

Some states have sports teams.
Many people watch basketball in Indiana.
Does your state have a sports team?

Lesson 3 — Review

Read and Think

1. Where are the laws for each state made? (Recall)
2. How are the states alike? (Synthesize)

Skills Check

Look at the map on page 161.
What city is south of Terre Haute?

163

Lesson 3 Review

Answers to Read and Think

1. Laws are made in the capital city.
2. States are alike in that they all have capital cities, state flowers, trees, and flags.

Answer to Skills Check

Evansville is south of Terre Haute.

Answer to Lesson Title Question

Ask the lesson title question found at the beginning of the lesson:
What makes each state special?
(Each state has its own capital city, flower, tree, and flag each of which makes the state special.)

Additional Practice

You may wish to assign the ancillary materials listed below.
Understanding the Lesson p. 48
Workbook p. 31

Reteaching Main Objective

★ *Recognize that each state has leaders who make decisions on the state level.*

● Describe the roles of state leaders as well as those of the President and the Congress.

● Have the students state who the description matches. Have them explain how they made their decision.

● Ask the students to identify any state-level issues that concern them. Discuss each issue with the class.

Review Master
Booklet, p. 48

UNDERSTANDING THE LESSON

NAME _____ UNIT
UNDERSTANDING THE LESSON **6**

Understanding Map Symbols   LESSON 3 CONTENT MASTER

✳ Every state has a state capital. The map symbol for a state capital is ✪. Write the name of the state capital of each of the states.

Boulder •
• Denver

COLORADO _____ Denver

Topeka •
Wichita •

KANSAS _____ Topeka

Fort Wayne •
• Indianapolis

INDIANA _____ Indianapolis

Richmond • • Norfolk

VIRGINIA _____ Richmond

Think and Do: What is the name of the capital of your state? Write its name on the back of this sheet.

48   Use with textbook pages 160–163.

What Are Our Country's Symbols?

Objectives

★1. **Demonstrate** an understanding of the concept of symbols.

2. **Name** four symbols of our country.

3. **Recognize** that the Statue of Liberty and the Liberty Bell are symbols of freedom.

1 STARTING THE LESSON

Motivation/ Prior Knowledge

■ Have the class sing the "Star-Spangled Banner" and say the Pledge of Allegiance.

■ Ask the students to listen carefully and find references to our flag in both.

■ Tell the students that the flag is very special to the people who live in our country.

Study the Vocabulary

NEW WORDS	DISCUSSION WORDS	ORAL VOCABULARY
symbol	*anthem*	*promise*
	pledge	
	freedom	
	statue	
	liberty	
	flag	
	eagle	

■ Explain to the students that a pledge is like a promise. Ask the students to think about important promises that they have honored. For example, a student may have promised to keep his or her room neat.

■ Have the students tell about promises they have fulfilled.

164

A **symbol** reminds us of something else.
There are symbols for our country.
The eagle is a symbol of our country.

164

Optional Activities

PREVIEWING LESSON VOCABULARY

NAME _____
PREVIEWING LESSON VOCABULARY   UNIT 6

Matching   LESSON 4 VOCABULARY MASTER

✱ A SYMBOL reminds us of something else.
The pictures below show some SYMBOLS.
The SYMBOLS remind us of the words in the
word box. Write the correct words from the
box under the SYMBOLS.

| gas   railroad crossing   school crossing   dollar |

school crossing   railroad crossing

dollar   gas

Think and Do: Think of another SYMBOL
you have seen. Draw it on the back of this sheet.

Use with textbook pages 164–169.   49

Review Master Booklet, p. 49

The flag is a symbol of our country too. Symbols say that our country is special to us.

165

Read and Discuss
Text pages 164–167

To help the students understand the value and importance of symbols, have them read pp. 164–167 and answer these questions.

1. **What bird is a symbol of our country?** (Eagle *p.164*)

2. **What is the purpose of symbols?** (To say that something is special. *p. 165*)

3. **What is our national anthem?** ("The Star-Spangled Banner," *p. 166*)

Thinking Critically Why do schools and offices all over the country display the American flag? (Analyze) (Answers may include that the people in those buildings are proud of our country.)

VISUAL THINKING SKILL

Analyzing the Photographs

■ Ask the students to look at the photographs on pp. 164–165 and answer this question. **What two symbols of our country are shown in different places?** (Eagle, flag)

Cooperative Learning

New Symbol Have the students work in groups of three to create and design a new symbol for our country.

Ask the students to brainstorm as a group and come up with an original symbol. Tell them this might be a plant, flower, animal, or something imaginary. Have them plan and name their symbol.

Have the groups draw and color their symbols. Have the groups think about special colors that they may wish to use in their designs.

● Have the groups think of ways that the symbols might be used. One member from each group should prepare a list.

● Have group representatives present the symbols to the rest of the class. Have the group members evaluate how well they listened to each other when planning their symbols. Create a display with the symbols.

Optional Activities

VISUAL THINKING SKILL

Analyzing the Photograph

■ Have the students look at the picture on p. 167. Then ask this question.

Why, do you think, is there a picture of a flag on the same page as the Pledge of Allegiance?

(Answers may include that people face the flag when they say the Pledge of Allegiance because their loyalty is directed towards the flag as a symbol of our country.)

The Star-Spangled Banner

Music by John Stafford Smith
Words by Francis Scott Key

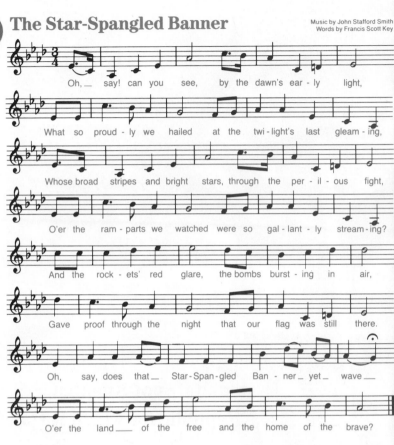

Oh, __ say! can you see, by the dawn's ear-ly light,

What so proud-ly we hailed at the twi-light's last gleam-ing,

Whose broad stripes and bright stars, through the per-il-ous fight,

O'er the ram-parts we watched were so gal-lant-ly stream-ing?

And the rock-ets' red glare, the bombs burst-ing in air,

Gave proof through the night that our flag was still there.

Oh, say, does that __ Star-Span-gled Ban-ner __ yet __ wave

O'er the land __ of the free and the home of the brave?

Words and songs can be symbols too.
We sing "The Star-Spangled Banner."
It is our national anthem.
We say the Pledge of Allegiance.

166

Symbol Mobile

● Give each student 5 four inch circles of paper, 5 pieces of yarn, and a coat hanger.

● Ask the students to write *Symbols of Our Country* on one of the circles and their own names on the reverse side.

● Have the students draw pictures of other symbols of our country on the remaining circles. Punch a hole in each circle.

● Tie the circle with the label on it to the center of the hanger. Attach the other circles to the hanger on either side of the centered circle. Hang the mobile.

166

Pledge of Allegiance to the Flag
of the United States

I pledge allegiance to the flag
of the United States of America
and to the Republic for which it stands,
one Nation under God, indivisible,
with liberty and justice for all.

167

To help student understand the concept of freedom, and how many of our symbols represent that, assign them one of the following activities described below.

◆ **EASY** Ask each student to draw a picture of either the Liberty Bell or the Statue of Liberty, write its name on the top and the word *Freedom* on the bottom of the paper.

◀▶ **AVERAGE** Have students make a collage about freedom. This may include symbols of freedom or pictures of people enjoying activities that illustrate the benefits of freedom in our country.

◀▮▶ **CHALLENGING** Ask each student to draw a picture of either the Liberty Bell, the Statue of Liberty, or any other symbol of freedom they can think of.

Ask them to write a few sentences below the picture explaining why this symbol stands for freedom.

Curriculum Connection

Music Review with the class two other popular American patriotic songs. Examples might be "America" or "America, the Beautiful."

● Discuss with the class the meanings of the words of these songs as well as "The Star-Spangled Banner."

● Have the students record all three songs on tape.

● Make a presentation to another class in which the meanings of the songs are outlined and the recording is played.

Writing to Learn

My Favorite Symbol   Ask each student to select one of the symbols from the lesson that he or she likes the best.

● Have the students write a story explaining why this symbol is their favorite.

● Ask the students to draw a picture of the symbol to accompany their story.

Optional Activities

Read and Discuss
Text pages 168–169

To help children understand that some of our country's symbols stand for the concept of freedom, ask them to read pp. 168–169, and answer the following questions.

1. **What are two symbols of our country that mean freedom?**
   (Statue of Liberty, Liberty Bell, *pp. 168–169*)

2. **Why did many people come to this country?**
   (To be free, *p. 168*)

3. **Where is the Liberty Bell located?**
   (Philadelphia, *p. 168*)

4. **Why was the Liberty Bell rung?**
   (To tell people that they would be free, *p. 168*)

   Thinking Critically Why, do you think, is the Statue of Liberty carrying a torch? (Hypothesize)
   (Answers may include to light up the area and welcome people at night. *p. 169*)

VISUAL THINKING SKILL

Analyzing the Photographs

■ Have the students look at the picture on p. 169.
Where is the Statue of Liberty standing?
(Answers may include in the water, ocean, harbor.)

Some symbols of our country mean freedom.
The Liberty Bell is a symbol of freedom.
People came to this country to be free.
The bell was rung to tell people that they would be free.
You can see the bell in Philadelphia.

168

Optional Activities

he Statue of Liberty is another symbol.
'he statue welcomes people to our country.
t reminds us of freedom.

---

esson 4

Review

Read and Think

1. What is a symbol? *(Recall)*

2. Where do you see symbols of our country? *(Analyze)*

Skills Check

Look at the pictures on pages 164 and 165.

Name the symbols of our country.

169

Lesson **4** Review

Answers to Read and Think

1. A symbol reminds us of something else.

2. Answers may include that you see symbols of our country at school, at home, in buildings and in special places.

Answer to Skills Check

The symbols are the the eagle and the flag. They are shown on coins, seals, and stamps.

Answer to Lesson Title Question

Ask the lesson title question found at the beginning of the lesson:

What are our country's symbols?

(Flag, eagle, song, pledge, Statue of Liberty, Liberty Bell)

Additional Practice

You may wish to assign the ancillary materials listed below.

Understanding the Lesson p. 50

Workbook pp. 32–33

Reteaching Main Objective

⭐ *Demonstrate an understanding of the concept of symbols.*

● Ask students to bring in from home actual objects or object with the symbols of the country or of their state. Examples might include coins, flags, stamps, miniature Statues of Liberty, and so on.

● Have the students set up a table display.

● Ask the students to name the display and invite other classes in to see it.

**Review Master
Booklet, p. 50**

UNDERSTANDING THE LESSON

NAME _____ U N I T

UNDERSTANDING THE LESSON **6**

Matching LESSON 4 CONTENT MASTER

✱ The pictures at the bottom of this page are symbols of our country. Cut out each picture and paste it in the correct box.

Liberty Bell	Statue of Liberty
American eagle	American flag

Think and Do: Draw one of the symbols of our country. Use the back of this sheet.

Statue of Liberty	American eagle
Liberty Bell	American flag

50 Use with textbook pages 164–169.

Optional Activities

169

What Are Natural Resources?

Objectives

★1. **Define** *natural resources* and **explain** how people use them.

2. **Recognize** the need to keep air and water clean.

1 STARTING THE LESSON

Motivation/ Prior Knowledge

■ Have a water party. Bring to class a container of fresh cold water and paper cups. Serve the water to the students.

■ Explain to the students that without water, no humans, plants, or animals could exist.

■ Discuss with the class how important it is to keep our water clean.

Study the Vocabulary

NEW WORDS	DISCUSSION WORDS	ORAL VOCABULARY
natural resources	*crops* *forest* *Kenya*	*drought*

Write the following list of words on the chalkboard:

pizza	air	socks
house	water	bus
football	trees	books
land	balloon	hot dogs

■ Ask the students to listen carefully as the list is read.

■ Have the students find the words from this list that are natural resources.

170

Lesson 5

What Are Natural Resources?

Our country has **natural resources**.
Air, water, and land are natural resources.
Farmers need air, water, and land to grow crops.

Optional Activities

PREVIEWING LESSON VOCABULARY

NAME _____   U N I T

PREVIEWING LESSON VOCABULARY   **6**

Matching   LESSON 5 VOCABULARY MASTER

✳ NATURAL RESOURCES are things found in nature. Land and water are NATURAL RESOURCES. Write the name of each NATURAL RESOURCE under its picture.

| trees | water | land | sun |

sun   trees

water   land

Think and Do: Draw a NATURAL RESOURCE on the back of this sheet.
Use with textbook pages 170–175.   51

Review Master Booklet, p. 51

Mike's mother works in a forest.

She takes care of the trees.

Trees are another natural resource.

Trees are used to make many things.

Mike has a pen pal named Jomo.

Jomo's family works with resources too.

171

Read and Discuss
Text pages 170–173

To emphasize the concept of natural resources and the need to preserve them, have the students read pp. 170–173 and answer the following questions.

1. **What are three natural resources that farmers need to grow crops?**
(Air, water, land, *p. 170*)

2. **What two natural resources need to be kept clean in order for people to live?**
(Air and water, *p. 173*)

3. **Why is the land important to Jomo's family?**
(They need the land to grow the corn which they eat and sell. They need to get a good crop in order to live. *p.172*)

Thinking Critically Why is it important for farmers to be able to grow crops? (Analyze)
(They supply food for the country. *p. 170*)

VISUAL THINKING SKILL

Analyzing the Photograph

■ Have the students look at the photographs on pp. 170–171.
What natural resources are being cared for in these pictures?
(Land and trees)

Curriculum Connection

Language Arts   Write the following lists of water words on the chalkboard. Practice reading the lists with the students.

List 1	List 2	List 3
shiny	drips	hose
slippery	gushes	faucet
icy	dribbles	pipe
murky	drains	ground
foamy	slides	crack
fresh	slips	spring
steamy	splashes	roof

● Ask a student to say a word from the first list, then say *water*. Ask the student to say a word from list two, then say *from the*. Then have them select a word from list three. An example is *Foamy water gushes from the pipe.*

● Ask the students to write sentences of their own and share them with the class.

Meeting Individual Needs

Concept:
Farms and Natural Resources

Natural resources are very important on a farm. Assign one of the activities below to emphasize this point.

◆ **EASY** Ask each student to draw a picture of a farm that has healthy animals and good crops.

◀▶ **AVERAGE** Have the students write a sentence about what happens to a farm when there isn't enough water to grow the crops. Explain that this is called a drought.

Ask them to draw a picture to accompany their sentence.

◀▮▶ **CHALLENGING** Ask each student to list three crops that can be grown on a farm and three animals that can be raised on a farm.

Have the students draw pictures of one crop and one type of animal.

VISUAL THINKING SKILL

Analyzing the Photograph

■ Have the students look at the photographs on page 172.
How does Kenya seem to be different from our country? How does it seem similar?
(Accept all reasonable answers.)

PEN PALS

Dear Mike,

My family grows corn on a small farm.
Many people grow corn in Kenya.
People eat corn with many meals.
My family eats most of the corn we grow
We sell some of the corn.
Our land is important to my family.

Your friend,

Jomo

172

Optional Activities

Writing to Learn

Writing a Letter Ask the students to write a letter to Jomo, the boy featured in the Pen Pal letter on p. 172.

● Have the students write two or three sentences telling something about their home and family that they think would interest Jomo.

For Your Information

Natural Resources in the News Ask the student to find articles and pictures from magazines and newspapers about the use and preservation of natural resources.

● Have them share their articles with the class.

● Ask the students to classify the articles according to t type of natural resource and create a bulletin board display.

People need clean air and water to live. Workers help to keep these resources clean. Each of us can help too.

Lesson 5 —————— Review ——————

Read and Think

1. Name some natural resources. (Recall)

2. What can you do to keep our air and water clean? (Evaluate)

Skills Check

Farmers use our natural resources.

Write a story about being a farmer.

Lesson 5 Review

Answers to Read and Think

1. Land, air, water, trees.

2. Accept all reasonable answers.

Answer to Skills Check

Stories should include a description of how farmers use land and water.

Answer to Lesson Title Question

Ask the question found at the beginning of the lesson:

What are natural resources?

(Land, air, and water are natural resources. We need natural resources to live.)

Additional Practice

You may wish to assign the ancillary materials listed below.

Understanding the Lesson p. 52
Workbook p. 34

Reteaching Main Objective

★ *Define* natural resources *and explain how people use them.*

● Have the students name air, land, and water as natural resources.

● Have each student fold an 8½″ × 11″ sheet of paper in thirds. Have them label the sections *Air*, *Water*, and *Land*.

● Below each label, have the students list the ways people use these resources. For example, we need water to drink and to grow crops.

● If the students also want to list ways that people can preserve the resources, have them add them to the bottom of the lists.

Review Master Booklet, p. 52

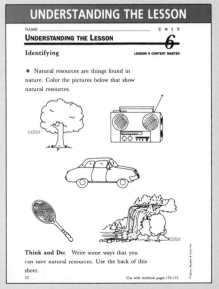

UNDERSTANDING THE LESSON

NAME _____

UNDERSTANDING THE LESSON

U N I T
6

Identifying

LESSON 5 CONTENT MASTER

✱ Natural resources are things found in nature. Color the pictures below that show natural resources.

color

color

Think and Do: Write some ways that you can save natural resources. Use the back of this sheet.

52

Use with textbook pages 170–175.

Optional Activities

CITIZENSHIP AND AMERICAN VALUES

Objectives

1. **Identify** reasons why we need trees.

2. **Identify** why we need to save our natural resources.

Guided Reading

To identify why we need trees and why it is important to save them, ask students the following questions after they read pp. 174–175.

1. **Why must we let some trees grow?**
(They help our land and our air. *p. 174*)

2. **Why do people save newspapers after they read them?**
(They can be used again to make new newspaper. *p. 175*)

How Can We Save Our Resources?

Trees are a natural resource.

We must use our trees carefully.

We need to let some trees grow.

They help our land and our air.

We need to use other trees to make things.

174

Optional Activities

Current Events

● Arrange a tour through a recycling plant in your area. Explain to the students where materials to be recycled came from, as well as where the finished product will be going after it leaves the plant.

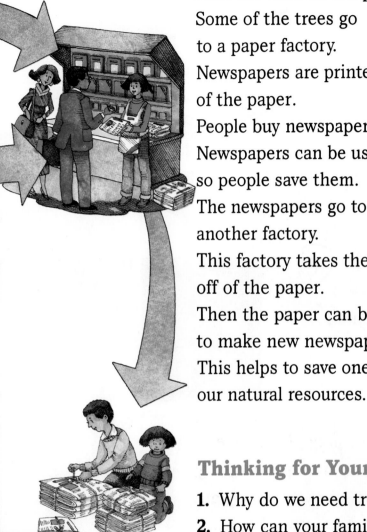

Find the trees in the picture.
Some of the trees go
to a paper factory.
Newspapers are printed on some
of the paper.
People buy newspapers to read.
Newspapers can be used again,
so people save them.
The newspapers go to
another factory.
This factory takes the ink
off of the paper.
Then the paper can be used
to make new newspapers.
This helps to save one of
our natural resources.

Thinking for Yourself

1. Why do we need trees?
2. How can your family help
   to save resources?

175

Answers to Thinking For Yourself

1. We need trees to help our land and our air, and also to make things like newspapers.

2. Answers may include saving newspapers and recycling them; planting new trees in their yard or in a park, buying and using things made from recycled paper, and so on.

or Your Information

Recycled paper is made into many things people use every day, including newspaper, tissue paper, paper towels, and even greeting cards.

Theodore Roosevelt made great strides to preserve our natural resources. During his presidency, there was a significant increase in the amount of land declared as national forests and parks. To honor his work, there is an island named after him in Washington, D.C. There are no cars allowed on the island. People must walk across a small footbridge to enter and leave the island.

Optional Activities

Using the New Words

The vocabulary terms in this review were introduced in the unit. Some students may have difficulty distinguishing between similar concepts. Discuss the meaning of each word in relation to the pictures before having the students match the words to the pictures.

Suggested Answers

1. G
2. D
3. F
4. C
5. B
6. E
7. A

Accept other responses if students can explain their choice.

A. Using the New Words

Find the picture that best matches each word.

1. law ____
2. ocean ____
3. state ____
4. symbol ____
5. natural resources ____
6. Congress ____
7. continents ____

A.

B.

C.

D.

E.

F.

Alabama

G.

176

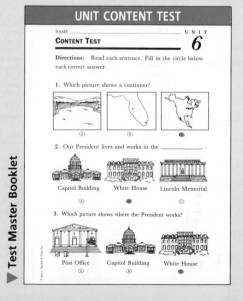

UNIT CONTENT TEST

NAME _____ U N I T
CONTENT TEST **6**

Directions: Read each sentence. Fill in the circle below each correct answer.

1. Which picture shows a continent?

Ⓐ   Ⓑ   Ⓒ

2. Our President lives and works in the _____.

Capitol Building   White House   Lincoln Memorial

3. Which picture shows where the President works?

Post Office   Capitol Building   White House
Ⓐ   Ⓑ   Ⓒ

► Test Master Booklet

UNIT CONTENT TEST

NAME _____ UNIT 6
CONTENT TEST (continued)

4. Which is a symbol for a state?

Ⓐ   Ⓑ   Ⓒ

5. One symbol of our country is a _____

Ⓐ   Ⓑ   Ⓒ

6. To what do we say a pledge?

Ⓐ   Ⓑ   Ⓒ

7. Which is a symbol of freedom?

Statue of Liberty   Post Office   White House
Ⓐ   Ⓑ   Ⓒ

► Test Master Booklet

Remembering
What You Read

Answer these questions about the unit.
1. The United States is on the continent of North America.
2. People vote for the leaders they want.
3. The flag and the eagle are seen in many places. The Statue of Liberty and the Liberty Bell are places that you must go to visit.

Summarizing the Unit

Tell the students to think of a trip they have taken with their families, relatives, or friends.

Have the students draw a picture of what they saw on their trip and discuss the picture with the class. Have the students identify where their special place is located.

B. Remembering What You Read

Answer these questions about the unit.
1. The United States is on which continent?
2. How does our country pick leaders?
3. Look at the pictures on this page. How are the symbols different?

C. Summarizing the Unit

Draw a picture of a place you have visited in our country.
Why is this place special to you?
In which state is your special place?

177

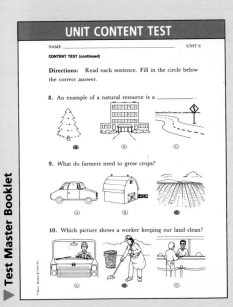

▶ Test Master Booklet

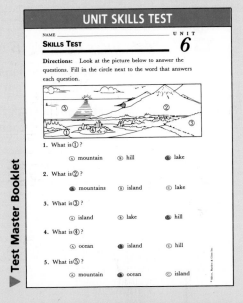

▶ Test Master Booklet

Objectives

1. **Understand** that the earth is made up of different landforms.

2. **Name** four landforms and their definitions.

Why Do I Need This Skill?

To help the students understand that the earth is made up of different types of land, ask these questions.

1. **What two things does the earth have?**
   (Water and land)

2. **What two things make landforms?**
   (Water and land)

Learning the Skill

To help the students recognize the four different types of landforms, have them answer these questions.

1. **Which landform is made of land with water all around it?**
   (Island)

2. **What is a lake?**
   (A body of water with land around it)

3. **What is the difference between a mountain and a hill?**
   (A mountain is much higher than a hill.)

SKILL TRACE:	Identifying Landforms	
INTRODUCE PE, p. 178	**PRACTICE** PE, p. 179 TE, p. 195 TE, p. U6-E	**TEST** Unit 6 Test, TMB

178

 A **Why Do I Need This Skill?**

The earth has water and land.
Water and land make landforms.
This lesson will help you name
landforms that you see.

B **Learning the Skill**

The picture shows four kinds of landforms.
An island is land with water all around it.
A lake is a body of water with land around it.
A hill is higher than the land around it.
A mountain is a very high hill.

178

Optional Activities

Curriculum Connection

Art Have the students bring in magazines to class.

- Ask the students to look through the magazines for photographs of the four different kinds of landforms.
- Ask each student to cut out pictures of different landforms and glue them on a piece of paper to make a collage.

C Practicing the Skill

Look at the pictures on this page.

1. Which picture shows a lake?
2. Which picture shows a hill?
3. Which picture shows an island?
4. Which picture shows a mountain?

b.

c.

d.

Practicing the Skill

Have the students use the letters below the pictures to indicate their answers to the questions.

1. b.
2. d.
3. c.
4. a.

Applying the Skill

In order to get to an island you have to go either on a boat or on an airplane. It is harder to get to an island because it is necessary to travel across water to get there.

D Applying the Skill

You are going on a trip to an island. Name some ways to get to the island. Why might going to an island be harder than going to a lake?

179

Reteaching Activity

- Review the four landforms with the class.
- Ask each student to write a story about a visit they took to either a hill, a mountain, an island or a lake.
- Have the students draw a picture to accompany the story.

179

Unit 7 Resource Center

Our Country's Holidays
(pp. 180–201)

Unit Theme: People gather throughout the year to celebrate holidays that mark important events in our country's history.

SILVER WINGS WORKSHOP: Let's Celebrate!

UNIT RESOURCES
Unit 7 Test

LESSON *1* Why Do We Celebrate Columbus Day?
(pp. 182–185)
Theme: Christopher Columbus led a voyage across the Atlantic Ocean. He encouraged others to explore the new land.

LESSON RESOURCES
Workbook, p. 35
Review Master Booklet
   Previewing Lesson Vocabulary,
    p. 53
   Understanding the Lesson, p. 54

LESSON *2* Why Is Thanksgiving Celebrated?
(pp. 190–193)
Theme: On Thanksgiving, people remember the things that they are grateful for, just as the Pilgrims were grateful for their food and the help of the Indians.

LESSON RESOURCES
Workbook, p. 36
Review Master Booklet
   Previewing Lesson Vocabulary,
    p. 55
   Understanding the Lesson, p. 56

LESSON *3* Who Are Some People We Honor?
(pp. 194–197)
Theme: George Washington, Abraham Lincoln, and Martin Luther King, Jr., all made important contributions to our country.

LESSON RESOURCES
Workbook, p. 37
Review Master Booklet
   Understanding the Lesson, p. 57

LESSON *4* What Is Flag Day?
(pp. 198–201)
Theme: Flag Day is the holiday on which we celebrate our flag.

LESSON RESOURCES
Workbook, p. 38
Review Master Booklet
   Understanding the Lesson, p. 58

PACING GUIDE

September UNIT	October UNIT	November UNITS	December UNIT	January UNIT	February UNIT	March UNITS	April UNIT	May UNIT
1	2	2–3	3	4	5	5–6	6	7

Annotated Bibliography

Books for Teachers

Barth, Edna. *Turkeys, Pilgrims and Indian Corn: The Story of the Thanksgiving Symbols.* Boston: Houghton Mifflin/Clarion, 1975. ISBN 0-395-28846-0. This resource book for teachers gives much information about the many different Thanksgiving foods, traditions, and symbols.

McElmeel, Sharron L. *My Bag of Book Tricks.* Englewood, CO: Teachers Ideas Press, 1979. ISBN 0-872-87722-1. This book categorizes books by themes and gives suggestions for literature-related activities to do with children.

Books for Read Aloud

Adler, David. *A Picture Book of Martin Luther King.* New York: Holiday House, 1989. ISBN 0-823-40770-5. This biography introduces Martin Luther King, his life, ideals, and all that he worked for.

DeLage, Ida. *Pilgrim Children on the Mayflower.* Champaign, IL: Garrard, 1980. ISBN 0-811-64315-8. The voyage of the *Mayflower* is told through the eyes of the children who were on board.

LITERATURE Read-Aloud D'Aulaire, Ingri and Edgar Parin. *Columbus.* Garden City, New York: Doubleday and Co., Inc., 1955. ISBN 0-385-24106-2. This biography discusses the four voyages of Columbus to the New World.

Filmstrips and Videos

Abraham Lincoln. Chicago: Society for Visual Arts. 12-minute filmstrip with cassette and guide. Based on the book by Ingri and Edgar Parin D'Aulaire, this filmstrip tells how Abraham Lincoln rose from a poor childhood on the American frontier and became the sixteenth president.

George Washington. Chicago: Society for Visual Arts. 8-minute filmstrip with cassette and guide. Based on the book by Ingri and Edgar Parin D'Aulaire, this filmstrip tells about George Washington's early life on a plantation, his years as a soldier and general, and his selection as our first president.

Here Comes Columbus Day. Mahwah, NJ: TROLL Associates. 6-minute video (VH026). Presents facts about Christopher Columbus's early life and voyage across the Atlantic to the New World.

Martin Luther King, Jr. Chicago: Society for Visual Arts. 11-minute filmstrip with cassette and guide. Presents the life and times of Martin Luther King and explains the significance of the national holiday honoring his birth.

Computer Software

TimeLiner: History in Perspective. Apple II. Cambridge, MA: Tom Snyder Productions.

Bulletin Board Idea

Student Activity

Have the students use pieces of string to connect each picture with the holiday it represents. Then have the students write what or whom we remember on each holiday.

The First Thanksgiving

How was the first Thanksgiving celebrated?

In Unit 7, the students will learn that holidays help us remember special times and special people. They will also learn that Thanksgiving helps us remember one day, long ago, when the European settlers and American Indians feasted together. In the following activities, students will learn more about the colonial setting of the first Thanksgiving.

SOCIAL STUDIES

Geography Display a map that shows both America and Europe. Help students find America and Europe on the map. Have volunteers point to these places on the map with their finger.

■ Remind the students that many Pilgrims came from England. Have the students find England on the map. Tell them that Plymouth is in southwest England and then point to it. Have the students find Massachusetts on the map. Ask a volunteer to

point to this place on the map with his or her finger. Then ask a volunteer to track the Pilgrims' route from England to America.

History Tell the students the story of the Pilgrims who first came to America, from their crossing on the *Mayflower* to the first Thanksgiving. (You may wish to read aloud the account, "Pilgrims on the Mayflower," from *A Child's History of America* written and illustrated by America's children; created and directed by Edward J. McGrath, Jr. (Boston, MA: Little, Brown & Co., Inc. 1975, ISBN 0-316-55934-2).

■ Have the students dramatize the story. Include adult, child, and baby Pilgrims; sailors; and Indians of all ages in the cast. Encourage the students to play their roles in appropriate costumes.

Economics From the time children in early America were about four years old, they helped their parents earn a living. Children worked both in the house and on the farm.

■ Have the students discuss the tasks that Pilgrims did at home and on the farm. List them on the chalkboard. The list could include wash-

ing, candle making, soap making, spinning, fishing, trapping, feeding animals, and chopping wood.

Settlers at Work In a class discussion, compare growing up in America today with growing up in America long ago. Ask the following questions.

1. Which people in your family help to earn a living? How do they each help?

2. How are the chores you do at home the same as the chores that children did long ago? How are they different?

3. How are your parents' chores at home the same as the chores that parents did long ago? How are they different?

LANGUAGE ARTS

Writing Directions Children in the New England colonies played games that were popular in England, such as blind man's bluff and leap frog. Have the students play these two games from colonial times. You may wish to divide the class in two groups for blind man's bluff.

■ Have the class dictate directions on how to play the games.

Writing a Letter Ask the students to imagine themselves as part of the group that celebrated the first Thanksgiving. Have them compose a letter to friends back home in England, describing the occasion. Write on the board the sentences that the students dictate. Have each student copy the letter and illustrate it.

SCIENCE

■ The Indians showed the Pilgrims how to grow corn, which became a major part of the Pilgrims' diet. One settler, having eaten quite a lot of this vegetable, remarked, "My bones are made of corn." Corn-husking bees were a favorite part of harvest time for children.

■ Explain the importance of corn to the Pilgrims' diet. Then have the students list the ways that corn can be prepared and write these on the chalkboard. Popcorn, corn on the cob, boiled corn, corn pudding, corn soup, corn bread are some of the ways corn can be prepared.

■ You may wish to have a corn-husking race followed by a snack of corn on the cob. (It is recommended that the teachers boil the corn.) The students may wish to prepare popcorn, corn bread, or corn soup at home and bring it in to share with the class.

ART

■ Have the students make construction-paper mosaics of the first Thanksgiving. Each student will need one piece of heavy paper for the backing, different colors of torn construction paper for the mosaic, a pencil to outline the scene, and glue to attach the colored paper to the backing.

■ Before the students begin, have them say what they might include in their mosaic. Indians and Pilgrims, corn on the cob, wild turkey, and people bowing their heads in prayer are some of the things the students may wish to include. List the students' ideas on the chalkboard.

Make and Use Clothespin Puppets

INSTRUCTIONS FOR THE TEACHER:

Focus   In this unit, "Our Country's Holidays," the students will learn about different holidays, why and how people celebrate holidays, and whom we honor on these holidays. It is important for the students to understand that holidays help us remember special times and special people. Have the students make a puppet theater and clothespin puppets to represent Columbus and his sailors on their voyage to the New World. To prepare for this activity, review with your class the concepts presented in Lesson 1, "Why Do We Celebrate Columbus Day?" Explain to the students that they will be putting on a puppet show about Columbus Day, an important American holiday.

Warm-Up Activity   Read to the students the excerpt from *Columbus*, by Ingri and Edgar Parin D'Aulaire (refer to pp. 186–189 in the student textbook). Sequence the story aloud with the students and write the following on the chalkboard.

1 Columbus and his crew sailed for many days in search of land.
2 A sailor spotted an object in the water.
3 Columbus changed his direction and sailed toward the object.
4 Columbus saw a strange light.
5 Columbus and his sailors found land on October 12, 1492.

Review this sequence with students by having them act out the events, using hand motions and impromptu dialogue. Tell the students that they will make puppets and a puppet theater to show the story of Columbus and his sailors looking for land.

ACTIVITY FOR THE STUDENTS:

Procedure Gather the following materials for this activity: several cardboard shoe boxes, one round wooden clothespin per student; glue, tape, sequins or glitter, felt strips, ribbon, fabric, markers, and construction paper for the class.

Making the Clothespin Puppet Have each student make his or her own clothespin puppet. Ask the students to decide if they will make a puppet of Columbus or of a sailor. Tell them to use the wooden clothespins for the bodies of the puppets. Hold a clothespin and help students grasp the concept of the item as a puppet. Show the students how to cut yarn for hair and how to glue each strand onto the top of the clothespin. Use small pieces of felt to make a hat and clothing. Help the students glue the felt pieces onto the clothespins. Let them dry. Then have the students make faces on the puppets with markers or sequins and let the clothespins dry.

Preparing the Puppet Theater Cut the bottom out of a shoe box. Have the students turn the box so that a long side is used as the floor of the stage. Have the students decorate the inside and outside of the box with construction paper, paint, and markers. You may wish to attach a piece of fabric to the back of the box for a backdrop.

Using the Clothespin Puppet Have the students help you summarize the story of Columbus that they heard earlier. Have the students work in small groups and use their puppets to role-play Columbus and his sailors on their voyage.

Follow-up Discussion Have students use sequencing skills to explain the steps they followed in making their clothespin puppets.

Then ask them to think of other holidays that they might dramatize with clothespin puppets. One suggestion is the first Thanksgiving. Read some descriptions of the first Thanksgiving to the students and ask them to sequence the events just as they did with Columbus's voyage. Write the events on the chalkboard as the students supply them in order. Then have the students decide what character or characters they will make. After the clothespin puppets are made, have the students dramatize the first Thanksgiving.

Extension Clothespin puppets may be used to help dramatize many of the concepts in social studies. You may wish to use this activity to develop the following topics: how family members interact, how people interact at school, wants and needs, and working together in communities. The students could write or orally plan skits about all these topics, deciding together on the characters and the activities. They could then make clothespin characters to fit the roles that they have planned.

Workbook Pages

U N I T
7

WHERE ARE THE SHIPS?

Observing

✳ Columbus led three ships across the Atlantic Ocean. Can you find the three ships in the picture below? Color the ships.

U N I T
7

GIVING THANKS

Following Directions

✳ Some things make you think of certain holidays. Color the spaces marked A brown. Color the spaces marked B with your favorite color. You will find a picture that shows something about Thanksgiving.

U N I T
7

WHO DO WE HONOR?

Using Illustrations

✳ Look at the pictures below. Then answer the questions. Circle the correct answer.

1. Who is shown on this coin?

   (Abraham Lincoln)   George Washington   Martin Luther King, Jr.

2. Which picture is shown on the coin above?

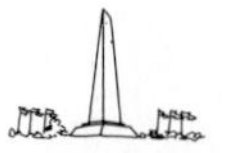

   Washington Monument 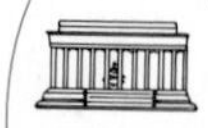   (Lincoln Memorial)   Statue of Liberty

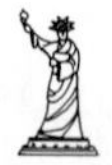

3. How much is the coin shown above worth?

   10¢   5¢   (1¢)

U N I T
7

THE AMERICAN FLAG

Observing

✳ The American flag is a symbol of our country. Each part of the flag has a special color. Color the flag below to make it look like a real flag. Use your classroom flag to help you.

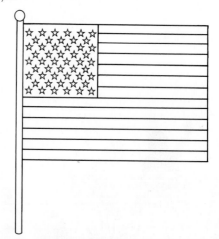

Alternating red and white stripes, beginning and ending with red. White stars on a blue background.

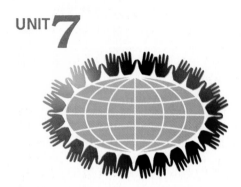

UNIT 7

MULTICULTURAL PERSPECTIVES

Before Columbus *(pages 182–185)*
Give your students an opportunity to see some aspects of American Indian culture that were in place prior to the arrival of Columbus.

Bring in books and photographs that depict Indian cultures across the United States before the arrival of Columbus. One such source is *Mysteries of the Ancient Americas* by the Editors of *Reader's Digest* (New York: Reader's Digest, 1986).

Explain to the students that there were many diverse groups of Indians. They had different kinds of homes and dressed differently, depending on where they lived. Select several groups of Indians and compare and contrast how they met their basic needs.

Thanksgiving *(pages 190–193)*
Explain to your students that Thanksgiving is a holiday that is celebrated in the United States. Families and friends usually get together on this holiday to share a special meal together.

Ask each student to think about the meal his or her family shares on Thanksgiving. Ask that each student write and illustrate a menu for that meal.

Compare the completed menus. Discuss the menus with the students. Draw to the students' attention any foods that are served that reflect a family's ethnicity or geographic origin.

Students may discuss how their families celebrate the day. Some students may not celebrate the holiday.

Unit 7 OUR COUNTRY'S HOLIDAYS

New Words

holiday

celebrate

feast

Pilgrims

American Indians

180

Optional Activities

Drawing Parades

● Have the students look at the picture of the parade on pp. 180–181. Discuss with the students some of the things they see, such as the special vehicles, the flags, and the spectators.

● Ask the students to recall a parade they have seen. Ask them what event or holiday was being celebrated, what they saw, and how they felt.

● Have the students draw pictures of the parades they remember and discuss them with the class.

181

Honoring People *(pages 194–197)*

Memorials, statues, and special days are some of the ways we honor people. Ask the students if they have ever been to a celebration to honor someone special.

Maya Lin, a Chinese-American architect, has designed two famous memorials. She designed the wall portion of the Vietnam Veterans Memorial in Washington, D.C. This memorial honors those people who served our country during the Vietnam War. The names of armed services personnel who were killed or who are missing in action are listed on the wall.

Maya Lin also designed the Civil Rights Memorial in Montgomery, Alabama. It notes some of the major events in the civil rights movement and the names of some individuals who died as a result of the movement. The memorial, which was dedicated in 1989, honors those people who have tried to make the country a better place for everyone to live.

Ask the students how they feel after they have visited a memorial or attended a ceremony that honors someone.

Optional Activities

Why Do We Celebrate Columbus Day?

Objectives

★1. **Tell** who Christopher Columbus was and explain the importance of his voyage.

2. **Explain** the difference between holidays and ordinary days.

3. **Identify** the following people and places: *Christopher Columbus, Atlantic Ocean,* and *Spain.*

1 STARTING THE LESSON

Motivation/ Prior Knowledge

■ Ask the students if any of them have ever moved. **How did their families get ready to move? What did they expect to find in their new area?**

■ Tell the students that today they are going to learn about Christopher Columbus. He went on a special trip to a new place long ago.

Study the Vocabulary

NEW WORDS	DISCUSSION WORDS	ORAL VOCABULARY
holiday celebrate	captain Spain Atlantic Ocean Christopher Columbus	explorer

■ Make a large chart with columns labeled *Holiday* and *Ways to Celebrate.* Have the students name holidays to be shown on the chart. Include Columbus Day. Define *celebrate* with the students and have them draw pictures to show how the holidays are celebrated in their families. Attach the pictures to the chart.

182

Lesson 1

Why Do We Celebrate Columbus Day?

Columbus Day is a **holiday**.
Holidays help us remember special times.
They help us remember special people too.
We remember Christopher Columbus
on Columbus Day.

182

Optional Activities

PREVIEWING LESSON VOCABULARY

NAME _____
PREVIEWING LESSON VOCABULARY U N I T **7**

Matching LESSON 1 VOCABULARY MASTER

✱ HOLIDAYS are special days. They help us remember important things and important people. On a HOLIDAY we CELEBRATE, or do special things. Match the pictures with the activities in the word box.

pledge	meal	parade

1. _____ parade

2. _____ pledge

3. _____ meal

Think and Do: We also CELEBRATE birthdays. Draw a gift you would like for your birthday. Use the back of this sheet.

Use with textbook pages 182–189. 53

Review Master
Booklet, p. 53

Christopher Columbus lived long ago. He lived in a country called Spain. Columbus was a sea captain. He led three ships across the Atlantic Ocean. Columbus was one of the first people to make this trip.

The Granger Collection

183

DEVELOPING THE LESSON

Read and Discuss
Text pages 182–185

Help the students define *holiday* and *celebrate* while learning about Christopher Columbus by having them read pp. 182–185 and answering these questions.

1. **What do holidays help us remember?** (Special people and times *p. 182*)
2. **What did Christopher Columbus do?** (He found new land. *p. 184*)
3. **When do we celebrate Columbus Day?** (October 12 *p. 185*)

   Thinking Critically Why, do you think, did other people come to the new land? (Hypothesize) (Answers may include that they wanted a new place to live. *p. 184*)

VISUAL THINKING SKILL

Interpreting the Photograph

■ Tell the students that a parade is one way to celebrate a holiday. Have the students look at the photograph on p. 182. Then ask this question.
How can you tell that the people are part of a parade?
(The people are wearing costumes; some of the people are carrying flags.)

Curriculum Connection

Art Give the students crayons and a white circle with an 8″ diameter. Have them draw the new land as seen through a porthole. Prepare a diluted blue paint mixture and have the students use a sponge to spread the paint over their pictures. Hang to dry.

Writing to Learn

Making a List Have the students pretend to be Christopher Columbus and prepare a list of supplies that are necessary for the trip.

For Your Information

● Columbus was sailing for the Indies, in the Far East, to find gold, silver, and jewels when he discovered the New World. That is why he named the people he found there Indians.

● Spain supported Columbus's venture by providing him with three ships, the *Nina*, the *Pinta*, and the *Santa Maria*. The voyage took Columbus and his crew over two months to make. Over the next ten years, Columbus made three more voyages to the New World, but he never found the treasures he sought.

Optional Activities

Meeting Individual Needs

Concept:
Recognizing Individuals' Talents

Help the students recognize that some types of gifts or talents are noticed and admired by others. Help the students learn to identify these gifts by completing one of the activities below.

◆**EASY** Have the students name family members who they feel are special and explain why. Encourage the students to name special abilities or characteristics that the people possess.

◀▶**AVERAGE** Have the students draw a picture of someone famous. Have them write a sentence or two about the person.

◀▮▶**CHALLENGING** Have the students each think of something that they could do that would make them famous. Have them draw a picture that shows why they are famous. Then have them write a story about their accomplishment and name a holiday in their honor.

GEOGRAPHY THEMES

Location

■ Have the students find the shapes of Spain and the Atlantic Ocean in the Dictionary of Places, on pp. 210–211. Then have them turn to the Atlas maps on pp. 208–209 to see the places in relation to each other. Show the students these places on a classroom globe, too, if one is available.

Columbus found new land near our country. Other people came to the new land after Christopher Columbus.

The Granger Collectio

Optional Activities

Role-Playing

● Have the students pretend to be Christopher Columbus and his crew. Prepare a large piece of cardboard for a boat and make a flag.

● Have the students discuss how the crew prepared the ship for the trip. Have them role-play loading the ship.

● Then have the students imagine how it felt to leave the port, to sail on calm seas, to sail on rough seas, to be desperate to find land, and to find land.

We **celebrate** Columbus Day on October 12.
We remember his famous trip.

Lesson 1

Review

Read and Think

1. Who was Christopher Columbus? (Recall)
2. Why would sailors go with Columbus?
(Hypothesize)

Skills Check

Look at the picture on page 184.
What did the ships need to move?

CLOSING THE LESSON

Answers to Read and Think

1. He was a sea captain from Spain who sailed to a new land.
2. Answers may include that they wanted to go on an adventure or that they wanted to go to another land.

Answer to Skills Check

The ships needed sails to move.

Answer to Lesson Title Question

Ask the lesson title question, found at the beginning of the lesson:
Why do we celebrate Columbus Day?
(We celebrate Columbus Day to remember Christopher Columbus as a brave sea captain who was one of the first people to sail across the Atlantic Ocean and as someone who inspired others to follow.)

Additional Practice

You may wish to assign the ancillary materials listed below.
Understanding the Lesson p. 54
Workbook p. 35

Reteaching Main Objective

⭐ *Tell who Christopher Columbus was and explain the importance of his voyage.*

● Have each student write a true sentence about Christopher Columbus or his trip. Then have each student write a false sentence about Columbus or the trip.

● Gather the sentences and read them aloud. Have the students stand if the sentence is true and sit down if the sentence is false.

Review Master Booklet, p. 54

UNDERSTANDING THE LESSON

NAME _____

UNDERSTANDING THE LESSON

UNIT 7

Recalling Facts

LESSON 1 CONTENT MASTER

✷ Read the sentences below. Circle the word or words that best complete each sentence.

1. We remember _____ on Columbus Day.

(Christopher Columbus)   George Washington   Martin Luther King, Jr.

2. Columbus Day is a _____.

summer day   (holiday)   school day

3. Columbus led _____ ships across the Atlantic Ocean.

two   four   (three)

4. We celebrate Columbus Day in _____.

(October)   July   November

Think and Do: Draw a picture of a ship. Use the back of this sheet.

54   Use with textbook pages 182–189.

Optional Activities

185

Thinking About Literature

Use the information below to help students better understand the literature selection found on pp. 186–189.

Selection Summary

This story tells the tale of Christopher Columbus and his desire to become a sailor, even as a young boy in Genoa, Italy.

He was a brave sailor who believed the world was round and not flat. He wanted to reach the Far East by sailing west.

Columbus's voyage was finally financed by King Ferdinand and Queen Isabella of Spain. They gave him three ships: the *Nina,* the *Pinta,* and the *Santa Maria.*

The voyage was long and difficult; finally Columbus and his men sighted land. However, Columbus had not reached the Far East but instead the new continent of America. Columbus found natives inhabiting this land whom he named "Indians".

The king and queen of Spain were impressed by Columbus's voyage, and Columbus, who was now considered a hero, was granted more ships and supplies to again try to reach the Far East. He made three more attempts; each time reaching different areas of America. Since he never reached the Far East, people soon lost interest in his voyages. Other sailors found a route to the Far East, and people soon forgot how courageous Columbus had been and that he had been the first to try.

FROM

COLUMBUS

BY INGRI AND EDGAR PARIN D'AULAIRE

This story tells about Columbus's trip.
The sailors are looking for land.
How do the sailors know that land is near?

Days went by; weeks went by. They sailed on and on
and saw nothing but the desolate sea and sky.
At last, one day, they spied a strange object in the water.
It was a carved stick.
Soon afterward a sailor fished up a branch
with buds and flowers.
The salty air seemed sweet and fragrant in their nostrils,
as if scented already by the spices of India.
Next day great flocks of land birds flew over the masts.
Land must be near.
For the first time Columbus changed his command.
He called, "To the southwest," and followed the birds.

186

Optional Activities

(187)

1. What are the sailors looking for?
   (They are looking for land.)

2. How many ships did Columbus have?
   (Columbus had three ships.)

Curriculum Connection

Literature   Have students build models of the three ships Columbus used on his voyage.

- Display pictures of old sailing vessels.

- Divide the class into three groups. Have each group make one of the three ships.

- Have students use milk cartons cut in half lengthwise for bottom of the ships. (They can be painted brown.) Use dowels or popsicle sticks for masts. Use construction paper for sails. Students can decorate with crayons or markers, if desired.

- Have students write the name of the ship on construction paper and glue the name on the ship.

Optional Activities

Guided Reading

1. **What did Columbus see late at night that let him know land was near?**
   (He saw a fire kindled by man.)

2. **What did the men on the *Pinta* do to signal to the other ships that land was ahead?**
   (They shot a cannon.)

Now every man was peering ahead.

Late at night, while Columbus stood at his lonely watch, staring through the dark, it seemed to him that one of the stars, low in the sky, looked different from the others.

It didn't twinkle.

It flickered like the flame of a candle.

It could not be a star.

It must be a fire kindled by man.

Columbus called his men.

They all saw it.

He ordered the anchors dropped so the ships would not hit a reef in the night.

Before dawn a cannon shot boomed.

It was a signal from the *Pinta,* which was ahead.

Her crew had seen breakers and a dark coast line.

It was Friday, October 12, 1492.

188

Optional Activities

What Do You Think?
Some adjectives that describe how Columbus felt might include *excited, happy, relieved, curious, thankful* and so on.

What Do You Think?

How, do you think, did Columbus feel when they found land?

189

Writing a Letter

Tell the students that Columbus needed a crew to take on his voyage. Tell them that the trip was dangerous, but Columbus was in search of riches.

Have the students pretend they are Columbus and write a letter to one of their friends persuading the friend to join the voyage. Have students read their letters and discuss them with the class.

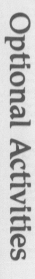

Optional Activities

What Do You Think?
Some adjectives that describe how Columbus felt might include *excited, happy, relieved, curious, thankful* and so on.

189

Why Is Thanksgiving Celebrated?

Objectives

★ **1. Explain** the origin of Thanksgiving.

2. Name four items to be thankful for.

3. Locate Europe on a map.

4. Identify the following people: the *Pilgrims* and the *American Indians*.

1 STARTING THE LESSON

Motivation/ Prior Knowledge

■ Ask the students to name occasions when other people have helped them to learn a new skill. Tell the students that this lesson explains one occasion long ago when one group needed the help of another group to survive.

Study the Vocabulary

NEW WORDS	DISCUSSION WORDS	ORAL VOCABULARY
Pilgrims *American Indians* *feast*	*thanked*	*knowledge* *survive* *harvest*

■ Have the students use the Picture Glossary on pp. 212–216 to look up the New Words.

■ Discuss the meaning of each word with the students. Encourage the students to use the pictures and the sentences from the glossary in their discussion.

■ Have the students imagine the needs of the Pilgrims when they first arrived. Review the basic needs of food, clothing, and shelter with the students.

Optional Activities

Lesson 2

Why Is Thanksgiving Celebrated?

The **Pilgrims** came to our country long ago.
They left their homes in Europe.
They wanted to live in a new land.

190

PREVIEWING LESSON VOCABULARY

NAME   U N I T
PREVIEWING LESSON VOCABULARY   **7**

Matching   LESSON 2 VOCABULARY MASTER

✱ The PILGRIMS came to live in America a long time ago. AMERICAN INDIANS are the people who were living here when the PILGRIMS came. The PILGRIMS and the INDIANS had a FEAST, or a big meal. Look at the pictures below. Write what each picture shows. Use the words you just learned.

1. _____ feast _____

2. _____ American Indians _____

3. _____ Pilgrims _____

Think and Do: Draw a picture of food you would like to eat at a feast. Use the back of this sheet.
Use with textbook pages 190–193.   55

Review Master Booklet, p. 55

The Pilgrims built homes and planted crops. **American Indians** were living in our country. They helped the Pilgrims with their crops.

Read and Discuss
Text pages 190–193

To help the students recognize the events which led to a holiday we still celebrate, have them read pp. 190–193 and answer the questions below.

1. **Who helped the Pilgrims grow their crops?**
   (American Indians *p. 191*)

2. **What did the Pilgrims thank God for on the first Thanksgiving?**
   (Food and friends *p. 192*)

3. **When is Thanksgiving celebrated?**
   (November *p. 193*)

   Thinking Critically How would you have felt coming to a new land as a Pilgrim? (Hypothesize)
   (Answers may include excited or scared. *p. 184*)

VISUAL THINKING SKILL

Analyzing the Drawing

■ The Indians knew that fortifying the soil would help the crops grow better. Have the students look at the picture on p. 191 and answer this question.
What are the Indians adding to the soil to help the crops grow?
(They are adding fish to the soil.)

Cooperative Learning

Creating a Map Have the students work in pairs to design a pioneer settlement. First have the students discuss what should be included in their settlement. One student should keep a list.

The students should decide how each item will be shown on a map and in the map key. Then they need to plan where each item will appear on their map. Finally, they should draw and color the map and map key.

- The pairs should each present their map to the class. They should explain why they positioned the buildings as they did.

- The pairs should evaluate how well they made decisions and how clearly they presented their map to the class.

- Display the maps in the classroom.

Optional Activities

Meeting Individual Needs

Concept:
Changing the Environment

To help the students visualize how civilization changes the environment, assign one of the activities below.

◆**EASY** Have the students paint a picture of a field and some trees. Let the picture dry. Then have the students add a house and some people playing to the picture.

◀▶**AVERAGE** Have the students work in small groups for this activity. Each group will start with several colors of clay. Let the students build an area with trees and a field. Then have the students remove some of the trees and put in a few houses. Have the students explain how their land area changed to make room for the houses.

◀▮▶**CHALLENGING** Have the students pretend to be Pilgrims. Ask each student to write a description of how the land was changed when he or she built a home and planted crops.

VISUAL THINKING SKILL

Analyzing a Photograph

■ Explain that people of today get together for Thanksgiving. Ask the students to look at the photograph on p. 193. Then ask this question.
How are these people celebrating Thanksgiving?
(They are getting together for a meal. They will be sharing their food. The man is holding a pie that the couple is bringing to the house.)

There was a **feast** when the crops were grown.
The Pilgrims and the Indians ate together.
The Pilgrims thanked God for their food.
They thanked God for their friends too.
This was the first Thanksgiving.

192

Optional Activities

For Your Information

● The Pilgrims traveled to America on a ship called The Mayflower. There were approximately 100 passengers aboard the ship. The word *pilgrim* means "persons traveling on a religious journey."

● The Pilgrims landed and settled in what we now know as Massachusetts. They named their colony Plymouth, which was the name of the port in England from which they had sailed.

Today Thanksgiving is a holiday in November. People remember what they are thankful for.

esson 2 ——— Review ———

Read and Think

1. Why did the Pilgrims have a feast? *(Recall)*

2. What are you thankful for? *(Evaluate)*

Skills Check

Think about the Pilgrims and the Indians.
Write a story about the first Thanksgiving.

Answers to Read and Think

1. The Pilgrims had a feast to celebrate the success of their crops and to thank God for the crop and their friends.

2. Answers will vary but may include family and friends.

Answer to Skills Check

Stories should describe the feast and how thankful the Pilgrims were.

Answer to Lesson Title Question

Ask the lesson title question, found at the beginning of the lesson:
Why is Thanksgiving celebrated?
(We celebrate the holiday today to remember the Pilgrims and the Indians and to give thanks for what we have.)

Additional Practice

You may wish to assign the ancillary materials listed below.
Understanding the Lesson p. 56
Workbook p. 36

Writing to Learn

Listing Reasons for Giving Thanks   Have the students trace their hands on white paper. Have them write a reason to be thankful in each finger. Color the hand to look like a turkey.

Reteaching Main Objective

⭐ ***Explain the origin of Thanksgiving.***

- Have the students discuss the first Thanksgiving and the events leading up to it. Then have the students assume the roles of Pilgrims and Indians and dramatize the series of events.

UNDERSTANDING THE LESSON

NAME _____   U N I T
UNDERSTANDING THE LESSON   **7**

Imagining a Scene   LESSON 2 CONTENT MASTER

✻ Circle the things that might have been part of the first Thanksgiving.

Think and Do: Draw a picture of a Thanksgiving feast someone might have at home now. Use the back of this sheet.

56   Use with textbook pages 190–193.

Review Master Booklet, p. 56

Optional Activities

Who Are Some People We Honor?

Objectives

★**1. Name** some of the people our country honors.

2. Correlate the people with their holidays.

3. State why *George Washington*, *Abraham Lincoln*, and *Martin Luther King, Jr.*, were important to our country.

4. Identify the following places: *England* and *Washington, D.C.*.

1 STARTING THE LESSON

Motivation/ Prior Knowledge

■ Ask the students to name school and local community leaders. Have the students state what these people do that makes them special.

■ Explain to the students that in this lesson they will be learning about people who were important in our country's history.

Study the Vocabulary

DISCUSSION WORDS	ORAL VOCABULARY
war	monument
President's Day	history
dream	leader

■ Ask the students to pretend that they are the President of the United States. Ask them to identify why the President has an important job.

■ Explain that this lesson contains some of the history of our country. Leaders and their solutions to the problems they faced make up a large part of our country's history. Tell the students that holidays and monuments are two ways to recognize important leaders.

Who Are Some People We Honor

Long ago laws for our country were made in England.

Our country wanted to make its own laws.

The countries could not agree, so there was a war.

George Washington helped our country win.

He became our first President.

194

Optional Activities

Giving Speeches

● Leaders often need to give speeches. It is important that they organize their thoughts first and speak clearly. Have the students each give a short speech about a person who is important to them.

● Have the students plan their speeches by listing three points about the person they are discussing.

● Allow the students to practice their speeches once. Then ask for the speeches to be presented to the class. Each speech should be limited to the prepared points.

Abraham Lincoln was another President.
Our country had a problem.
Some states did not want to be part
of our country.
President Lincoln kept our country together.

The Granger Collection

195

Read and Discuss
Text pages 194–197

Have the students read pp. 194–197. Then ask the questions below to help the students understand the contributions the leaders made to our country's history.

1. **What holiday remembers Washington and Lincoln?**
   (Presidents' Day *p. 196*)

2. **How did these Presidents help our country?**
   (Washington helped us win a war, and Lincoln kept our country together. *pp. 194–195*)

3. **What dream did Martin Luther King, Jr., have for our country?**
   (For everyone to be treated fairly *p. 197*)

   Thinking Critically What, do you think, makes a person a good leader?
   (Evaluate)
   (Answers may include that the person cares about other people and makes good decisions. *pp. 194–197*)

   Thinking Critically How, do you think, do the monuments shown on p. 196 honor our leaders?
   (Hypothesize)
   (Answers may include that they remind us of the important contributions these leaders made in the history of our country. *pp. 194–197*)

Identifying Landforms On pp. 178–179 the students learned to identify hills, mountains, islands, and lakes. Ask the students to use this information to do the activity below.

● Have the students plan an outdoor monument for someone they respect. The students should draw a picture of the monument and place it near a lake, on a hill, on a mountain, or on an island. Have the students explain why they chose their locations.

For Your Information

● George Washington served two consecutive terms (1789–1797). The capital city was located first in New York City and then in Philadelphia during this time span.

● Abraham Lincoln, our sixteenth president, served during the Civil War. The Gettysburg Address and his second inaugural address are part of his memorial in Washington, D.C.

● Martin Luther King, Jr., is recognized for his efforts to end racial discrimination. He encouraged and led nonviolent demonstrations.

Optional Activities

195

Meeting Individual Needs

Concept:
Understanding Time Relationships

To understand history, the students must be able to distinguish between the past, the present, and the future. Assign one of the activities below to help develop this concept.

◆ EASY Have the students prepare a series of pictures for a TV viewer as described in the How To article on p. U1-E–F. One picture should show a before school activity. The second picture should show the students' present work, and the third picture should show something that the students will do after school. Have the students show the pictures and narrate them.

◀▶ AVERAGE Have the students draw pictures of something that they did yesterday, that they have already done today, and that they will do tomorrow. Have them label the pictures *Before*, *Now*, and *After* and write one or two sentences to describe each picture.

◀▮▶ CHALLENGING Have the students draw three pictures to depict events over the course of a lifetime. The first picture should show the students as infants, the second picture should show them now, and the last picture should show them as adults. Have the students write about each picture.

GEOGRAPHY THEMES

Location

■ Have the students locate Washington, D.C., on the map on pp. 206–207 and answer this question.
What states are near Washington, D.C.?
(Answers should include Virginia, Maryland, and West Virginia.)

■ Tell the students that England is a part of the United Kingdom. Have the students turn to the map on p. 209 and answer this question.
What country is closer to the United Kingdom—France or Romania?
(France is closer.)

Our country is proud of Lincoln and Washington.
We remember them on Presidents' Day.
There are special places to honor them in Washington, D.C.

196

Optional Activities

Writing to Learn

Describing People Have the students write a statement about themselves and their accomplishments as if they were one of the leaders described in this lesson.

● Have the students read their statements aloud and ask the other members of the class to name the person described in each statement.

Martin Luther King, Jr., was another leader.
He wanted everyone to be treated fairly.
There is a holiday to remember his dream.

Lesson 3

Review

Read and Think

1. Whom do we remember on Presidents' Day?
2. How do we show we are proud of people?

Skills Check

Look at the pictures on pages 194 and 196.
What symbol of our country do you see on both pages?

197

Lesson 3 Review

Answers to Read and Think
1. We remember George Washington and Abraham Lincoln on Presidents' Day.
2. Answers may include that we name a holiday after them, have a parade for them, or build a monument named for them.

Answer to Skills Check
There are flags on both pages.

Answer to Lesson Title Question

Ask the lesson title question, found at the beginning of the lesson:
Who are some people we honor?
(Answers should include George Washington, Abraham Lincoln, and Martin Luther King, Jr.)

Additional Practice

You may wish to assign the ancillary materials listed below.
Understanding the Lesson p. 57
Workbook p. 37

Reteaching Main Objective

⭐ *Name some of the people our country honors.*

- Select one of the leaders discussed in this lesson. Have the students try to guess the identity of the leader by asking questions that can be answered by a yes or a no.
- The students must try to identify the leader in less than 20 questions. Repeat this process with the other leaders mentioned in the lesson.

Review Master Booklet, p. 57

UNDERSTANDING THE LESSON

NAME _____
UNDERSTANDING THE LESSON   U N I T **7**

Recognizing Famous People   LESSON 3 CONTENT MASTER

✱ Look at the pictures below. On the lines, write each important person's name. Use the words in the box below.

| George | Lincoln | King |

This person's name is
_____
_____George_____ Washington.

This person's name is Martin
_____
Luther _____King_____ , Jr.

This person's name is
_____
Abraham _____Lincoln_____

Think and Do: Write your full name. Use the back of this sheet.
Use with textbook pages 194–197.   57

What Is Flag Day?

Objectives

★**1. Describe** the American flag and **explain** its design.
2. Tell how we honor the flag.
3. Identify Betsy Ross.

1 STARTING THE LESSON

Motivation/ Prior Knowledge

■ Ask the students to stand and say the Pledge of Allegiance while they face our flag. Remind the students that our flag is a symbol of our country. Tell the students that they will learn about our flag in this lesson.

Study the Vocabulary

DISCUSSION WORDS	ORAL VOCABULARY
Flag Day	*respect*
fly	
Betsy Ross	

■ Tell the students that Flag Day is a special holiday to honor our flag. Explain that people use the phrase *fly the flag* to describe hanging a flag.

■ Tell the students that *respect* means "to think that something or someone is very important." Have the students name people and items that they respect. List their answers on the chalkboard.

■ Write the word *respect* vertically on the chalkboard. After each letter, write a word that starts with that letter and defines *respect*. Copy the completed diagram and display it in the classroom.

198

Lesson 4

What Is Flag Day?

We celebrate Flag Day on June 14.
We honor the American flag.
Many homes fly our flag on the holiday.

198

Optional Activities

Cooperative Learning

Making Decisions Have the students work in pairs. Give each pair a piece of blue paper and 50 beans and ask them to design a new arrangement of stars for our flag. One student should keep track of the ideas tried.

● Have the pairs decide on the design each likes best and glue the beans in place. Have the pairs list the reasons they like their design.

● Have the students explain why they chose their design and evaluate how well they planned them.

The first flag was made by hand.
Some people think that Betsy Ross made the first flag.
The flag was planned by our first Congress.
The colors red, white, and blue were picked.
Congress wanted stars and stripes on the flag.

The Granger Collection

199

Read and Discuss
Text pages 198–201

To help the students understand the development of the flag's design and its meaning, have the students read pp. 199–201 and answer these questions.

1. **What do the stars and stripes mean on our flag?**
   (There is a star per state and a stripe for each of the first 13 states. *p. 200*)

2. **Who was Betsy Ross?**
   (Some people think she sewed the first flag. *p. 199*)

   Thinking Critically How do people show respect for our flag? (Analyze)
   (Answers may include standing and saluting the flag. *p. 201*)

VISUAL THINKING SKILL

Interpreting a Photograph

■ Explain that sewing machines were not available when the first flag was made. Have the students look at the photograph on p. 199 and answer this question.
How was the first flag made?
(The pieces were sewn together by hand.)

Graphic Organizer

● To help the students organize the information they have learned about our flag, draw this graphic organizer on the chalkboard. Fill in the headings for each category. Let the students supply the answers.

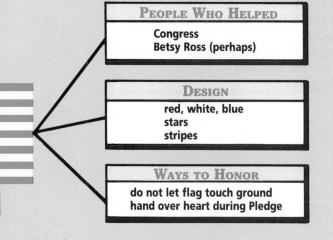

OUR FLAG

PEOPLE WHO HELPED
Congress
Betsy Ross (perhaps)

DESIGN
red, white, blue
stars
stripes

WAYS TO HONOR
do not let flag touch ground
hand over heart during Pledge

Optional Activities

Concept:
Honoring Our Flag

Review the following guidelines for honoring the flag with the students.

The flag should never touch the ground.

Face the flag when The Star-Spangled Banner is played.

Place your right hand over your heart to salute the flag.

◆ **EASY** Let one student hold the flag aloft each day when the Pledge of Allegiance is recited. Have the other members of the class face the flag and hold their hands over their hearts.

◀▮▶ **AVERAGE** Have the students visit a kindergarten class. Each student should have a partner from the kindergarten class. The first-grade students should show their partners how to salute the flag. Then have the students explain the other general rules about handling the flag.

◀▮▶ **CHALLENGING** Have the students draw a picture showing one way that people can honor the flag. Have the students write below the picture the rule and when it is used.

VISUAL THINKING SKILL

Interpreting the Photograph

■ Tell the students that some families fly a flag near their homes. Have the students look at the photograph on p. 201 and answer this question.
How is this family treating the flag with respect?
(They are facing the flag and not letting it touch the ground.)

Long ago our country only had 13 states. The first flag had 13 stars and 13 stripes. Today our flag still has 13 stripes. They remind us of the first 13 states. Now there are 50 stars on our flag. There is a star for each state.

200

Optional Activities

For Your Information

● On June 14, 1777, the Second Continental Congress enacted the Flag Resolution, which said the American Flag would have 13 alternating red and white stripes and 13 stars on a field of blue. This is why we celebrate Flag Day on June 14th.

Writing to Learn

Planning a Flag Have the students list the types of decisions that they would need to make in order to plan a flag. Then have the students plan and draw a flag.

Our flag is a symbol
of our country.
We are proud of our
country on Flag Day.

Lesson 4

—— Review ——

Read and Think

1. What did the first flag look like? **(Recall)**

2. What kind of flag would you make for our country?
   (Hypothesize)

Skills Check

Look at the pictures on page 200.
How are the flags alike?

201

3 CLOSING THE LESSON

Lesson 4 Review

Answers to Read and Think
1. It had 13 stars and 13 stripes.

2. Accept answers with explanations.

Answer to Skills Check
The flags have the same colors, and they both contain stars, stripes, and a blue rectangle.

Answer to Lesson Title Question

Ask the lesson title question, found at the beginning of the lesson:
What is Flag Day?
(Flag Day is a holiday that honors the American flag. It is celebrated on June 14. It is a holiday when many people fly their flags.)

Additional Practice

You may wish to assign the ancillary materials listed below.
Understanding the Lesson p. 58
Workbook p. 38

Reteaching Main Objective

⭐ *Describe the American flag and explain its design.*

● Have the students make a flag from a 12″ × 18″ piece of paper. Prepare a list with the names of the states. Have the students glue the names onto the flag in place of the stars. Have them draw in the stripes for the flag and write the name of a colony in each stripe. Have the students state what the stars and stripes represent.

Review Master Booklet, p. 58

UNDERSTANDING THE LESSON

NAME _____
UNDERSTANDING THE LESSON

UNIT 7

Recalling Facts   LESSON 4 CONTENT MASTER

✶ Read each question below about our flag.
Circle the picture that answers each question.

1. What does the American flag look like today?

2. What colors make up the American flag?
   red   red   red
   white   yellow   white
   green   blue   blue

3. On what date do we celebrate Flag Day?
   JUNE   JULY   JANUARY

Think and Do: Draw a picture of the first flag. Use the back of this sheet.

58   Use with textbook pages 198–201.

Optional Activities

201

The vocabulary terms in this review were introduced in the unit. Some students may have difficulty distinguishing between similar concepts. Discuss the meaning of each word in relation to the pictures before having the students match the words to the pictures.

Suggested Answers

1. B
2. D
3. E
4. C
5. A

Accept other responses if students can explain their choice.

UNIT **7** PUTTING IT ALL TOGETHER

A. Using the New Words

Find the picture that best matches each word.

1. American Indians _____
2. celebrate _____
3. Pilgrims _____
4. holiday _____
5. feast _____

A.

B.

C.

D.

E.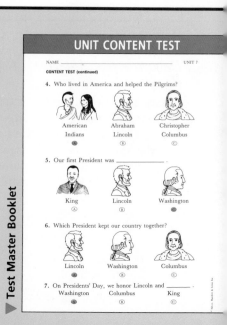

UNIT CONTENT TEST

NAME _____ U N I T
CONTENT TEST **7**

Directions: Read each sentence. Fill in the circle below the correct answer.

1. Who sailed from Spain and discovered a new land?

   George Washington · Christopher Columbus · Abraham Lincoln

2. Which picture shows people celebrating?

3. Who left Europe long ago to live in our country?

   American Indians · Pilgrims · Abraham Lincoln

▶ Test Master Booklet

UNIT CONTENT TEST

NAME _____ UNIT 7
CONTENT TEST (continued)

4. Who lived in America and helped the Pilgrims?

   American Indians · Abraham Lincoln · Christopher Columbus

5. Our first President was _____.

   King · Lincoln · Washington

6. Which President kept our country together?

   Lincoln · Washington · Columbus

7. On Presidents' Day, we honor Lincoln and _____.

   Washington · Columbus · King

▶ Test Master Booklet

B. Remembering What You Read

Answer these questions about the unit.

1. Why do people celebrate holidays?
2. Name some ways people celebrate holidays.
3. How are the people we honor alike?
   How are they different?

C. Summarizing the Unit

Write a story about your favorite holiday.
How do you celebrate the holiday?
Draw a picture of your celebration.

203

Remembering What You Read

Answer these questions about the unit.

1. People celebrate holidays to help remember special times and special people.

2. Answers may include parades, parties, special meals, decorating their home with symbols of the holiday, and so on.

3. The people we honor all did things to help the people of our country. They are different in that they lived at different times and helped people in different ways.

Summarizing the Unit

Discuss with the students some of the ways they celebrate different holidays.

Tell them each to write a story about their favorite holiday. Have them include why it is their favorite and how they celebrate it.

Have the students draw a picture to go along with the story.

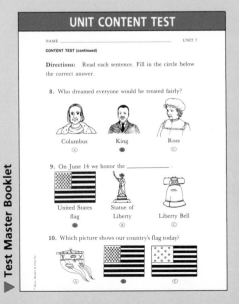

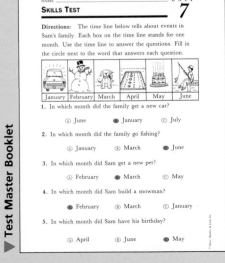

Objectives

1. **Read** and **comprehend** the information contained on a time line.

2. **Sequence** a series of events to prepare a time line.

3. **Create** a time line using information from their own experiences.

Why Do I Need This Skill?

Time lines allow people to show information graphically. Ask the students the following questions to clarify their understanding.

1. **What is an event?**
   (An event is something that has happened.)

2. **What do time lines show?**
   (Time lines show the order of events.)

Learning the Skill

Have the students look at the time line on p. 204. Then have them answer these questions.

1. **What events are shown on the time line?**
   (Born, new dog, new house, new baby, school)

2. **How much time does each box mean?**
   (One year)

3. **What is the last event on the time line?**
   (School)

SKILL TRACE:	Understanding Time Lines	
INTRODUCE PE, p. 204	**PRACTICE** PE, p. 205 TE, pp. 204– 205	**TEST** Unit 7 Test, TMB

204

 Why Do I Need This Skill?

Time lines show when events happened.
Some things happened long ago.
Some things just happened.
Time lines help us see the order of events.

 Learning the Skill

Look at the time line on this page.
It shows important events in Mary's family.
The time line starts when Mary was born.
Each box is one year on this time line.
Mary was one when her family got a dog.

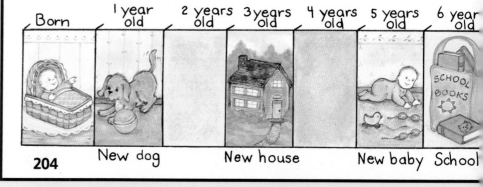

204

Optional Activities

Create a Seasonal Time Line

● Have the students work together to create a time line on large roll paper. Divide the time line into four sections: winter, spring, summer, and fall.

● Have the students draw or cut out pictures from magazines that represent each season. Have the students attach the pictures to the correct section of the time line.

● Have the students make labels for each section and a title for the time line. Have the students compare the pictures associated with each season.

C Practicing the Skill

This time line shows holidays during the school year.

Each box is one month on this time line.

The first holiday is Columbus Day.

What holiday comes in June?

September	October	November	December	January
	Columbus Day	Thanksgiving		Martin Luther King, Jr., Day

February	March	April	May	June
Presidents' Day				 Flag Day

D Applying the Skill

Make a time line of your life.

Make each box stand for one year.

Put at least one event in each box.

205

Reteaching Activity

List on the chalkboard the special activities that your class participates in each week. Music class, gym class, and library time are a few examples.

Have the students draw a time line with each box representing one school day. Have the students draw pictures for the special activities in the correct boxes.

Optional Activities

Using a Time Line

Practicing the Skill

Have the students look at the time line on p. 205 to answer these questions. This time line is shown in two segments so that it is easier for the students to read.

1. **How much time does one box mean on this time line?**
   (One month)

2. **What months are shown on this time line?**
   (September, October, November, December, January, February, March, April, May, and June.)

3. **What holiday comes in February?**
   (Presidents' Day)

Have the students answer the question in the text.
Flag Day comes in June.

For students having difficulty with the concept, you may wish to assign the Reteaching activity.

Applying the Skill

Have the students choose at least one significant event that occurred during each year of their life.

Have the students draw a time line on a piece of construction paper with a box for each year of their lives.

Have the students draw a picture in each box to represent the event that occurred during that year.

Display the time lines.

ATLAS

Russia

ARCTIC OCEAN

Alaska

Canada

Anchorage

Juneau

C a n a d a

Seattle

Olympia

Portland

Washington

Salem

Helena

Montana

Oregon

Billings

Boise

Idaho

Pocatello

Wyoming

Casper

PACIFIC

Carson City

West Valley

Salt Lake City

Cheyenne

Sacramento

Nevada

Utah

River

Denver

OCEAN

Colorado

Colorado

Colorado Springs

← West

California

Las Vegas

Colorado

Los Angeles

Santa Fe

Arizona

Albuquerque

Phoenix

New Mexico

Pearl City ・ Honolulu

Tucson

Hawaii

PACIFIC OCEAN

M e x i c o

THE UNITED STATES OF AMERICA

MAP KEY

⊛ National capital

✪ State capitals

● Other cities

ATLAS

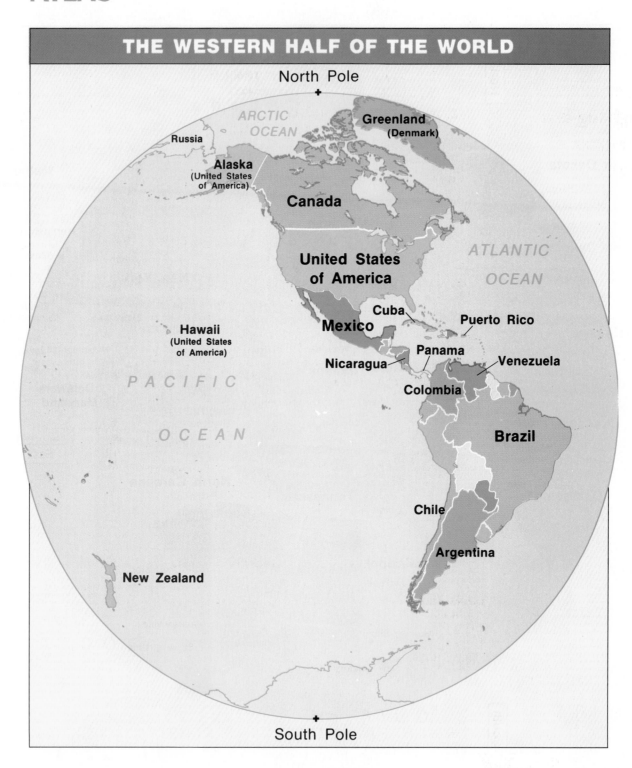

THE WESTERN HALF OF THE WORLD

North Pole

ARCTIC
OCEAN

Greenland
(Denmark)

Russia

Alaska
(United States
of America)

Canada

United States
of America

ATLANTIC

OCEAN

Cuba

Hawaii
(United States
of America)

Mexico

Puerto Rico

Panama

Nicaragua

Venezuela

Colombia

PACIFIC

Brazil

OCEAN

Chile

New Zealand

Argentina

South Pole

THE EASTERN HALF OF THE WORLD

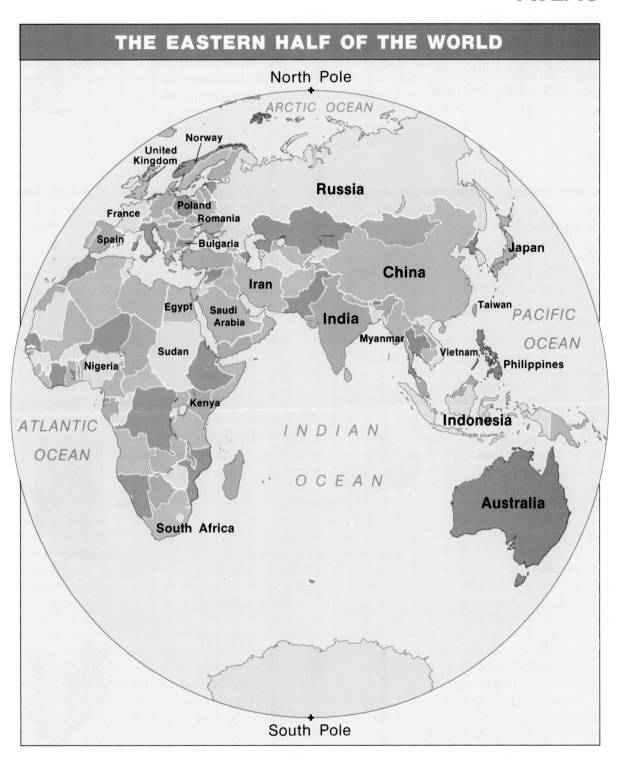

North Pole

ARCTIC OCEAN

Norway

United Kingdom

Russia

France

Poland

Romania

Bulgaria

Spain

Japan

Iran

China

Egypt

Saudi Arabia

India

Taiwan

PACIFIC

Sudan

Myanmar

OCEAN

Nigeria

Vietnam

Philippines

Kenya

INDIAN

Indonesia

ATLANTIC

OCEAN

OCEAN

Australia

South Africa

South Pole

DICTIONARY OF PLACES

You can find each of these places on a map in your book. The page numbers tell you where the maps are.

Atlantic Ocean
The large body of water along the eastern coast of the United States. Page 151

Canada
The country just to the north of the United States. Page 151

Chile
A country in South America that borders on the Pacific Ocean. Page 208

England
The part of the United Kingdom where laws for our country used to be made. Page 209

Europe
The continent that the Pilgrims came from. Page 153

Indiana
A state that borders on Lake Michigan. Page 161

Kenya
A country in Africa that borders on the Indian Ocean. Page 209

DICTIONARY OF PLACES

London
The capital city of the United Kingdom. Page 209

Spain
The country that Christopher Columbus sailed from. Page 209

Mexico
The country just to the south of the United States. Page 151

United States of America
Our country, which stretches from the Atlantic Ocean to the Pacific Ocean. Pages 156–157

North America
The continent that our country is part of. Page 151

Washington, D.C.
Our country's capital city. Page 157

Philadelphia
A large city in Pennsylvania where the Liberty Bell is found. Page 207

West Virginia
A state in the eastern part of the United States. Page 157

PICTURE GLOSSARY

alike

Twins look **alike**. Page 18

alone

Sometimes Jim works **alone**. Page 26

American Indians

American Indians knew how to grow crops. Page 191

apartment

My new **apartment** is in a tall building. Page 67

bar graph

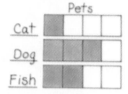

This **bar graph** tells about pets. Page 80

celebrate

We **celebrate** my birthday each year. Page 185

change

Moving was a **change** for my family. Page 38

city

A **city** is a busy place. Page 139

212

PICTURE GLOSSARY

clothing

Pants are one kind of **clothing**. Page 61

community

My **community** has many stores. Page 126

Congress

Congress makes laws for all of us. Page 158

continent

Our country is part of a **continent**. Page 150

D

different

Sue and Mike look **different**. Page 19

directions

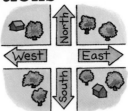

There are four main **directions**. Page 120

F

factory

This **factory** makes books. Page 96

family

My **family** is a special group of people. Page 34

farm

We have animals on our **farm**. Page 50

PICTURE GLOSSARY

feast

We had a **feast** on Thanksgiving. Page 192

food

There are many kinds of **food** to eat. Page 60

G **globe**

You can find our country on a **globe**. Page 24

goods

Many **goods** are made in factories. Page 92

group

This **group** will play together. Page 26

H **holiday**

The Fourth of July is a **holiday**. Page 182

L **law**

The **law** says to stop at a red light. Page 158

M **map**

I need a **map** to find Jim's house. Page 44

map key

The **map key** will help me find the house. Page 44

N

natural resources

Trees and water are **natural resources**. Page 170

needs

Food is one of our **needs**.
Page 60

neighbor

I wave to my **neighbor** every day. Page 118

neighborhood

My friends live in my **neighborhood**. Page 118

O

ocean

I like to watch the waves in the **ocean**. Page 150

P

pictograph

The **pictograph** tells about going to school. Page 98

Pilgrims

The **Pilgrims** sailed to our country. Page 190

R

rule

My class made a **rule** about the crayons. Page 12

PICTURE GLOSSARY

school

I learn many things in **school**. Page 4

service

The dentist gives a **service**. Page 94

shelter

We are looking for a new **shelter**. Page 61

state

West Virginia is a **state**.

Page 157

symbol

The eagle is a **symbol** of our country. Page 164

table

This **table** shows different kinds of clothing. Page 142

travel

I like to **travel** on airplanes. Page 108

wants

Bikes and skates are **wants** for some children.

Page 62

CREDITS

Front cover: *Background* Greg Nikas/VIESTI ASSOCIATES, INC; *inset m., b.* SuperStock

Back cover: *t.* Jean Kugler/FPG International; *m.* FourBy-Five/SuperStock; *b.* SuperStock

Logo art: Denman Hampson

Maps: Maryland Cartographics, Inc.

Contributing artists: Lori Bernero: 56, 57, 204, 205; Alex Bloch: 50, 51, 52, 53, 190, 191, 192; Suzanne Clee: 2, 29, 32, 58, 86, 87, 90, 112, 113, 116, 148, 176, 177, 180, 203; Olivia Cole: 42, 43, 146, 147, 212, 216; Michele Epstein: 18, 20, 21, 48, 124, 172; Simon Galkin: 178, 179; Ron LeHew: 140, 141, 142, 143; Lisa O'Hanlon: 54, 55, 88, 89, 92, 115, 144, 176; Claudia Sargent: 44, 45, 80, 98; Joan Slater: 130; Susan Swan: 4, 47, 48, 85, 124, 135, 172, 193; Courtesy of the United States Postal Service: 164, 165, 166, 167, 168, 169; Lane Yerkes: 174, 175.

Photographs

All photographs by Silver Burdett Ginn (SBG) unless otherwise noted.

Contents: iii: *b.* Cheryl Griffin for SBG. iv: *t.* Ken Kerbs for SBG; *b.* After Image/Robert Rathe. v: *b.* Alan Pitcairn/Grant Heilman Photography.

Unit 1 6–7: Cheryl Griffin for SBG. 16, 17: Angelo Santaniello for SBG. 24: *t.* NASA.

Unit 2 32–33: Pete Turner/The Image Bank. 35: *t.* Kamyar Samoul; *b.* Michael Paras for SBG. 36: *b.* Cheryl Griffin for SBG. 46: *t.* © Walter Hodges/Westlight; *b.* Gabe Palmer/Mug Shots. 47: Cheryl Griffin for SBG. 48: *b.* Kamyar Samoul. 49: Ken Kerbs for SBG. 54: *m.r.* Larry Lefever/Grant Heilman Photography; *b.l.* Ellis Herwig/Stock, Boston.

Unit 3 60: Ken Kerbs for SBG. 61: *t.* Dario Perla/After Image; *b.* Cheryl Griffin for SBG. 62: *l.* Ken Kerbs for SBG; *r.* Dan DeWilde for SBG. 63: Bob Yellen for SBG. 64: Len Speir. 65: Trevor's Campaign. 66: *t.* Kamyar Samoul. 67: *t.r.* Mike MeDici for SBG; *b.* J. Gerard Smith for SBG. 68: *t.* Ray Pfortner/Peter Arnold, Inc.; *b.* E.R. Degginger. 69: *t.* David Barned/West Light; *b.* Tom Walker/Allstock. 76: Courtesy of Super Foodtown, Cedar Knolls, NJ. 78: *t.* Alan Pitcairn/Grant Heilman Photography; *b.* Grant Heilman Photography. 82:

J. Gerard Smith for SBG. 83: *t.* Courtesy of Whistles, Summit, N.J.

Unit 4 92: *l.* Marvin S. Wolf/After Image; *r.* Victoria Beller-Smith for SBG. 93: *t.* Richard Pasley/Stock, Boston; *b.* John Zoiner. 94: *b.* Dan DeWilde for SBG. 95: UPS and UPS in shield design are registered trademarks of United Parcel Service of America, Inc. Used by permission. 96: John Zoiner. 97: *t.l.* Robert Rathe/After Image; *t.r.* Ken Kerbs for SBG; *b.* Rob Nelson/Stock, Boston. 99: Frank Fischer. 100–106: SBG, Courtesy of Converse Sneaker Factory. 108: *l.* North Wind Picture Archives; *r.* Culver Pictures, Inc. 110: *t.l.* Michael Medford/The Image Bank. 111: © 1982 Paul Shambroom/Photo Researchers, Inc. 112: *t.l.* John Zoiner; *b.r.* Kamyar Samoul. 114: SBG, Courtesy of Converse Sneaker Factory.

Unit 5 118: Richard Hutchings for SBG. 119 *b.* Stacy Pick/Stock, Boston. 124: *t.l.* Karl Kummels/Superstock; *m.l.* Manley Photo/Superstock; *b.l.* David Phillips; *r.* Eric Wheater/The Image Bank. 126: Dan DeWilde for SBG. 128: *r.* Robert Frerck/Odyssey Prod. 129: Dan DeWilde for SBG. 135: *t.r.* Kamyar Samoul. 136 *t.* Pam Hasegawa. 137: Audrey Gottlieb/Monkmeyer Press. 138: *t.r.* Robert Frerck/Odyssey Prod.; *b.* Larry Lefever/Grant Heilman Photography. 139: *l.* Superstock; *r.* J. Gerard Smith for SBG. 144: *m.r.* Kamyar Samoul.

Unit 6 148, 149: Douglas Faulkner/Photo Researchers, Inc. 150: David Lucas for SBG. 155: *t.* UPI/Bettmann Newsphotos; *b.* Stock, Boston. 158: H. Markel/Gamma Liaison. 159: Rhoda Pollack. 160: George Schwartz/Alpha. 162: *t.r.* Derek Fell; *b.* Steve Solum/Bruce Coleman, Inc. 163: Sports Information Office at Indiana University. 164: *m.* Leonard Lee Rue/Monkmeyer Press; *b.* Courtesy of U.S. Dept. of State; 168: Superstock. 169: *t.* Alan Pitcairn/Grant Heilman Photography; *r.* Berenholtz/The Stock Market. 170: Herman Kokojan/Black Star. 171: Forest Service. 172: *t.l.* E. Botts; *t.r.* J.C. Carton/Bruce Coleman; *m.* Bill Ruth/Bruce Coleman; *b.* Luis Villota/The Stock Market. 173: John Zoiner. 176: *m.* Stan Osolinski/The Stock Market; *r.* Rick Strange/International Stock Photo; *b.* H. Markel/Gamma Liaison.

Unit 7 181–182 Craig Blovin/F/Stop Pictures. 182, 196: Kamyar Samoul. 197: Mike Smith/FPG. 198: George A. Robinson/F/Stop Pictures. 200: *t.* Stock, Boston. 202: *t., m.l.* The Bettmann Archive; *m.r.* Kamyar Samoul.

PROGRAM SCOPE & SEQUENCE CHART

I. Acquiring and Providing Information

	Grade 1	2	3	4	5	6/7
A. Map and Globe Skills						
Understanding directions: up, down, left, right, North, South, East, West	●	●	●	●	●	●
Understanding the globe	●	●	●	●	●	●
Understanding cardinal directions	●	●	●	●	●	●
Using the globe to explain night and day				●	●	●
Comparing maps and the globe	●	●	●	●	●	●
Comparing maps with photographs	●	●	●	●	●	●
Understanding symbols	●	●	●	●	●	●
Understanding the legend (key)	●	●	●	●	●	●
Identifying landforms	●	●	●	●	●	●
Understanding relative size		●	●	●	●	●
Understanding latitude: Equator				●	●	●
Arctic Circle				●	●	●
Antarctic Circle				●	●	●
Tropic of Cancer				●	●	●
Tropic of Capricorn				●	●	●
Understanding longitude: Prime Meridian			●	●	●	●
Understanding continents and oceans	●	●	●	●	●	●
Understanding hemispheres			●	●	●	●
Understanding intermediate directions			●	●	●	●
Understanding the compass rose			●	●	●	●
Understanding scale			●	●	●	●
Using scale to measure distance			●	●	●	●
Understanding coordinates (grid system)			●	●	●	●

T1

	Grade 1	2	3	4	5	6/7
A. Map and Globe Skills (continued)						
Understanding elevation tints				●	●	●
Understanding contour lines				●	●	●
Understanding special-purpose maps:						
Relief map				●	●	●
Population map				●	●	●
Product map			●	●	●	●
Precipitation map				●	●	●
Physical-Political map			●	●	●	●
Road map			●	●	●	●
Historical map			●	●	●	●
Understanding movements of the earth: rotation, revolution				●	●	●
Understanding time zones				●	●	●
Understanding seasons		●	●	●	●	●
Understanding map projections				●	●	●
B. Graphic Skills						
Understanding charts	●	●	●	●	●	●
Understanding diagrams	●	●	●	●	●	●
Understanding graphs:						
Pictograph	●	●	●	●	●	●
Pie graph		●	●	●	●	●
Bar graph	●	●	●	●	●	●
Line graph			●	●	●	●
Climograph			●	●	●	●
Understanding time lines	●	●	●	●	●	●
Understanding cartoons					●	●
C. Learning Social Studies [Reading Skills] **1. Vocabulary**						
Using context clues (synonym, antonym, definition) to understand word meanings	●	●	●	●	●	●
Using illustrations or objects to understand word meanings	●	●	●	●	●	●
Using a dictionary or glossary to understand word meanings	●	●	●	●	●	●
Classifying and categorizing words (semantic maps and feature analysis)	●	●	●	●	●	●
Understanding the multiple meanings of words		●	●	●	●	●
Recognizing roots and affixes			●	●	●	●

	1	2	3	4	5	6/7
1. Vocabulary (continued)						
Understanding denotations and connotations of words			•	•	•	•
Identifying abbreviations and acronyms			•	•	•	•
Understanding etymology			•	•	•	•
2. Comprehension						
Understanding stated facts and details	•	•	•	•	•	•
Inferring unstated ideas	•	•	•	•	•	•
Understanding main ideas and details:						
Identifying stated main ideas	•	•	•	•		•
Generating unstated main ideas	•	•	•	•	•	•
Identifying details that support main ideas	•	•	•	•	•	•
Using headings and prereading questions to aid in main idea identification	•	•	•	•	•	•
Understanding sequence	•	•	•	•	•	•
Understanding cause and effect	•	•	•	•	•	•
Making and verifying predictions	•	•	•	•	•	•
Drawing conclusions	•	•	•	•	•	•
Understanding word referents				•	•	•
Relating text information to prior knowledge	•	•	•	•	•	•
Recognizing an author's purpose				•	•	•
Distinguishing fact from opinion			•	•	•	•
Understanding an author's point of view				•	•	•
Detecting bias:						
Propaganda techniques				•	•	•
Emotionally laden words				•	•	•
Evaluating arguments:						
Detecting illogical reasoning				•	•	•
Detecting faulty generalizations				•	•	•
Recognizing comprehension breakdowns					•	•
Employing reading comprehension fix-up strategies (summarizing, paraphrasing, rereading/retelling)		•	•	•	•	•
Recognizing and understanding the characteristics of various text types (informational/expository, narrative, historical fiction, biography/autobiography, journal/diary, essay, letter, speech, legend/myth)	•	•	•	•	•	•
Recognizing and using various text structures to aid comprehension (description, simple listing, sequence/time order, cause/effect, problem/solution, explanation, comparison/contrast, definition/examples)	•	•	•	•	•	•

	Grade					
	1	**2**	**3**	**4**	**5**	**6/7**
D. Speaking and Listening						
Listening to and following oral directions	●	●	●	●	●	●
Preparing and giving oral reports	●	●	●	●	●	●
Preparing and engaging in a debate			●	●	●	●
Expressing a point of view	●	●	●	●	●	●
Critical listening: Recognize a speaker's purpose/point of view			●	●	●	●
Distinguishing fact from opinion			●	●	●	●
Detecting bias (propaganda, emotionally laden words)			●	●	●	●
Evaluating oral arguments (illogical reasoning, faulty generalizations)			●	●	●	●
E. Study Skills						
Alphabetical order	●	●	●	●	●	●
Understanding and following written directions	●	●	●	●	●	●
Understanding and using book parts (table of contents, glossary, index, bibliography, appendices, gazetteer, footnotes)	●	●	●	●	●	●
Understanding and using graphic and typographical features (boldface, headings, captions, dictionary respellings)	●	●	●	●	●	●
Understanding and using textbook study features (prereading questions, graphic organizers, preview statements, summary statements, postreading questions)	●	●	●	●	●	●
Learning and using a study/reading technique		●	●	●	●	●
Note-taking			●	●	●	●
Outlining a selection			●	●	●	●
Summarizing a chapter or section	●	●	●	●	●	●
Skimming for main ideas	●	●	●	●	●	●
Scanning for specific facts or ideas			●	●	●	●
Adjusting reading rate to accommodate the purpose for reading, a reader's prior knowledge, and the difficulty/content of the material			●	●	●	●
F. Reference Skills						
Using the community as a resource	●	●	●	●	●	●
Selecting and using the appropriate resources: Atlas and gazetteer	●	●	●	●	●	●
Encyclopedia			●	●	●	●
Dictionary and thesaurus		●	●	●	●	●
Newspaper and periodicals		●	●	●	●	●

	1	2	3	4	5	6/7
F. Reference Skills (continued)						
Other resources (almanac, vertical files, telephone book, films, audio and video recordings, art, artifacts, microfiche)			●	●	●	●
Using a manual and electronic card catalog			●	●	●	●
Using a computer to run instructional and reference software			●	●	●	●

II. Organizing and Using Information

Grade

	1	2	3	4	5	6/7
A. Writing Skills						
Report writing		●	●	●	●	●
Writing a biography/autobiography			●	●	●	●
Writing a journal/diary	●	●	●	●	●	●
Writing book reports			●	●	●	●
Persuasive writing (editorials, commentaries, opinions)			●	●	●	●
Writing letters: Friendly letter	●	●	●	●	●	●
Business letter			●	●	●	●
Writing other forms common to social studies (essay, historical fiction, legend, myth, news report, research paper, speech, bibliography)			●	●	●	●
B. Thinking Skills						
Making observations	●	●	●	●	●	●
Classifying information	●	●	●	●	●	●
Interpreting information	●	●	●	●	●	●
Analyzing information	●	●	●	●	●	●
Summarizing information	●	●	●	●	●	●
Synthesizing information	●	●	●	●	●	●
Hypothesizing information	●	●	●	●	●	●
Evaluating information	●	●	●	●	●	●
Applying information	●	●	●	●	●	●

III. Interpersonal Skills

	1	2	3	4	5	6/7
A. Personal Skills						
Being sensitive to needs, problems and aspirations of others	●	●	●	●	●	●
Being courteous to others	●	●	●	●	●	●
Accepting and giving constructive feedback	●	●	●	●	●	●
Developing friendships	●	●	●	●	●	●
Developing respect for others as individuals (not stereotyping)	●	●	●	●	●	●
B. Group Interaction Skills						
Listening to differing views	●	●	●	●	●	●
Participating in group discussions	●	●	●	●	●	●
Participating in making decisions in a group setting	●	●	●	●	●	●
Being able to lead	●	●	●	●	●	●
Showing willingness to follow	●	●	●	●	●	●
Showing skills in persuading, compromising, debating, negotiating, and solving conflicts	●	●	●	●	●	●

IV. Citizenship

	1	2	3	4	5	6/7
A. Social and Political Participation Skills						
Keeping informed on social issues	●	●	●	●	●	●
Showing commitment toward the improvement of society	●	●	●	●	●	●
Showing willingness to work to influence those in power to preserve and extend justice, freedom, equality, and human rights	●	●	●	●	●	●
Working with others towards the solution of social problems	●	●	●	●	●	●
B. American Beliefs and Values						
Respecting the multicultural nature of our society	●	●	●	●	●	●
Abiding by the majority rule	●	●	●	●	●	●
Respecting and protecting the rights of the minorities	●	●	●	●	●	●
Respecting peaceful solutions	●	●	●	●	●	●
Respecting society's rules and laws	●	●	●	●	●	●
Striving for equality and freedom for all	●	●	●	●	●	●

B. American Beliefs and Values (continued)

	1	2	3	4	5	6/7
Working for the common good	●	●	●	●	●	●
Recognizing and protecting the rights of the individual	●	●	●	●	●	●
Recognizing and protecting the freedom of the individual	●	●	●	●	●	●
Recognizing the responsibilities of the individual in a democracy	●	●	●	●	●	●
Developing pride in one's own work	●	●	●	●	●	●
Accepting the dignity in all occupations	●	●	●	●	●	●
Developing good work and job habits	●	●	●	●	●	●

C. Seven Strands of Citizenship

	1	2	3	4	5	6/7
Participate in the democratic process	●	●	●	●	●	●
Develop patriotism and American values	●	●	●	●	●	●
Develop an awareness of and skills in interdependence	●	●	●	●	●	●
Develop an awareness of and skills in resolving social issues	●	●	●	●	●	●
Develop an awareness of and skills in relating to public officials	●	●	●	●	●	●
Learn how to use resources wisely	●	●	●	●	●	●
Develop strong personal integrity and positive self-image	●	●	●	●	●	●

V. Life Skills

	1	2	3	4	5	6/7
Practicing pedestrian safety	●	●	●	●		
Reading traffic signs	●	●	●	●		
Being able to say full name and address	●	●	●			
Explaining fire drill procedures	●	●	●			
Being able to tell when and how to call for fire and police help	●	●	●	●		
Using a telephone	●	●	●	●	●	●
Being able to dial emergency telephone numbers	●	●	●	●	●	●
Budgeting and banking		●	●	●	●	●
Addressing an envelope		●	●	●	●	●
Using a telephone directory		●	●	●	●	●
Reading a schedule	●	●	●	●	●	●
Reading a calendar	●	●	●	●	●	●
Filling out forms and applications		●	●	●	●	●
Reading newspaper ads		●	●	●	●	●
Using leisure time appropriately	●	●	●	●	●	●

TEACHER NOTES

TEACHER NOTES

TEACHER NOTES

TEACHER NOTES

TEACHER NOTES

TEACHER NOTES

TEACHER NOTES